ROMANS

A BEGINNING-INTERMEDIATE GREEK READER

ROMANS

A BEGINNING-INTERMEDIATE GREEK READER

ADAM W. JONES ◆ CARMEN A. PILANT

GLOSSAHOUSE
WILMORE, KY
www.glossahouse.com

Romans: A Beginning-Intermediate Greek Reader

GlossaHouse, LLC
110 Callis Circle
Wilmore, KY 40390

Publisher's Cataloging-in-Publication Data

Jones, Adam W. and **Carmen A. Pilant**

Romans : a beginning-intermediate Greek reader / Adam W. Jones and Carmen A. Pilant Wilmore, KY: GlossaHouse, ©2022.

xxiv, 180 pages ; 22 cm.– (Accessible Greek resources and online studies series. Tier 3)

ISBN: 978-1-63663-0182 (paperback)

1. Bible. Romans – Translating. 2. Bible. Romans – Terminology. 3. Greek language, Biblical – Grammar. 4. Bible. – New Testament – Greek – Language, style. I. Title. II. Series.

Library of Congress Control Number: 2022918591

Greek Paradigm Charts by J. Klay Harrison in consultation with Fredrick J. Long

Cover Design by T. Michael W. Halcomb

Book Layout and volume editing by Fredrick J. Long

The fonts used to create this work are available from www.linguistsoftware.com/lgku.htm.

This Series is dedicated to all who have struggled to make Greek a regular part of their study of Scripture.

Contents

AGROS

ACCESSIBLE GREEK RESOURCES AND ONLINE STUDIES

SERIES EDITORS

GlossaHouse
Wilmore, KY

AGROS

The Greek term ἀγρός is a field where seeds are planted and growth occurs. It also can denote a small village or community that forms around such a field. The type of community envisioned here is one that attends to Holy Scripture, particularly one that encourages the use of biblical Greek. Accessible Greek Resources and Online Studies (AGROS) is a tiered curriculum suite featuring innovative readers, grammars, specialized studies, and other exegetical resources to encourage and foster the exegetical use of biblical Greek. The goal of AGROS is to facilitate the creation and publication of innovative and inexpensive print and digital resources for the exposition of Scripture within the context of the global church. The AGROS curriculum includes five tiers, and each tier is indicated on the book's cover: Tier 1 (Beginning I), Tier 2 (Beginning II), Tier 3 (Intermediate I), Tier 4 (Intermediate II), and Tier 5 (Advanced). There are also two resource tracks: Conversational and Translational. Both involve intensive study of morphology, grammar, syntax, and discourse features. The conversational track specifically values the spoken word, and the enhanced learning associated with speaking a language in actual conversation. The translational track values the written word and encourages analytical study to aide in understanding and translating biblical Greek and other Greek literature. The two resource tracks complement one another and can be pursued independently or together.

ABBREVIATIONS

1st	first person
2nd	second person
3rd	third person
F,ϝ	*vau* or digamma (an old Greek letter)
abl.	ablative
abs.	absolute, absolutely
acc.	accusative
act.	active
add.	additional, additionally
adj.	adjective
adv.	adverb, adverbial, adverbially
alt.	alternately
ans.	answer
ante.	antecedent
aor.	aorist
app.	apposition, appositional
art.	article
attrib.	attributive, attributively
aug.	augment
BDAG	Bauer, F., F. W. Danker, et al., eds. *A Greek-English Lexicon of the New Testament and Other Early Christian Literature*. 3rd ed. Chicago: University of Chicago Press, 2000.
beg.	beginning
btw.	between
cmpd.	compound
comp.	comparative, comparatively
conj.	conjunction
constr.	construct, construction.
correl.	correlative
corresp.	corresponding, correspondingly
dat.	dative
dem.	demonstrative

dep.	deponent
diph.	diphthong
dir.	direct
dissim.	dissimilate, dissimilation
ditrans.	ditransitive (trivalent)
ECM	Aland, Barbara, Kurt Aland, Gerd Mink and Klaus Wachtel, eds. *Novum Testamentum Graecum: Editio Critica Maior*, vol. 4: *Catholic Letters*. 4 installments. Stuttgart: Deutsche Biblegesellschaft, 1997–2005.
e.g.	exempli gratia, Latin: "for example"
em.	emendation
emph.	emphatic
encl.	enclitic
equiv.	equivalent
euphem.	euphemism
fem.	feminine
fig.	figurative, figuratively
fut.	future
gen.	genitive, genitival
GNT	Greek New Testament
hist.	historical
Holmes	Michael W. Holmes
imper.	impersonal (avalent)
impf.	imperfect
impv.	imperative
indef.	indefinite
indic.	indicative
indir.	indirect
inf.	infinitive
init.	initial
instr.	instrumental
inter.	interrogative
intrans.	intransitive (monovalent)
irreg.	irregular

L&N	Louw, Johannes P., and Eugene A. Nida, eds. *Greek-English Lexicon of the New Testament: Based on Semantic Domains*. 2 vols. 2nd ed. New York: United Bible Societies, 1989.
length.	lengthen, lengthened
lit.	literally
loc.	locative
LSJ	Liddell, Henry G., R. Scott, H. S. Jones, and R. McKenzie, eds. *A Greek-English Lexicon*. Rev. 9th ed. Oxford: Clarendon, 1996.
masc.	masculine
mid.	middle
metaph.	metaphor, metaphorical
MH	morphology help
Mounce	Mounce, William D. *The Morphology of Biblical Greek*. Grand Rapids: Zondervan, 1994.
Muraoka	Muraoka, T. *A Greek-English Lexicon of the Septuagint*. Louvain: Peeters, 2009.
neg.	negative, negate(d)
neut.	neuter
Newman	Newman, Barclay M., ed. *A Concise Greek-English Dictionary of the New Testament*. Stuttgart: Deutsche Bibelgesellschaft, 1993.
nom.	nominative, nominal
NA	Greek text of the NA^{27} and UBS^{4}
NA^{27}	Aland, Barbara, K. Aland, J. Karavidopoulos, C. M. Martini, and B. M. Metzger, eds. *Novum Testamentum Graece*. 27th ed. Stuttgart: Deutsche Bibelgesellschaft, 1993.
NA^{28}	Aland, Barbara, K. Aland, J. Karavidopoulos, C. M. Martini, B. M. Metzger, and Institute for New Testament Textual Research, eds. *Novum Testamentum Graece*, 28th ed. Stuttgart: Deutsche Bibelgesellschaft, 2012.

NIV	Goodrich, Richard J., and Albert L. Lukaszewski, eds., *A Reader's Greek New Testament*. Grand Rapids: Zondervan, 2003.
NRSV	New Revised Standard Version
occ.	occur, occurrence
obj.	object
opt.	optative
paren.	parenthetical
pass.	passive
per.	person, personal
periphr.	periphrastic
pf.	perfect, perfective
pl.	plural
plpf.	pluperfect
pos.	positive
poss.	possessive
post.	postcedent
prec.	preceding
pred.	predicate
pref.	prefix, prefixed
prep.	preposition, prepositional
pres.	present
pron.	pronoun
prtc.	participle
reduc.	reduction
redupl.	reduplicate, reduplication
ref.	reference
reflex.	reflexive
rel.	relative
RP	Robinson, Maurice A., and William G. Pierpont, eds. *The New Testament in the Original Greek: Byzantine Textform*. Southborough, MA: Chilton, 2005.
SBL	Society of Biblical Literature

SBLGNT	Holmes, Michael W. *The Greek New Testament: SBL Edition*. Atlanta: Society of Biblical Literature, 2010. http://sblgnt.com/.
SBLGNT^{app}	Apparatus of SBLGNT
sg.	singular
Smyth	Smyth, Herbert Weir. *Greek Grammar*. Revised by Gordon M. Messing. Harvard Press, 1984.
subj.	subjunctive
subst.	substantival, substantive
suf.	suffix, suffixed
superl.	superlative
suppl.	suppletive
syn.	synonym
TDNT	Friedrich, Gerhard, and Gerhard Kittel, eds. *Theological Dictionary of the New Testament*. 10 vols., tr. by G. W. Bromiley. Grand Rapids: Eerdmans, 1964–76.
TH	Translation Help
TLNT	Spicq, Ceslas. *Theological Lexicon of the New Testament*. 3 vols. Peabody, MA: Hendrickson, 1994.
TR	Textus Receptus ("Received Text")
trans.	transitive (divalent)
translit.	transliteration (of a loan word into Greek)
Treg	Tregelles, Samuel Prideaux. *The Greek New Testament, Edited from Ancient Authorities, with their Various Readings in Full, and the Latin Version of Jerome*. London: Bagster; Stewart, 1857–1879.
Treg^{marg}	margin of Treg
Trenchard	Trenchard, Warren C. *Complete Vocabulary Guide to the Greek New Testament*. Rev. ed. Grand Rapids: Zondervan, 1998.
UBS^{4}	Aland, B., K. Aland, J. Karavidopoulos, C. M. Martini, and B. M. Metzger, eds. *The Greek New Testament*. 4th rev. ed. New York: United Bible Societies, 2006.
voc.	vocative

WH	Hort, Fenton John Anthony, and Brooke Foss Westcott. *The New Testament in the Original Greek.* 2 vols. Cambridge: Macmillan, 1881.
WH^{app}	*Appendix* (vol. 2 of WH)
WH^{marg}	margin of WH
Works (TJ)	Jackson, Thomas, ed. *The Works of the Rev. John Wesley, M.A.* 14 vols. Grand Rapids: Baker, 1978.

Preface to the GlossaHouse Beginning-Intermediate Readers

And men who speak the Latin tongue, of whom are those I have undertaken to instruct, need two other languages for the knowledge of Scripture, Hebrew and Greek, that they may have recourse to the original texts if the endless diversity of the Latin translators throw them into doubt.

—Saint Augustine, *De Doctrina Christiana* 2.11.16

Do I understand Greek and Hebrew? Otherwise, how can I undertake, (as every Minister does,) not only to explain books which are written therein, but to defend them against all opponents? Am I not at the mercy of everyone who does understand, or even pretends to understand, the original? For which way can I confute his pretense? Do I understand the language of the Old Testament? critically? at all? Can I read into English one of David's Psalms, or even the first chapter of Genesis? Do I understand the language of the New Testament? Am I a critical master of it? Have I enough of it even to read into English the first chapter of St. Luke? If not, how many years did I spend at school? How many at the University? And what was I doing all those years? Ought not shame to cover my face?

—John Wesley, "An Address to the Clergy," *Works* (TJ) X:491.

PREFACE

Learning Koinē Greek can be a daunting task. Some students learn just enough to fulfill degree requirements and then forget most of what they learned. This is a sad fact, especially since many people would love such an opportunity to read Scripture in the original languages. Forgetting Greek may not be intentional, yet it is a reality for numerous students. While many resources are available that teach the grammatical basics of Koinē Greek, the beginning student is often still not able to read their Greek New Testament (GNT). Beginning students are often hindered from reading the GNT due to a lack of vocabulary or unfamiliarity with Koinē Greek syntax and idioms.

GlossaHouse's *Beginning-Intermediate Greek Readers* are Tier 3 resources that assume the completion of beginning NT Greek instruction. These readers are designed to build confidence and encourage reading the GNT by providing vocabulary glosses, morphological explanations, and translation helps, while also assisting the student to transition from beginning into intermediate Greek studies. By carefully working through these Greek readers, students will find value interacting with the GNT and see how grammatical classifications affect meaning and translation in context.

Any student who uses GlossaHouse's *Beginning-Intermediate Greek Readers* of the Greek New Testament will be able to apply her/his beginning Greek education and read from the GNT. By doing so, it is hoped that the GNT might become a part of daily reading and proclamation. Interpreters, pastors, and students will find these readers beneficial for careful investigation of the GNT.

J. Klay Harrison

May 2013

How to Use This Beginning-Intermediate Reader

GlossaHouse's *Beginning-Intermediate Greek Readers* are designed to be a user-friendly guide for reading the GNT. They provide footnotes with textual helps for each vocabulary word occurring 49 times or less. Additionally, each chapter is introduced with a vocabulary list of these infrequent words that occur within each chapter of the biblical book. The list is sorted by word frequency as found in the chapter, arranged from most to least frequent occurrences. Additionally, footnotes contain morphological helps for more difficult lexical forms. Occasionally, too, students will see footnotes about the textual variants between the SBLGNT and other GNT critical editions. More information is provided below about these features.

The Greek Text

The main Greek text of GlossaHouse's *Beginning-Intermediate Greek Readers* is *The Greek New Testament: SBL Edition* (SBLGNT), copyright 2010 Society of Biblical Literature and Logos Bible Software [ISBN 978-1-58983-535-1]. The SBLGNT text can be found online at http://sblgnt.com.

The Text-Critical Apparatus

The SBLGNT is a critical edition of the GNT and includes a text-critical apparatus explained in the "Introduction to the SBLGNT," found online at https://sblgnt.com/about/introduction/. This introduction expounds not only how the SBLGNT text was assembled but also how to understand the text-critical information found at the end of each chapter of the biblical text of this reader. The "Introduction to the SBLGNT," written by Michael Holmes, the editor of the SBLGNT, is also found in the print edition and electronic editions of *The Greek New Testament: SBL Edition.*

The text-critical markings found in the SBLGNT point the reader to the apparatus that occurs at the end of each chapter. For an explanation of the text critical marks and the apparatus, please see "Introduction to the SBLGNT" found at https://sblgnt.com/about/introduction/.

THE FOOTNOTES

For ease of reading, this reader uses footnotes as a guide through the GNT. The footnotes potentially provide four categories of information: lexical aid, morphology help (MH), translation help (TH), and NA (NA27/UBS4) and NA28 variants. Each category is described below.

1. If a Greek word occurs 49 times or less in the SBLGNT, then lexical aid is provided in a footnote. Each Greek word is provided in lexical (dictionary) form. Thus, all verbs are presented in **pres. act. indic. 1st sg**. conjugation. Pronouns and adjectives are shown in **nom. sg. masc.** form followed by the **nom. sg. fem.** and **nom. sg. neut.** endings. The lexical form for a noun is the **nom. sg.** full inflection followed by the **gen. sg.** ending and then the respective article, indicating gender. After the word's lexical form, glosses are found in italics. These glosses are general meanings for the Greek word, so they are not comprehensive of the word's complete lexical range. Since words only have meaning in context, there are times when a standard gloss is not appropriate for adequate contextual translation. In these instances, a contextual gloss will be suggested in a bold italic font following a semicolon. For example, consider footnote 11 below.

   [11] λόγος, ου, ὁ, *word, speech, matter;* ***concept***.

   In this footnote, the Greek word in question is a form of λόγος. Since λόγος is a noun, the fully inflected nom. sg. masc. form (λόγος) is provided. Then follows the gen. ending (ου), which lets the reader know this is a 2nd declension noun. The article (ὁ) is given in nom. sg. masc. inflected form. Since ὁ is masc., the article then indicates λόγος is a masc. noun. Thus, the entire lexical form is λόγος, ου, ὁ. Then, to translate λόγος, the lexical aid suggests using one of the following standard glosses: *word, speech, matter*. However, it appears these standard glosses do not capture the contextual meaning of λόγος. So, the lexical aid also provides a gloss befitting this particular context. Thus, here it is suggested that λόγος may be translated as ***concept***.

2. Morphology Help (MH) may also be provided in the footnotes. These notes supply potentially difficult parsing, explain word formation, and clarify any morphological issues. For example, consider footnote 12 below.

[12] MH: fut. act. indic. 2nd pl. from μένω = μεν (root) + εσ (tense formative) + ετε (thematic 2nd pl. ending) › μεν + εετε (σ btw. two vowels elides) › μενεῖτε (vowels contract; ε + ε = εῖ).

The abbreviation MH indicates that morphological help follows. The particular word in question is μενεῖτε. The parsing is given along with the lexical form. Then, a detailed explanation shows step-by-step how the inflected verb was formed.

3. One also may find Translation Help (TH) in the footnotes. These offer brief explanations for difficult grammar, idioms, morphology, and syntax. For example, consider footnote 13 below.

[13] TH: λόγου is dir.obj. of ἀκούει.

The initials TH identify that what follows is a translation help. λόγου is the word in question within the main Greek text. The TH is telling the reader that λόγου is functioning as the direct object of the verb ἀκούει.

Students should be aware that at times certain phrases will be placed in front of the verb for various reasons. Although it is beyond the purpose of this reader to discuss prominence and emphasis, there will be some Translation Helps marking the Greek wordage as "fronted."

4. Differences in wording between the SBLGNT, NA, and NA[28] may also be found in the footnotes. This will typically be indicated by "NA has" (or "NA[28] has") and then the textual difference. Although some of these variants are presented in the text-critical apparatus found in the Appendix I, they are included in the footnotes for sake of quick reference. Thus, consider footnote 14 below.

    [14] NA has ῥῆμα.

    Here the reader is informed that the NA Greek texts have ῥῆμα where the SBLGNT has something different.

THE VOCABULARY AND GLOSSES

The beginning Koinē Greek student should learn every word that occurs in the GNT 50 times or more (310 words). The GlossaHouse Beginning-Intermediate Greek Readers include glosses for these high frequency words in Appendices II and III. They are listed both by frequency (for vocabulary retention) and in alphabetical order (for quick reference). Every word that occurs 49 times or less in the SBLGNT will be glossed in the footnote section of the GlossaHouse Beginning-Intermediate Greek Readers. Additionally, each chapter is introduced with a vocabulary list of these glossed words that occur within the chapter. The list is sorted by word frequency as found in the chapter, arranged from most to least frequent in the SBLGNT. All word frequencies are based upon lexical occurrences in the SBLGNT, not the NA or NA[28].

The goal in establishing vocabulary glosses is to provide accurate yet concise glosses for every word. Knowing that words only have meaning in context, standard glosses will not suffice for every word occurrence. Such is the limit of a gloss. Whenever a standard gloss does not fix the context, a contextual gloss will be available in a footnote.

All glosses are a collaborative effort between the author(s), AGROS Editorial Board, and Babel Lexicography (BabLex). These glosses are the result of independent research and the consultation of numerous resources, which include but are not limited to Newman, BDAG, Muraoka, LSJ, L&N, TDNT, TLNT, and Trenchard.

The Appendices

The Appendices will typically include three sections: Appendix I: Vocabulary 50 Times or More Sorted by Frequency, Appendix II: Vocabulary 50 Times or More Arranged Alphabetically, and Appendix III: Koinē Greek Paradigm Charts. Each appendix is described below. However, for the Beginning-Intermediate Greek Readers for the Catholic Letters (James, 1–2 Peter, 1–3 John, and Jude) will include an additional apparatus that shows differences between the SBLGNT and ECM (*Novum Testamentum Graecum: Editio Critica Maior*). This short apparatus is from the SBLGNT and will be entitled "Appendix: The SBLGNT in comparison to ECM."

Appendix I: Vocabulary 50 Times or More Sorted by Frequency. In order to best serve the Koinē Greek student, all vocabulary assumed as known has been sorted from most to least frequent and is included in Appendix I. The frequency of occurrences for each word is based upon the SBLGNT and not the NA. These 310 words, which occur 50 times or more in the SBLGNT, are available for students wanting to learn or refresh their basic Greek vocabulary.

Appendix II: Vocabulary 50 Times or More Arranged Alphabetically. All vocabulary occurring 50 times or more in the SBLGNT is assumed as known to readers. However, these vocabulary words are included and arranged alphabetically in Appendix II.

Appendix III: Koinē Greek Paradigm Charts. These paradigm charts will be a helpful resource to students who have difficulty parsing words or who just need a refresher about Greek word formations. The *Koinē Greek Paradigm Charts* were created by J. Klay Harrison in consultation and with assistance from Fredrick J. Long.

ROMANS

A BEGINNING-INTERMEDIATE GREEK READER

ΠΡΟΣ ΡΩΜΑΙΟΥΣ

ROMANS 1

New Vocabulary by Frequency [Chapter, Book, SBLGNT Occurrences]

ἁγιωσύνη, ης, ἡ, *holiness* [1, 1, 3]
ἀγνοέω, *I am unaware, ignorant (of)* [1, 6, 22]
ἀδιαλείπτως, *constantly, without ceasing* [1, 1, 4]
ἀδικία, ας, ἡ, *unrighteousness, injustice* [3, 7, 25]
ἀδόκιμος, ον, *not approved, worthless* [1, 1, 8]
ἀΐδιος, ον, *eternal* [1, 1, 2]
ἀκαθαρσία, ας, ἡ, *impurity, immorality* [1, 2, 10]
ἀλαζών, όνος, ὁ, *boastful* [1, 1, 2]
ἀλλάσσω, *I exchange* [1, 1, 6]
ἀναπολόγητος, ον, *without excuse* [1, 2, 2]
ἀνάστασις, εως, ἡ, *resurrection* [1, 2, 42]
ἀνελεήμων, ον, *unmerciful, ruthless* [1, 1, 1]
ἀνόητος, ον, *foolish, unintelligent* [1, 1, 6]
ἀντιμισθία, ας, ἡ, *penalty* [1, 1, 2]
ἄξιος, ία, ον, *deserving, worthy* [1, 2, 41]
ἀόρατος, όν, *invisible, unseen* [1, 1, 5]
ἀπειθής, ές, *disobedient* [1, 1, 6]
ἀποκαλύπτω, *I reveal, make fully known* [2, 3, 26]
ἀπολαμβάνω, *I receive, take away* [1, 1, 10]
ἀποστολή, ης, ἡ, *apostleship* [1, 1, 4]
ἄρσην, εν, ενος, *male, man* [3, 3, 9]
ἀσέβεια, ας, ἡ, *ungodliness, impiety* [1, 2, 6]
ἄστοργος, ον, *unloving, heartless* [1, 1, 2]
ἀσύνετος, ον, *foolish, senseless* [2, 3, 5]
ἀσύνθετος, ον, *untrustworthy, faithless* [1, 1, 1]
ἀσχημοσύνη, ης, ἡ, *shameless acts* [1, 1, 2]
ἀτιμάζω, *I dishonor, shame* [1, 2, 7]
ἀτιμία, ας, ἡ, *shame, dishonor, disgrace* [1, 2, 7]
ἄφθαρτος, ον, *immortal, imperishable* [1, 1, 8]
ἀφορίζω, *I set apart, appoint* [1, 1, 10]
ἄχρι, *until* [1, 4, 49]
βάρβαρος, ον, *barbarian, non-Greek, uncivilized* [1, 1, 6]
γνωστός, ή, όν, *what can be known* [1, 1, 15]
γονεύς, έως, ὁ, *parent* [1, 1, 20]
δέομαι, *I ask, request, plead* [1, 1, 22]
δεῦρο, *now, the present time* [1, 1, 9]

διαλογισμός, *reasoning* [1, 2, 14]
δικαίωμα, ατος, τό, *requirement, righteous deed* [1, 5, 10]
διότι, *because, for* [2, 4, 23]
δοκιμάζω, *I test (to see if something is genuine), approve* [1, 4, 22]
δόλος, ου, ὁ, *deceit* [1, 1, 11]
εἰκών, όνος, ἡ, *image* [1, 2, 23]
ἐκκαίω, *I am inflamed* [1, 1, 1]
Ἕλλην, ηνος, ὁ, *Greek, civilized* [2, 6, 25]
ἐπαισχύνομαι, *I am ashamed (of)* [1, 2, 11]
ἐπιγινώσκω, *I know* [1, 1, 44]
ἐπίγνωσις, εως, ἡ, *knowledge, recognition* [1, 3, 20]
ἐπιθυμία, ας, ἡ, *desire, lust* [1, 5, 38]
ἐπιποθέω, *I long for, desire* [1, 1, 9]
ἔρις, ιδος, ἡ, *strife* [1, 2, 9]
ἑρπετόν, οῦ, τό, *reptile* [1, 1, 4]
εὐλογητός, ή, όν, *blessed, praised* [1, 2, 8]
εὐοδόω, *I succeed, am able to* [1, 1, 4]
εὐχαριστέω, *I give thanks* [2, 5, 38]
ἐφευρετής, οῦ, ὁ, *inventor* [1, 1, 1]
θειότης, ητος, ἡ, *divine nature* [1, 1, 1]
θεοστυγής, ές, *God-hater* [1, 1, 1]
θῆλυς, εια, υ, *female, woman* [2, 2, 5]
καθήκω, *I am fitting, am appropriate* [1, 1, 2]
καθοράω, *I perceive, discern* [1, 1, 1]
κακία, ας, ἡ, *malice, wickedness* [1, 1, 11]
κακοήθεια, ας, ἡ, *malice* [1, 1, 1]
καταγγέλλω, *I make known, announce, proclaim* [1, 1, 18]
κατάλαλος, ου, ὁ, *slanderer* [1, 1, 1]
κατεργάζομαι, *I do, commit* [1, 11, 22]
κατέχω, *I restrain, hold back* [1, 2, 17]
κλητός, ή, όν, *called* [3, 4, 10]
κτίζω, *I create* [1, 1, 15]
κτίσις, εως, ἡ, *creation* [2, 7, 19]
κωλύω, *I prevent, hinder* [1, 1, 23]
λατρεύω, *I serve* [2, 2, 21]
μάρτυς, ρος, ὁ, *witness* [1, 1, 35]
ματαιόω, *I render worthless* [1, 1, 1]
μεστός, ή, όν, *full* [1, 2, 9]
μεταδίδωμι, *I impart, give, share* [1, 2, 5]
μεταλλάσσω, *I exchange* [2, 2, 2]
μνεία, ας, ἡ, *mention, memory* [1, 1, 7]

μωραίνω, *I make foolish* [1, 1, 4]
νοέω, *I understand, think through carefully* [1, 1, 14]
νοῦς, ός, ὁ, *mind, way of thinking* [1, 6, 24]
ὁμοίωμα, ατος, τό, *likeness* [1, 4, 6]
ὁμοίως, *likewise, in the same way* [1, 1, 31]
ὀργή, ῆς, ἡ, *wrath* [1, 12, 36]
ὄρεξις, εως, ἡ, *desire, lust* [1, 1, 1]
ὁρίζω, *I appoint, designate* [1, 1, 8]
ὀφειλέτης, ου, ὁ, *debtor, one who is under obligation* [1, 3, 7]
πάθος, ους, τό, *passion* [1, 1, 3]
πάντοτε, *always* [1, 1, 41]
πετεινόν, ή, όν, *bird* [1, 1, 14]
πλάνη, ης, ἡ, *deceit, error* [1, 1, 10]
πλεονεξία, ας, ἡ, *greediness* [1, 1, 10]
πνευματικός, ή, όν, *spiritual* [1, 3, 26]
ποίημα, ατος, τό, *that which is made, creation* [1, 1, 2]
πολλάκις, *often, many times* [1, 1, 18]
πονηρία, ας, ἡ, *wickedness, sinfulness* [1, 1, 7]
ποτέ, *at last* [1, 3, 29]
πράσσω, *I do, engage in* [2, 10, 38]
προεπαγγέλλω, *I promise beforehand* [1, 1, 2]
πρόθυμος, ον, *eager* [1, 1, 3]
προσευχή, ῆς, ἡ, *prayer* [1, 3, 36]
προτίθημι, *I intend, plan* [1, 2, 3]
πως, *somehow, perhaps* [1, 1, 12]
Ῥώμη, ης, ἡ, *Rome* [2, 2, 8]
σεβάζομαι, *I worship, revere* [1, 1, 1]
σκοτίζω, *I become dark, darken* [1, 2, 5]
σοφός, ή, όν, *wise, intelligent* [2, 3, 19]
σπέρμα, τος, τό, *seed, offspring, descendant* [1, 9, 43]
στηρίζω, *I strengthen, establish* [1, 1, 13]
συμπαρακαλέω, *I am mutually encouraged, comforted* [1, 1, 1]
συνευδοκέω, *I approve of* [1, 1, 6]
σωτηρία, ας, ἡ, *salvation* [1, 5, 46]
τετράπους, ουν, *four footed* [1, 1, 3]
ὑβριστής, οῦ, ὁ, *insolent* [1, 1, 2]
ὑπακοή, ῆς, ἡ, *obedience* [1, 6, 14]
ὑπερήφανος, ου, ὁ, *arrogant, proud* [1, 1, 5]
φανερός, ά, όν, *evident, visible* [1, 3, 18]
φανερόω, *I reveal, make known* [1, 2, 48]
φάσκω, *I claim, assert* [1, 1, 3]

φθαρτός, ή, όν, *perishable* [1, 1, 6]
φθόνος, ου, ὁ, *envy, jealousy* [1, 1, 9]
φόνος, ου, ὁ, *murder* [1, 1, 9]
φυσικός, ή, όν, *natural* [2, 2, 3]
φύσις, εως, ἡ, *nature* [1, 7, 14]
χάρισμα, ατος, τὸ, *gift* [1, 6, 17]
χρῆσις, εως, ἡ, *relations* [2, 2, 2]
ψεῦδος, ους, τό, *lie* [1, 1, 10]
ψιθυριστής, οῦ, ὁ, *gossiper* [1, 1, 1]

ΠΡΟΣ ΡΩΜΑΙΟΥΣ

1.1 Παῦλος[1] δοῦλος[2] ⸂Χριστοῦ Ἰησοῦ⸃, κλητὸς[3] ἀπό-
στολος, ἀφωρισμένος[4] εἰς[5] εὐαγγέλιον θεοῦ **2** ὃ[6]
προεπηγγείλατο[7] διὰ τῶν προφητῶν αὐτοῦ ἐν γραφαῖς
ἁγίαις **3** περὶ τοῦ υἱοῦ αὐτοῦ, τοῦ γενομένου[8] ἐκ
σπέρματος[9] Δαυὶδ[10] κατὰ σάρκα, **4** τοῦ ὁρισθέντος[11] υἱοῦ
θεοῦ ἐν δυνάμει κατὰ πνεῦμα ἁγιωσύνης[12] ἐξ
ἀναστάσεως[13] νεκρῶν, Ἰησοῦ Χριστοῦ[14] τοῦ κυρίου ἡμῶν,
5 δι᾽ οὗ[15] ἐλάβομεν[16] χάριν καὶ ἀποστολὴν[17] εἰς[18]
ὑπακοὴν[19] πίστεως ἐν πᾶσιν τοῖς ἔθνεσιν ὑπὲρ[20] τοῦ
ὀνόματος αὐτοῦ, **6** ἐν οἷς[21] ἐστε καὶ[22] ὑμεῖς κλητοὶ[23]

---

[1] TH: 1:1-7 is one verbless sentence so a verb needs to be supplied. Readers are introduced to the recipient of the letter in v. 7, which is the best place to supply a verb (“writing”); *Paul … writing to all.*

[2] TH: δοῦλος is in app. to Παῦλος.

[3] κλητός, ή, όν, *called.* TH: attrib. adj. modifier of ἀπόστολος in app. to Παῦλος.

[4] ἀφορίζω, *I set apart, appoint.* MH: ἀφ (prep. aspirated from the rough breathing mark) + ὁριδ › ἀφωριδ (redupl. of ο + stem) + μεν (pf. pass. prtc. tense formative) + ος (nom. sg. masc. ending) › ἀφωρισμένος (δ + μ = σμ). TH: ἀφωρισμένος is a subst. prtc. in app. to Παῦλος.

[5] TH: εἰς is indicating purpose; *for.*

[6] TH: ὃ is a rel. prn. referring to the ante. εὐαγγέλιον; *which.*

[7] προεπαγγέλλω, *I promise beforehand.* MH: liquid verb stem is προεπαγγειλ.

[8] TH: τοῦ γενομένου is an attrib. adj. modifying τοῦ υἱοῦ.

[9] σπέρμα, ατος, τό, *seed, offspring, descendant.*

[10] TH: Δαυὶδ is indeclinable functioning here as a genitive.

[11] ὁρίζω, *I appoint, designate.* MH: the root is ὁριδ; δ + θ = σθ. TH: ὁρισθέντος is an attrib. adj. modifying τοῦ υἱοῦ.

[12] ἁγιωσύνη, ης, ἡ, *holiness.*

[13] ἀνάστασις, εως, ἡ, *resurrection.*

[14] TH: Ἰησοῦ Χριστοῦ is in app. to τοῦ υἱοῦ.

[15] TH: οὗ is a rel. prn. referring to the ante. Ἰησοῦ Χριστοῦ.

[16] MH: 2nd aor. of λαμβάνω; aor. tense stem is λαβ.

[17] ἀποστολή, ης, ἡ, *apostleship.*

[18] TH: εἰς is indicating purpose; *for.*

[19] ὑπακοή, ῆς, ἡ, *obedience.*

[20] TH: ὑπὲρ is indicating advantage; *for the sake of.*

[21] TH: οἷς is a rel. prn. referring to the ante. τοῖς ἔθνεσιν; with ἐν, *among whom.*

[22] TH: καὶ is additive; *also.*

[23] κλητός, ή, όν, *called.* TH: pred. adj. to the subject ὑμεῖς.

Ἰησοῦ Χριστοῦ,[1] **7** πᾶσιν τοῖς οὖσιν[2] ἐν Ῥώμῃ[3] ἀγαπητοῖς[4]
θεοῦ, κλητοῖς[5] ἁγίοις· χάρις ὑμῖν[6] καὶ εἰρήνη ἀπὸ θεοῦ
πατρὸς[7] ἡμῶν καὶ κυρίου Ἰησοῦ Χριστοῦ.

8 Πρῶτον μὲν εὐχαριστῶ[8] τῷ θεῷ μου διὰ Ἰησοῦ
Χριστοῦ ⸀περὶ πάντων ὑμῶν, ὅτι ἡ πίστις ὑμῶν
καταγγέλλεται[9] ἐν ὅλῳ τῷ κόσμῳ. **9** μάρτυς[10] γάρ μού
ἐστιν ὁ θεός, ᾧ λατρεύω[11] ἐν τῷ πνεύματί μου ἐν τῷ
εὐαγγελίῳ τοῦ υἱοῦ αὐτοῦ, ὡς ἀδιαλείπτως[12] μνείαν[13]
ὑμῶν ποιοῦμαι[14] **10** πάντοτε[15] ἐπὶ τῶν προσευχῶν[16] μου,
δεόμενος[17] εἴ πως[18] ἤδη ποτὲ[19] εὐοδωθήσομαι[20] ἐν[21] τῷ
θελήματι τοῦ θεοῦ ἐλθεῖν[22] πρὸς ὑμᾶς. **11** ἐπιποθῶ[23] γὰρ

---

[1] TH: Ἰησοῦ Χριστοῦ is a gen. of possession; *belonging to Jesus Christ.*

[2] MH: pres. act. prtc. dat. pl. masc. of εἰμί. TH: subst. prtc.; *to the ones who are.*

[3] Ῥώμη, ης, ἡ, *Rome.*

[4] TH: ἀγαπητοῖς is a dat. in app. to τοῖς οὖσιν.

[5] κλητός, ή, όν, *called.* TH: attrib. adj. modifier of ἁγίοις in app. to τοῖς οὖσιν.

[6] TH: ὑμῖν should be read after εἰρήνη; *to you all.*

[7] TH: πατρὸς is in app. to θεοῦ.

[8] εὐχαριστέω, *I give thanks.* TH: εὐχαριστέω takes a dat. dir. obj.

[9] καταγγέλλω, *I make known, announce, proclaim.*

[10] μάρτυς, ρος, ὁ, *witness.* TH: μάρτυς, a fronted pred. nom. to the subject ὁ θεός.

[11] λατρεύω, *I serve.* TH: λατρεύω takes a dat. dir. obj. Here, the dir. obj. ᾧ precedes the verb and is a rel. pron. whose ante. is ὁ θεός.

[12] ἀδιαλείπτως, *constantly, without ceasing.*

[13] μνεία, ας, ἡ, *mention, memory.*

[14] MH: the contract verb (ποιε) contracts with the connecting vowel (ε + ο = ου).

[15] πάντοτε, *always.*

[16] προσευχή, ῆς, ἡ, *prayer.*

[17] δέομαι, *I ask, request, plead.*

[18] πώς, *somehow, perhaps.*

[19] ποτέ, *at last.* TH: εἴ πως ἤδη ποτὲ, *if somehow now at last.*

[20] εὐοδόω, *I succeed, am able to.* MH: The ο lengthens to ω before the tense formative.

[21] TH: ἐν is instrumental; *by.*

[22] MH: aor. act. inf. of ἔρχομαι. TH: complementary inf. with εὐοδωθήσομαι.

[23] ἐπιποθέω, *I long for, desire.* MH: the root (ἐπιποθε) ends in a vowel, so the connecting vowel contracts (ε + ω = ω).

ἰδεῖν[1] ὑμᾶς, ἵνα τι μεταδῶ[2] χάρισμα[3] ὑμῖν πνευματικὸν[4]
εἰς τὸ στηριχθῆναι[5] ὑμᾶς, **12** τοῦτο δέ ἐστιν συμπαρα-
κληθῆναι[6] ἐν ὑμῖν διὰ τῆς ἐν ἀλλήλοις πίστεως ὑμῶν τε
καὶ[7] ἐμοῦ. **13** οὐ θέλω δὲ ὑμᾶς[8] ἀγνοεῖν,[9] ἀδελφοί,
ὅτι πολλάκις[10] προεθέμην[11] ἐλθεῖν[12] πρὸς ὑμᾶς, καὶ
ἐκωλύθην[13] ἄχρι[14] τοῦ δεῦρο[15], ἵνα τινὰ καρπὸν σχῶ[16] καὶ
ἐν ὑμῖν καθὼς καὶ[17] ἐν τοῖς λοιποῖς ἔθνεσιν.
14 Ἕλλησίν[18] τε καὶ βαρβάροις[19], σοφοῖς[20] τε καὶ ἀνοήτοις[21]

---

[1] MH: aor. act. inf. of ὁράω; Fίδ (aor. tense stem) + ειν (aor. act. inf. ending) › ἰδεῖν (F was not used in the Koine era). TH: complementary inf. with ἐπιποθῶ.

[2] μεταδίδωμι, *I impart, give, share.* MH: aor. act. subj. 1st sg. of μεταδίδωμι = μετα (prep) + δο (aor. tense stem) + ω (lenth. connecting vowel) + ω (1st sg. ending) › μεταδῶ (ο + ω = ω).

[3] χάρισμα, ατος, τό, *gift.*

[4] πνευματικός, ή, όν, *spiritual.*

[5] στηρίζω, *I strengthen, establish.* MH: aor. pass. inf. The root is στηριγ; γ + θ = χθ. TH: εἰς τὸ + inf. indicates purpose; *in order to strengthen.*

[6] συμπαρακαλέω, *I am mutually encouraged, comforted.* MH: aor. pass. inf.; aor. tense stem is συμπαρακλη.

[7] TH: τε καὶ, *both … and.*

[8] TH: acc. subject of the inf. ἀγνοεῖν.

[9] ἀγνοέω, *I am unaware, ignorant (of).* TH: complementary inf. with θέλω.

[10] πολλάκις, *often, many times.*

[11] προτίθημι, *I intend, plan.* MH: the root of τίθημι is θε; προ (prep.) + ε (aug.) + θε (aor. tense stem) + μην (aor. mid. indic. 1st sg. ending) › προεθέμην.

[12] MH: aor. act. inf. of ἔρχομαι; aor. tense stem is ἐλθ. TH: complementary inf. with προεθέμην.

[13] κωλύω, *I prevent, hinder.*

[14] ἄχρι, *until.*

[15] δεῦρο, *now, the present time.*

[16] MH: from ἔχω; the root is σεχ; σεχ › σχ (aor. tense stem; ε drop due to ablaut) + ω (lengthened connecting vowel) + – (aor. act. subj. 1st sg. ending) › σχῶ.

[17] TH: καὶ … καὶ, *both … and.*

[18] Ἕλλην, ηνος, ὁ, *Greek; civilized.*

[19] βάρβαρος, ον, *barbarian, non-Greek; uncivilized.*

[20] σοφός, ή, όν, *wise, intelligent.*

[21] ἀνόητος, ον, *foolish, unintelligent.*

ὀφειλέτης[1] εἰμί· **15** οὕτως τὸ κατ᾽ ἐμὲ πρόθυμον[2] καὶ[3]
ὑμῖν τοῖς[4] ἐν Ῥώμῃ[5] εὐαγγελίσασθαι.[6]

16 Οὐ γὰρ ἐπαισχύνομαι[7] τὸ ⸀εὐαγγέλιον, δύναμις[8] γὰρ
θεοῦ ἐστιν εἰς[9] σωτηρίαν[10] παντὶ τῷ πιστεύοντι[11],
Ἰουδαίῳ τε πρῶτον καὶ Ἕλληνι·[12] **17** δικαιοσύνη γὰρ θεοῦ
ἐν αὐτῷ ἀποκαλύπτεται[13] ἐκ[14] πίστεως εἰς[15] πίστιν,
καθὼς γέγραπται· Ὁ δὲ δίκαιος ἐκ πίστεως ζήσεται.

18 Ἀποκαλύπτεται[16] γὰρ ὀργὴ[17] θεοῦ ἀπ᾽ οὐρανοῦ ἐπὶ
πᾶσαν ἀσέβειαν[18] καὶ ἀδικίαν[19] ἀνθρώπων τῶν[20] τὴν
ἀλήθειαν ἐν[21] ἀδικίᾳ[22] κατεχόντων,[23] **19** διότι[24] τὸ γνωστὸν[25]

---

[1] ὀφειλέτης, ου, ὁ, *debtor, one who is under obligation.* TH: pred. nom. to the implied subject of εἰμί.

[2] πρόθυμος, ον, *eager.* TH: τὸ agrees with πρόθυμον (subject), bracketing the prep. phrase κατ᾽ ἐμὲ; *My eagerness is …*

[3] TH: καὶ is additive; *also.*

[4] TH: τοῖς nominalizes the prep. phrase ἐν Ῥώμῃ; *to those in Rome.*

[5] Ῥώμη, ης, ἡ, *Rome.*

[6] MH: aor. mid. inf.; the root ends in δ; δ + σ = σ. TH: inf. is functioning as the dir. obj. of the implied verb; *my eagerness is to preach the gospel.*

[7] ἐπαισχύνομαι, *I am ashamed (of).*

[8] TH: δύναμις is fronted and is a pred. nom. to the implied subject of the verb ἐστιν; *it is the power.*

[9] TH: εἰς indicates purpose; *for.*

[10] σωτηρία, ας, ἡ, *salvation.*

[11] TH: τῷ πιστεύοντι is a subst. prtc.; with παντὶ, *to everyone who believes.*

[12] Ἕλλην, ηνος, ὁ, *Greek; civilized.*

[13] ἀποκαλύπτω, *I reveal, make fully known.*

[14] TH: ἐκ is being used to indicate means; *by.*

[15] TH: εἰς is being used to indicate purpose; *for.*

[16] ἀποκαλύπτω, *I reveal, make fully known.*

[17] ὀργή, ῆς, ἡ, *wrath.*

[18] ἀσέβεια, ας, ἡ, *ungodliness, impiety.*

[19] ἀδικία, ας, ἡ, *unrighteousness, injustice.*

[20] TH: τῶν agrees with the subst. prtc. κατεχόντων, bracketing both τὴν ἀλήθειαν and ἐν ἀδικίᾳ; *those who suppress the truth by unrighteousness.*

[21] TH: ἐν is instrumental; *by.*

[22] ἀδικία, ας, ἡ, *unrighteousness, injustice.*

[23] κατέχω, I *restrain, hold back,* ***suppress.***

[24] διότι, *because, for.*

[25] γνωστός, ή, όν, *what can be known.*

τοῦ θεοῦ[1] φανερόν[2] ἐστιν ἐν αὐτοῖς, ὁ θεὸς γὰρ αὐτοῖς
ἐφανέρωσεν[3]. **20** τὰ γὰρ ἀόρατα[4] αὐτοῦ ἀπὸ κτίσεως[5]
κόσμου τοῖς ποιήμασιν[6] νοούμενα[7] καθορᾶται[8], ἥ τε
ἀΐδιος[9] αὐτοῦ δύναμις καὶ θειότης[10], εἰς τὸ εἶναι[11] αὐτοὺς
ἀναπολογήτους[12], **21** διότι[13] γνόντες[14] τὸν θεὸν οὐχ ὡς
θεὸν ἐδόξασαν ἢ ηὐχαρίστησαν[15], ἀλλὰ ἐματαιώ-θησαν[16]
ἐν τοῖς διαλογισμοῖς[17] αὐτῶν καὶ ἐσκοτίσθη[18]
ἡ ἀσύνετος[19] αὐτῶν καρδία· **22** φάσκοντες[20] εἶναι σοφοὶ[21]

---

[1] TH: τοῦ θεοῦ is an objective gen.; *about God.*

[2] φανερός, ά, όν, *evident, visible.*

[3] φανερόω, *I reveal, make known.* MH: ο lengthens to ω before tense formative.

[4] ἀόρατος, όν, *invisible, unseen.* TH: ἀόρατα is a subst. adj.; *invisible things/attributes.*

[5] κτίσις, εως, ἡ, *creation.*

[6] ποίημα, ατος, τό, *that which is made, creation.*

[7] νοέω, *I understand, think through carefully.* MH: the root (νοε) ends in a vowel, so the connecting vowel contracts (ε + ο = ου).

[8] καθοράω, *I perceive, discern.* MH: the root (καθορα) ends in a vowel, so the connecting vowel contracts (α + ε = α).

[9] ἀΐδιος, ον, *eternal.*

[10] θειότης, ητος, ἡ, *divine nature.* TH: ἥ τε ἀΐδιος αὐτοῦ δύναμις καὶ θειότης is an attrib. adj. phrase. αὐτοῦ appears after ἀΐδιος, which is modifying both δύναμις and θειότης. These two nom. are in app. to the subject ἀόρατα; *both his eternal power and divine nature.*

[11] TH: εἰς τὸ + inf. is indicating result; *so that they are.*

[12] ἀναπολόγητος, ον, *without excuse.*

[13] διότι, *because, for.*

[14] TH: γνόντες is a prtc. of concession; *though they knew.*

[15] εὐχαριστέω, *I give thanks.* MH: ε lengthens to η before tense formative.

[16] ματαιόω, *I render worthless.* MH: ο lengthens to ω before tense formative.

[17] διαλογισμός, *reasoning.*

[18] σκοτίζω, *I become dark, darken.* MH: the root is σκοτιδ; δ + θ = σθ.

[19] ἀσύνετος, ον, *foolish, senseless.* TH: ἀσύνετος is an attrib. adj. modifying καρδία; *their foolish heart.*

[20] φάσκω, *I claim, assert.* TH: φάσκοντες is a participle of concession; *although they claimed.*

[21] σοφός, ή, όν, *wise, intelligent.*

ἐμωράνθησαν[1], **23** καὶ ἤλλαξαν[2] τὴν δόξαν τοῦ ἀφθάρτου[3]
θεοῦ ἐν[4] ὁμοιώματι[5] εἰκόνος[6] φθαρτοῦ[7] ἀνθρώπου καὶ
πετεινῶν[8] καὶ τετραπόδων[9] καὶ ἑρπετῶν[10].

24 ⸀Διὸ παρέδωκεν[11] αὐτοὺς ὁ θεὸς ἐν[12] ταῖς ἐπι-
θυμίαις[13] τῶν καρδιῶν αὐτῶν εἰς ἀκαθαρσίαν[14] τοῦ
ἀτιμάζεσθαι[15] τὰ σώματα αὐτῶν ἐν ⸀αὐτοῖς, **25** οἵτινες[16]
μετήλλαξαν[17] τὴν ἀλήθειαν τοῦ θεοῦ ἐν[18] τῷ ψεύδει[19], καὶ
ἐσεβάσθησαν[20] καὶ ἐλάτρευσαν[21] τῇ κτίσει[22] παρὰ[23] τὸν
κτίσαντα,[24] ὅς ἐστιν εὐλογητὸς[25] εἰς τοὺς αἰῶνας· ἀμήν.

---

[1] μωραίνω, *I make foolish*. MH: aor. tense stem is μωραν.

[2] ἀλλάσσω, *I exchange*. MH: aor. tense stem is ἀλλαγ; γ + σ = ξ.

[3] ἄφθαρτος, ον, *immortal, imperishable*.

[4] TH: when ἐν follows ἀλλάσσω; *I exchange … for*.

[5] ὁμοίωμα, ατος, τό, *likeness*.

[6] εἰκών, όνος, ἡ, *image*.

[7] φθαρτός, ή, όν, *perishable*.

[8] πετεινόν, ή, όν, *bird*.

[9] τετράπους, ουν, *four footed*. TH: τετραπόδων is a subst. adj.; *four-footed animals*.

[10] ἑρπετόν, οῦ, τό, *reptile*.

[11] MH: from παραδίδωμι. The root is παραδο. The ο lengthens to ω before tense formative. δίδωμι belongs to a small group of verbs called "*kappa* aorists."

[12] TH: ἐν is functioning like εἰς; *to*.

[13] ἐπιθυμία, ας, ἡ, *desire, lust*.

[14] ἀκαθαρσία, ας, ἡ, *impurity, immorality*.

[15] ἀτιμάζω, *I dishonor, shame*. TH: τοῦ + inf. can indicate result; τοῦ ἀτιμάζεσθαι τὰ σώματα αὐτῶν, *resulting in their bodies being dishonored*.

[16] TH: οἵτινες is a rel. prn. referring to the ante. ἀνθρώπων in v. 18; *they*.

[17] μεταλλάσσω, *I exchange*. MH: the aor. tense stem is μεταλλαγ; γ + σ = ξ.

[18] TH: when ἐν follows μεταλλάσσω; *I exchange … for*.

[19] ψεῦδος, ους, τό, *lie*.

[20] σεβάζομαι, *I worship, revere*. MH: the root is σεβαδ; δ + θ = σθ.

[21] λατρεύω, *I serve*.

[22] κτίσις, εως, ἡ, *creation*.

[23] TH: παρὰ is functioning comparatively indicating exclusion; *instead of*.

[24] κτίζω, *I create*. TH: subst. prtc. *the Creating One*

[25] εὐλογητός, ή, όν, *blessed, praised*.

26 Διὰ τοῦτο παρέδωκεν αὐτοὺς ὁ θεὸς εἰς πάθη[1]
ἀτιμίας[2]· αἵ τε[3] γὰρ θήλειαι[4] αὐτῶν μετήλλαξαν[5] τὴν
φυσικὴν[6] χρῆσιν[7] εἰς[8] τὴν παρὰ[9] φύσιν[10], **27** ὁμοίως[11] τε
καὶ[12] οἱ ἄρσενες[13] ἀφέντες[14] τὴν φυσικὴν[15] χρῆσιν[16] τῆς
θηλείας[17] ἐξεκαύθησαν[18] ἐν τῇ ὀρέξει[19] αὐτῶν εἰς
ἀλλήλους, ἄρσενες[20] ἐν[21] ἄρσεσιν[22] τὴν ἀσχημοσύνην[23]
κατεργαζόμενοι[24] καὶ τὴν ἀντιμισθίαν[25] ἣν[26] ἔδει τῆς
πλάνης[27] αὐτῶν ἐν ʽἑαυτοῖς ἀπολαμβάνοντες.[28]

---

[1] πάθος, ους, τό, *passion.*

[2] ἀτιμία, ας, ἡ, *shame, dishonor, disgrace.* TH: attrib. gen.; *shameful passions.*

[3] TH: τε connects this clause to the parallel τε clause in v. 27; *both … and.*

[4] θῆλυς, υ, *female.*

[5] μεταλλάσσω, *I exchange.* MH: the aor. tense stem is μεταλλαγ; γ + σ =ξ.

[6] φυσικός, ή, όν, *natural.*

[7] χρῆσις, εως, ἡ, *relations.*

[8] TH: when εἰς follows μεταλλάσσω; *I exchange … for.*

[9] TH: παρὰ is indicating opposition; *against.*

[10] φύσις, εως, ἡ, *nature.* TH: χρῆσιν is implied here; τὴν παρὰ φύσιν, *the relations against nature.*

[11] ὁμοίως, *likewise, in the same way.*

[12] TH: καὶ is ascensive; *also.*

[13] ἄρσην, εν, *male, man.*

[14] MH: aor. act. prtc. nom. pl. masc. from ἀφίημι.

[15] φυσικός, ή, όν, *natural.*

[16] χρῆσις, εως, ἡ, *relations.*

[17] θῆλυς, υ, *female.*

[18] ἐκκαίω, *I am inflamed.* MH: the root is ἐκκαF; the *digamma* F becomes υ in tenses other than pres. When the aug. is added, the κ of the prep. becomes ξ.

[19] ὄρεξις, εως, ἡ, *desire, lust.*

[20] ἄρσην, εν, *male, man.*

[21] TH: ἐν is indicating association; *with.*

[22] ἄρσην, εν, *male, man.*

[23] ἀσχημοσύνη, ης, ἡ, *shameless acts.*

[24] κατεργάζομαι, *I do, commit, bring about.*

[25] ἀντιμισθία, ας, ἡ, *penalty.*

[26] TH: rel. pron. refers to ἀντιμισθίαν; ἣν ἔδει, *which is due.*

[27] πλάνη, ης, ἡ, *deceit, error.*

[28] ἀπολαμβάνω, *I receive, take away.*

28 Καὶ καθὼς οὐκ ἐδοκίμασαν [1] τὸν θεὸν ἔχειν ἐν
ἐπιγνώσει,[2] παρέδωκεν αὐτοὺς ὁ θεὸς εἰς ἀδόκιμον[3] νοῦν,
[4] ποιεῖν τὰ μὴ καθήκοντα,[5] **29** πεπληρωμένους [6] πάσῃ
⸀ἀδικίᾳ[7] πονηρίᾳ[8] πλεονεξίᾳ[9] κακίᾳ[10], μεστοὺς[11] φθόνου[12]
φόνου [13] ἔριδος [14] δόλου [15] κακοηθείας, [16] ψιθυριστάς, [17]
30 καταλάλους,[18] θεοστυγεῖς,[19] ὑβριστάς,[20] ὑπερηφάνους,[21]
ἀλαζόνας, [22] ἐφευρετὰς [23] κακῶν, γονεῦσιν [24] ἀπειθεῖς, [25]
31 ἀσυνέτους,[26] ἀσυνθέτους,[27] ⸀ἀστόργους,[28] ἀνελεήμονας·[29]

---

[1] δοκιμάζω, *I test, approve, **see fit***. MH: the root is δοκιμαδ; δ + σ = σ.

[2] ἐπίγνωσις, εως, ἡ, *knowledge, recognition*. TH: τὸν θεὸν ἔχειν ἐν ἐπιγνώσει, *to acknowledge God*.

[3] ἀδόκιμος, ον, *not approved, worthless*.

[4] νοῦς, ός, ὁ, *mind, way of thinking*.

[5] καθήκω, *I am fitting, am appropriate*. TH: καθήκοντα is a participle functioning substantivally; τὰ μὴ καθήκοντα, *what ought not be done*.

[6] MH: the ο of πληρόω lengthens to ω before the tense formative.

[7] ἀδικία, ας, ἡ, *unrighteousness, injustice*.

[8] πονηρία, ας, ἡ, *wickedness, sinfulness, **evil***.

[9] πλεονεξία, ας, ἡ, *greediness*.

[10] κακία, ας, ἡ, *malice, wickedness*.

[11] μεστός, ή, όν, *full*.

[12] φθόνος, ου, ὁ, *envy, jealousy*.

[13] φόνος, ου, ὁ, *murder*.

[14] ἔρις, ιδος, ἡ, *strife*.

[15] δόλος, ου, ὁ, *deceit*.

[16] κακοήθεια, ας, ἡ, *malice*.

[17] ψιθυριστής, οῦ, ὁ, *gossiper*.

[18] κατάλαλος, ου, ὁ, *slanderer*.

[19] θεοστυγής, ές, *God-hater*.

[20] ὑβριστής, οῦ, ὁ, *insolent*.

[21] ὑπερήφανος, ου, ὁ, *arrogant, proud*.

[22] ἀλαζών, όνος, ὁ, *boastful*.

[23] ἐφευρετής, οῦ, ὁ, *inventor*.

[24] γονεύς, έως, ὁ, *parent*.

[25] ἀπειθής, ές, *disobedient*.

[26] ἀσύνετος, ον, *foolish, senseless*.

[27] ἀσύνθετος, ον, *untrustworthy, faithless*.

[28] ἄστοργος, ον, *unloving, heartless*.

[29] ἀνελεήμων, ον, *unmerciful, ruthless*.

32 οἵτινες[1] τὸ δικαίωμα[2] τοῦ θεοῦ ἐπιγνόντες,[3] ὅτι οἱ τὰ
τοιαῦτα πράσσοντες[4] ἄξιοι[5] θανάτου εἰσίν, οὐ μόνον
αὐτὰ ποιοῦσιν ἀλλὰ καὶ[6] συνευδοκοῦσιν[7] τοῖς πράσσουσιν.[8]

1:1 **Χριστοῦ Ἰησοῦ** Treg NA28] Ἰησοῦ Χριστοῦ WH RP
1:1 **Χριστοῦ Ἰησοῦ** Treg NA28] Ἰησοῦ Χριστοῦ WH RP
8 **περὶ** WH Treg NA28] ὑπὲρ RP
16 **εὐαγγέλιον** WH Treg NA28] + τοῦ χριστοῦ RP
19 **θεὸς γὰρ** WH Treg NA28] γὰρ θεὸς RP
19 **θεὸς γὰρ** WH Treg NA28] γὰρ θεὸς RP
24 **Διὸ** WH Treg NA28] + καὶ RP
- **αὐτοῖς** WH Treg NA28] ἑαυτοῖς RP
27 **ἑαυτοῖς** Treg NA28 RP] αὑτοῖς WH
29 **ἀδικίᾳ** WH Treg NA28] + πορνείᾳ RP
31 **ἀστόργους** WH Treg NA28] + ἀσπόνδους RP

---

1 TH: οἵτινες is a rel. prn. referring to the ante. ἀνθρώπων in v. 18; *they.*
2 δικαίωμα, ατος, τό, *requirement, righteous deed.*
3 ἐπιγινώσκω, *I know.* MH: the root is ἐπιγνο. TH: ἐπιγνόντες is a prtc. implying concession; *although they know.*
4 πράσσω, *I do, engage in,* ***practice.*** TH: subst. prtc.; οἱ τὰ τοιαῦτα πράσσοντες, *those who practice such things.*
5 ἄξιος, ία, ον, *deserving, worthy.*
6 TH: καὶ is additive; *also.*
7 συνευδοκέω, *I approve of.* TH: takes dative dir. obj.
8 πράσσω, *I do, engage in,* ***practice.*** TH: subst. prtc.; dative dir. obj.

ROMANS 2

New Vocabulary by Frequency [Chapter, Book, SBLGNT Occurrences]

ἀγνοέω, *I do not know, do not realize* [1, 6, 22]
ἀδικία, ας, ἡ, *unrighteousness, injustice* [1, 7, 25]
ἀκροατής, οῦ, ὁ, *hearer* [1, 1, 4]
ἀκροβυστία, ας, ἡ, *uncircumcision* [4, 11, 20]
ἁμαρτάνω, *I sin, do wrong* [2, 7, 43]
ἀμετανόητος, ον, *unrepentant* [1, 1, 1]
ἀναπολόγητος, ον, *without excuse* [1, 2, 2]
ἀνόμως, *lawless, without law* [2, 2, 2]
ἀνοχή, ῆς, ἡ, *forbearance, tolerance* [1, 2, 2]
ἀπειθέω, *I disobey, am disobedient* [1, 5, 14]
ἀποδίδωμι, *I repay, render* [1, 3, 48]
ἀποκάλυψις, εως, ἡ, *revelation* [1, 2, 17]
ἀπολογέομαι, *I defend* [1, 1, 10]
ἀτιμάζω, *I dishonor, shame* [1, 2, 7]
ἀφθαρσία, ας, ἡ, *immortality* [1, 1, 7]
ἄφρων, ον, *foolish* [1, 1, 11]
βδελύσσομαι, *I abhor, detest* [1, 1 ,2]
βλασφημέω, *I speak impiously, blaspheme* [1, 3, 34]
γνῶσις, εως, ἡ, *knowledge* [1, 3, 29]
γράμμα, ατος, τό, *letter* [2, 3, 14]
γραπτός, ή, όν, *written* [1, 1, 1]
διαφέρω, *I carry over, excel in* [1, 1, 13]
δικαιοκρισία, ας, ἡ, *righteous judgment, just verdict* [1, 1, 1]
δικαιόω, *I justify, declare righteous* [1, 15, 39]
δικαίωμα, ατος, τό, *requirement, righteous deed* [1, 5, 10]
δοκιμάζω, *I test, approve* [1, 4, 22]
εἴδωλον, ου, τό, *idol, image* [1, 1, 11]
ἐκφεύγω, *I escape* [1, 1, 8]
Ἕλλην, ηνος, ὁ, *Greek, civilized* [2, 6, 25]
ἐνδείκνυμι, *I show, point out* [1, 3, 11]
ἔπαινος, ου, ὁ, *praise, approval* [1, 2, 11]
ἐπαναπαύομαι, *I rely on, rest upon* [1, 1, 2]
ἐπονομάζω, *I call, name* [1, 1, 1]
ἐργάζομαι, *I work, labor, do* [1, 4, 41]
ἐριθεία, ας, ἡ, *selfish ambition* [1, 1, 7]
θησαυρίζω, *I store up, gather* [1, 1, 8]

θλῖψις, εως, ἡ, *affliction, tribulation* [1, 5, 45]
θυμός, οῦ, ὁ, *passion, anger, rage* [1, 1, 18]
ἱεροσυλέω, *I rob temples* [1, 1, 1]
κατακρίνω, *I pronounce a sentence on* [1, 4, 17]
καταφρονέω, *I treat with contempt, have little regard for* [1, 1, 9]
κατεργάζομαι, *I do, commit, bring about* [1, 11, 22]
κατηγορέω, *I speak against, accuse* [1, 1, 23]
κατηχέω, *I teach, instruct* [1, 1, 8]
καυχάομαι, *I boast* [2, 5, 35]
κλέπτω, *I steal* [2, 3, 13]
κρίμα, ατος, τό, *judgment* [2, 6, 27]
κρυπτός, ή, όν, *hidden, secret* [2, 2, 17]
λογίζομαι, *I regard, consider* [2, 19, 40]
λογισμός, οῦ, ὁ, *thought, reasoning* [1, 1, 2]
μακροθυμία, ας, ἡ, *patience, steadfastness* [1, 2, 14]
μετάνοια, ας, ἡ, *repentance* [1, 1, 22]
μεταξύ, *between, in the midst of* [1, 1, 9]
μοιχεύω, *I commit adultery* [2, 3, 15]
μόρφωσις, εως, ἡ, *form, embodiment* [1, 1, 2]
νήπιος, ία, ον, *infant, child* [1, 1, 14]
ὁδηγός, οῦ, ὁ, *guide, leader* [1, 1, 5]
ὀργή, ῆς, ἡ, *wrath* [3, 12, 36]
παιδευτής, οῦ, ὁ, *educator, instructor* [1, 1, 2]
παράβασις, εως, ἡ, *transgression* [1, 3, 7]
παραβάτης, ου, ὁ, *transgressor* [2, 2, 5]
περιτομή, ῆς, ἡ, *circumcision* [6, 15, 36]
πλοῦτος, ου, ὁ, *wealth, riches* [1, 5, 22]
ποιητής, οῦ, ὁ, *doer, one who does something* [1, 1, 6]
πράσσω, *I do, engage in* [4, 10, 38]
προσωπολημψία, ας, ἡ, *partiality* [1, 1, 4]
σεαυτοῦ, ῆς, *yourself* [4, 6, 43]
σκληρότης, ητος, ἡ, *hardness, stubbornness* [1, 1, 1]
σκότος, ους, τό, *darkness* [1, 2, 30]
στενοχωρία, ας, ἡ, *distress, trouble* [1, 2, 4]
συμμαρτυρέω, *I bear witness with* [1, 3, 3]
συνείδησις, εως, ἡ, *conscience* [1, 3, 30]
τελέω, *I fulfill, complete* [1, 2, 28]
τιμή, ῆς, ἡ, *honor* [2, 6, 41]
ὑπομονή, ῆς, ἡ, *endurance, perseverance* [1, 6, 32]
φανερός, ά, όν, *evident, visible* [2, 3, 18]
φυλάσσω, *I keep, guard* [1, 1, 31]

φύσις, εως, ἡ, *nature* [2, 7, 14]
χρηστός, ή, όν, *reputable, kind* [1, 1, 7]
χρηστότης, ητος, ἡ, *kindness, generosity* [1, 5, 10]
ὦ, *O!, Oh* [2, 4, 17]
ὠφελέω, *I help, am of use* [1, 1, 15]

2.1 Διὸ ἀναπολόγητος[1] εἶ, ὦ[2] ἄνθρωπε πᾶς ὁ κρίνων·[3]
ἐν[4] ᾧ γὰρ κρίνεις τὸν ἕτερον, σεαυτὸν[5] κατακρίνεις,[6] τὰ
γὰρ αὐτὰ[7] πράσσεις[8] ὁ κρίνων·[9] **2** οἴδαμεν δὲ ὅτι τὸ
κρίμα[10] τοῦ θεοῦ ἐστιν κατὰ ἀλήθειαν ἐπὶ τοὺς τὰ
τοιαῦτα πράσσοντας.[11] **3** λογίζῃ[12] δὲ τοῦτο, ὦ[13] ἄνθρωπε ὁ
κρίνων[14] τοὺς τὰ τοιαῦτα πράσσοντας[15] καὶ ποιῶν αὐτά,[16]
ὅτι σὺ ἐκφεύξῃ[17] τὸ κρίμα[18] τοῦ θεοῦ; **4** ἢ τοῦ πλούτου[19]
τῆς χρηστότητος[20] αὐτοῦ καὶ τῆς ἀνοχῆς[21] καὶ
τῆς μακροθυμίας[22] καταφρονεῖς,[23] ἀγνοῶν[24] ὅτι τὸ

---

[1] ἀναπολόγητος, ον, *without excuse.*

[2] ὦ, *O!, Oh.* TH: ὦ + voc. occurs 8 times in the NT, 3 times in Romans. It emphasizes the direct address. ὦ ἄνθρωπε, *O person.*

[3] TH: the nom. phrase πᾶς ὁ κρίνων is in app. to the voc. ἄνθρωπε; *O person, everyone who judges.*

[4] TH: ἐν is indicating manner; with ᾧ, *by which standards.*

[5] σεαυτοῦ, ῆς, *yourself.*

[6] κατακρίνω, *I pronounce a sentence on,* ***condemn.***

[7] TH: τὰ … αὐτὰ is indentical (i.e., "same") use of αὐτός; *the same things.*

[8] πράσσω, *I do, engage in,* ***practice.***

[9] TH: ὁ κρίνων is in app. to the 2nd nom. sg. pron. implied as the subject of πράσσεις; *you, the one judging, practice ….*

[10] κρίμα, ατος, τό, *judgment.*

[11] πράσσω, *I do, engage in,* ***practice.***

[12] λογίζομαι, *I regard, consider,* ***think.***

[13] ὦ, *O!, Oh.* TH: ὦ + voc. occurs 8 times in the NT, 3 times in Romans. It emphasizes the direct address. ὦ ἄνθρωπε, *O person.*

[14] TH: the phrase ὁ κρίνων is in app. to the voc. ἄνθρωπε; *O person who judges.*

[15] πράσσω, *I do, engage in,* ***practice.***

[16] TH: ὦ ἄνθρωπε ὁ κρίνων τοὺς τὰ τοιαῦτα πράσσοντας καὶ ποιῶν αὐτά, *O person who judges the ones doing such things and also does them.*

[17] ἐκφεύγω, *I escape.* MH: γ + σ = ξ.

[18] κρίμα, ατος, τό, *judgment.*

[19] πλοῦτος, ου, ὁ, *wealth, riches.*

[20] χρηστότης, ητος, ἡ, *kindness, generosity.*

[21] ἀνοχή, ῆς, ἡ, *forbearance, tolerance.*

[22] μακροθυμία, ας, ἡ, *patience, steadfastness.* TH: πλούτου, ἀνοχῆς, and μακροθυμίας are gen. dir. obj. of καταφρονεῖς.

[23] καταφρονέω, *I treat with contempt, have little regard for.*

[24] ἀγνοέω, *I do not know, do not realize.* MH: the root (ἀγνοε) ends in a vowel, so the connecting vowel contracts (ε + ω = ω).

χρηστὸν[1] τοῦ θεοῦ εἰς μετάνοιάν[2] σε ἄγει; **5** κατὰ δὲ τὴν
σκληρότητά [3] σου καὶ ἀμετανόητον [4] καρδίαν
θησαυρίζεις [5] σεαυτῷ [6] ὀργὴν [7] ἐν ἡμέρᾳ ὀργῆς [8] καὶ
⸀ἀποκαλύψεως[9] δικαιοκρισίας[10] τοῦ θεοῦ, **6** ὃς ἀποδώσει[11]
ἑκάστῳ κατὰ τὰ ἔργα αὐτοῦ· **7** τοῖς[12] μὲν καθ᾽ ὑπομονὴν[13]
ἔργου ἀγαθοῦ δόξαν καὶ τιμὴν [14] καὶ ἀφθαρσίαν [15]
ζητοῦσιν ζωὴν αἰώνιον·[16] **8** τοῖς[17] δὲ ἐξ ἐριθείας[18] καὶ
⸀ἀπειθοῦσι [19] τῇ ἀληθείᾳ πειθομένοις δὲ τῇ ἀδικίᾳ [20]
⸂ὀργὴ [21] καὶ θυμός [22]⸃, **9** θλῖψις [23] καὶ στενοχωρία,[24] ἐπὶ
πᾶσαν ψυχὴν ἀνθρώπου τοῦ κατεργαζομένου[25] τὸ κακόν,

---

[1] χρηστός, ή, όν, *reputable, kind*. TH: when used as a subst.; *kindness*.
[2] μετάνοια, ας, ἡ, *repentance*.
[3] σκληρότης, ητος, ἡ, *hardness, stubbornness*.
[4] ἀμετανόητος, ον, *unrepentant*.
[5] θησαυρίζω, *I store up, gather*.
[6] σεαυτοῦ, ῆς, *yourself*.
[7] ὀργή, ῆς, ἡ, *wrath*.
[8] ὀργή, ῆς, ἡ, *wrath*.
[9] ἀποκάλυψις, εως, ἡ, *revelation*.
[10] δικαιοκρισία, ας, ἡ, *righteous judgment, just verdict*.
[11] ἀποδίδωμι, *I repay, render*. MH: The root is δο. The ο lengthens to ω before the tense formative.
[12] TH: τοῖς is the art. for prtc. ζητοῦσιν.
[13] ὑπομονή, ῆς, ἡ, *endurance, perseverance*.
[14] τιμή, ῆς, ἡ, *honor*.
[15] ἀφθαρσία, ας, ἡ, *immortality*. TH: δόξαν … τιμὴν … ἀφθαρσίαν are dir. obj. for the prtc. ζητοῦσιν.
[16] TH: the acc. phrase ζωὴν αἰώνιον serves as the dir. obj. for the verb ἀποδώσει from the previous verse.
[17] TH: τοῖς is the art. for the two prtc., ἀπειθοῦσι and πειθομένοις.
[18] ἐριθεία, ας, ἡ, *selfish ambition*.
[19] ἀπειθέω, *I disobey, am disobedient*.
[20] ἀδικία, ας, ἡ, *unrighteousness, injustice*.
[21] ὀργή, ῆς, ἡ, *wrath*.
[22] θυμός, οῦ, ὁ, *passion, anger, rage*. TH: ὀργὴ καὶ θυμός are the subjects; *wrath and anger are for the ones*.
[23] θλῖψις, εως, ἡ, *affliction, tribulation*.
[24] στενοχωρία, ας, ἡ, *distress, trouble*. TH: this is a verbless sentence, so a verb needs to be supplied; *will come*.
[25] κατεργάζομαι, *I do, commit, bring about*.

Ἰουδαίου τε πρῶτον καὶ Ἕλληνος·[1] **10** δόξα δὲ καὶ τιμὴ[2]
καὶ εἰρήνη παντὶ τῷ ἐργαζομένῳ[3] τὸ ἀγαθόν, Ἰουδαίῳ τε
πρῶτον καὶ Ἕλληνι·[4] **11** οὐ γάρ ἐστιν προσωπολημψία[5]
παρὰ τῷ θεῷ.

12 Ὅσοι γὰρ ἀνόμως[6] ἥμαρτον,[7] ἀνόμως[8] καὶ[9]
ἀπολοῦνται·[10] καὶ ὅσοι ἐν νόμῳ ἥμαρτον,[11] διὰ νόμου
κριθήσονται·[12] **13** οὐ γὰρ οἱ ἀκροαταὶ[13] ⸀νόμου δίκαιοι[14]
παρὰ ⸀τῷ θεῷ, ἀλλʼ οἱ ποιηταὶ[15] ⸀νόμου δικαιωθήσονται.[16]
14 ὅταν γὰρ ἔθνη τὰ μὴ νόμον ἔχοντα[17] φύσει[18] τὰ[19] τοῦ
νόμου ⸀ποιῶσιν,[20] οὗτοι νόμον μὴ ἔχοντες ἑαυτοῖς εἰσιν
νόμος·[21] **15** οἵτινες ἐνδείκνυνται[22] τὸ ἔργον τοῦ νόμου
γραπτὸν[23] ἐν ταῖς καρδίαις αὐτῶν, συμμαρτυρούσης[24]

---

[1] Ἕλλην, ηνος, ὁ, *Greek; civilized.*
[2] τιμή, ῆς, ἡ, *honor.*
[3] ἐργάζομαι, *I work, labor, do.*
[4] Ἕλλην, ηνος, ὁ, *Greek; civilized.*
[5] προσωπολημψία, ας, ἡ, *partiality.* TH: προσωπολημψία is a pred. nom. to the implied subject of ἐστιν.
[6] ἀνόμως, *lawlessly, without law.*
[7] ἁμαρτάνω, *I sin, do wrong.* MH: 2nd aor.; root is ἁμαρτ.
[8] ἀνόμως, *lawlessly, without law.*
[9] TH: καὶ is additive; *also.*
[10] MH: fut. stem of ἀπόλλυμι = ἀπολ + εσ (tense formative) + ονται (3rd pl. ending) › ἀπολοῦνται (intervocalic σ drops out; ε + ο = ου).
[11] ἁμαρτάνω, *I sin, do wrong.* MH: 2nd aor.; root is ἁμαρτ.
[12] MH: from κρίνω; ν drops out in fut. pass.
[13] ἀκροατής, οῦ, ὁ, *hearer.*
[14] TH: δίκαιοι is a pred. adj. to the subject οἱ ἀκροαταὶ.
[15] ποιητής, οῦ, ὁ, *doer, one who does something.*
[16] δικαιόω, *I justify, declare righteous.* MH: the ο lengthens to ω before the ending.
[17] TH: τὰ … ἔχοντα is attrib. to the subject ἔθνη.
[18] φύσις, εως, ἡ, *nature.*
[19] TH: τὰ substantivizes τοῦ νόμου; *the (things) of the law.*
[20] MH: pres. act. subj. 3rd pl.
[21] TH: νόμος is a pred. nom. to the subject οὗτοι
[22] ἐνδείκνυμι, *I show, point out.* MH: pres. mid. indic. 3rd pl.
[23] γραπτός, ή, όν, *written.*
[24] συμμαρτυρέω, *I bear witness with.* MH: the root (συμμαρτυρε) ends in a vowel, so the connecting vowel contracts (ε + ου = ου).

αὐτῶν τῆς συνειδήσεως [1] καὶ μεταξὺ [2] ἀλλήλων τῶν
λογισμῶν[3] κατηγορούντων[4] ἢ καὶ[5] ἀπολογουμένων,[6] **16** ἐν
⸂ἡμέρᾳ ὅτε⸃ ⸀κρίνει[7] ὁ θεὸς τὰ κρυπτὰ[8] τῶν ἀνθρώπων
κατὰ τὸ εὐαγγέλιόν μου διὰ ⸂Χριστοῦ Ἰησοῦ⸃.

17 ⸂Εἰ δὲ⸃ σὺ Ἰουδαῖος ἐπονομάζῃ[9] καὶ ἐπαναπαύῃ[10]
⸀νόμῳ καὶ καυχᾶσαι[11] ἐν θεῷ **18** καὶ γινώσκεις τὸ θέλημα
καὶ δοκιμάζεις[12] τὰ διαφέροντα[13] κατηχούμενος[14] ἐκ τοῦ
νόμου, **19** πέποιθάς[15] τε σεαυτὸν[16] ὁδηγὸν[17] εἶναι τυφλῶν,
φῶς τῶν [18] ἐν σκότει, [19] **20** παιδευτὴν [20] ἀφρόνων, [21]
διδάσκαλον νηπίων, [22] ἔχοντα τὴν μόρφωσιν [23] τῆς

---

[1] συνείδησις, εως, ἡ, *conscience*. TH: τῆς συνειδήσεως is the subject of the gen. abs. construction with συμμαρτυρούσης.

[2] μεταξύ, *between, in the midst of.*

[3] λογισμός, οῦ, ὁ, *thought, reasoning.*

[4] κατηγορέω, *I speak against, accuse*. MH: the root (κατηγορε) ends in a vowel, so the connecting vowel contracts (ε + ο = ου).

[5] TH: καὶ is ascensive; *even.*

[6] ἀπολογέομαι, *I defend.* MH: the root (ἀπολογε) ends in a vowel, so the connecting vowel contracts (ε + ο = ου).

[7] TH: futuristic pres.; *will judge.*

[8] κρυπτός, ή, όν, *hidden, secret.*

[9] ἐπονομάζω, *I call, name.*

[10] ἐπαναπαύομαι, *I rely on, rest upon.*

[11] καυχάομαι, *I boast.* MH: καυχα (pres. tense stem) + ε (connecting vowel) + σαι (2nd sg. mid./pass. ending) = καυχᾶσαι (α + ε = α; in this instance, the intervocalic σ did not drop out as expected with 2nd sg. mid./pass. contract verbs).

[12] δοκιμάζω, *I test, approve.*

[13] διαφέρω, *I carry over, excel in,* ***am superior***. TH: subst. adj. prtc.; *the superior things.*

[14] κατηχέω, *I teach, instruct*. MH: the root (κατηχε) ends in a vowel, so the connecting vowel contracts (ε + ο = ου).

[15] MH: 2nd pf. of πείθω; pf. tense stem is ποιθ.

[16] σεαυτοῦ, ῆς, *yourself.* TH: subject of the inf. εἶναι.

[17] ὁδηγός, οῦ, ὁ, *guide, leader.*

[18] TH: τῶν substantivizes the prep. phrase ἐν σκότει; *the ones in darkness.*

[19] σκότος, ους, τό, *darkness.*

[20] παιδευτής, οῦ, ὁ, *educator, instructor.*

[21] ἄφρων, ον, *foolish.*

[22] νήπιος, ία, ον, *infant, child.*

[23] μόρφωσις, εως, ἡ, *form, embodiment.*

γνώσεως [1] καὶ τῆς ἀληθείας ἐν τῷ νόμῳ— **21** ὁ οὖν
διδάσκων ἕτερον σεαυτὸν[2] οὐ διδάσκεις; ὁ κηρύσσων μὴ
κλέπτειν[3] κλέπτεις;[4] **22** ὁ λέγων μὴ μοιχεύειν[5] μοιχεύεις;[6]
ὁ βδελυσσόμενος[7] τὰ εἴδωλα[8] ἱεροσυλεῖς;[9] **23** ὃς ἐν νόμῳ
καυχᾶσαι,[10] διὰ τῆς παραβάσεως[11] τοῦ νόμου τὸν θεὸν
ἀτιμάζεις; [12] **24** τὸ γὰρ ὄνομα τοῦ θεοῦ δι᾽ ὑμᾶς
βλασφημεῖται[13] ἐν τοῖς ἔθνεσιν, καθὼς γέγραπται.

25 Περιτομὴ[14] μὲν γὰρ ὠφελεῖ[15] ἐὰν νόμον πράσσῃς·[16]
ἐὰν δὲ παραβάτης [17] νόμου ᾖς, ἡ περιτομή [18] σου
ἀκροβυστία [19] γέγονεν.[20] **26** ἐὰν οὖν ἡ ἀκροβυστία[21] τὰ
δικαιώματα[22] τοῦ νόμου φυλάσσῃ,[23] ⸀οὐχ ἡ ἀκροβυστία[24]

---

[1] γνῶσις, εως, ἡ, *knowledge.*

[2] σεαυτοῦ, ῆς, *yourself.*

[3] κλέπτω, *I steal.*

[4] κλέπτω, *I steal.*

[5] μοιχεύω, *I commit adultery.*

[6] μοιχεύω, *I commit adultery.*

[7] βδελύσσομαι, *I abhor, detest.*

[8] εἴδωλον, ου, τό, *idol, image.*

[9] ἱεροσυλέω, *I rob temples.*

[10] καυχάομαι, *I boast.* MH: καυχα (pres. tense stem) + ε (connecting vowel) + σαι (2nd sg. mid./pass. ending) = καυχᾶσαι (α + ε = α; in this instance, the intervocalic σ did not drop out as expected with 2nd sg. mid./pass. contract verbs).

[11] παράβασις, εως, ἡ, *transgression.*

[12] ἀτιμάζω, *I dishonor, shame.*

[13] βλασφημέω, *I slander, blaspheme.* MH: the root (βλασφημε) ends in a vowel, so the connecting vowel contracts (ε + ε = ει).

[14] περιτομή, ῆς, ἡ, *circumcision.*

[15] ὠφελέω, *I help, am of use.*

[16] πράσσω, *I do, engage in, **practice.*** MH: subj. mood has length. connecting vowel; ε › η.

[17] παραβάτης, ου, ὁ, *transgressor.* TH: pred. nom. to the subject of ᾖς.

[18] περιτομή, ῆς, ἡ, *circumcision.*

[19] ἀκροβυστία, ας, ἡ, *uncircumcision.*

[20] MH: 2nd pf. of γίνομαι. The root (γεν) becomes γον due to ablaut.

[21] ἀκροβυστία, ας, ἡ, *uncircumcision, **uncircumcised.***

[22] δικαίωμα, ατος, τό, *requirement, righteous deed.*

[23] φυλάσσω, *I keep, guard, **obey.*** TH: subj. mood in conditional sentence.

[24] ἀκροβυστία, ας, ἡ, *uncircumcision.*

αὐτοῦ εἰς περιτομὴν[1] λογισθήσεται;[2] **27** καὶ κρινεῖ[3] ἡ ἐκ
φύσεως[4] ἀκροβυστία[5] τὸν νόμον τελοῦσα[6] σὲ τὸν[7] διὰ
γράμματος[8] καὶ περιτομῆς[9] παραβάτην[10] νόμου. **28** οὐ γὰρ
ὁ ἐν τῷ φανερῷ[11] ’Ιουδαῖός[12] ἐστιν, οὐδὲ ἡ ἐν τῷ φανερῷ[13]
ἐν σαρκὶ περιτομή·[14] **29** ἀλλ’ ὁ ἐν τῷ κρυπτῷ[15] ’Ιουδαῖος,[16]
καὶ περιτομὴ[17] καρδίας ἐν πνεύματι οὐ γράμματι,[18] οὗ
ὁ ἔπαινος[19] οὐκ ἐξ ἀνθρώπων ἀλλ’ ἐκ τοῦ θεοῦ.

---

[1] περιτομή, ῆς, ἡ, *circumcision.*

[2] λογίζομαι, *I regard, consider.* MH: the stem ends in δ; δ + θ = σθ.

[3] MH: since the root (κριν) ends in ν, the fut. tense formative is εσ. κριν + εσ + ε (3rd sg. ending) = κρινεε (intervocalic σ drops out) › κρινει (ε + ε = ει).

[4] φύσις, εως, ἡ, *nature.*

[5] ἀκροβυστία, ας, ἡ, *uncircumcision,* ***uncircumcised.***

[6] τελέω, *I fulfill, complete.* MH: the root (τελε) ends in a vowel, so the connecting vowel contracts (ε + ου = ου). TH: adj. prtc. is attrib. to ἀκροβυστία.

[7] TH: τὸν is the art. for παραβάτην and is in app. to σὲ; *you, the … transgressor.*

[8] γράμμα, ατος, τό, *letter.*

[9] περιτομή, ῆς, ἡ, *circumcision.*

[10] παραβάτης, ου, ὁ, *transgressor.*

[11] φανερός, ά, όν, *evident, visible.* TH: ἐν τῷ φανερῷ, *by what is visible.*

[12] TH: ’Ιουδαῖός is a pred. nom. to the implied subject of ἐστιν; *someone is a Jew.*

[13] φανερός, ά, όν, *evident, visible.* TH: ἐν τῷ φανερῷ ἐν σαρκὶ, *visible in the flesh*; these two prep. phrases are attributive modifiers of ἡ … περιτομή.

[14] περιτομή, ῆς, ἡ, *circumcision.* TH: περιτομή is a pred. nom. to subject of the implied verb ἐστιν.

[15] κρυπτός, ή, όν, *hidden, secret,* ***not seen.*** TH: ἐν τῷ κρυπτῷ, *by what is not seen.*

[16] TH: ’Ιουδαῖός is a pred. nom. to subject of the implied verb ἐστιν; *someone is a Jew in secret.*

[17] περιτομή, ῆς, ἡ, *circumcision.* TH: "is" should be supplied after περιτομὴ.

[18] γράμμα, ατος, τό, *letter.*

[19] ἔπαινος, ου, ὁ, *praise, approval.* TH: "is" should be supplied after ἔπαινος.

2:5 ἀποκαλύψεως WH Treg NA28] + καὶ RP
8 ἀπειθοῦσι WH Treg NA28] + μὲν RP
- **ὀργὴ καὶ θυμός** WH Treg NA28] θυμὸς καὶ ὀργή RP
- **ὀργὴ καὶ θυμός** WH Treg NA28] θυμὸς καὶ ὀργή RP

13 ⸀**νόμου** WH Treg NA28] τοῦ νόμου RP
- **τῷ** WH NA28 RP] – Treg
- ⸀**νόμου** WH Treg NA28] τοῦ νόμου RP

14 ποιῶσιν WH Treg NA28] ποιῇ RP
16 ἡμέρᾳ ὅτε Treg NA28 RP] ᾗ ἡμέρᾳ WH
16 ἡμέρᾳ ὅτε Treg NA28 RP] ᾗ ἡμέρᾳ WH
- **κρίνει** WH NA28] κρινεῖ Treg RP
- **Χριστοῦ Ἰησοῦ** WH NA28] Ἰησοῦ Χριστοῦ Treg NIV RP
- **Χριστοῦ Ἰησοῦ** WH NA28] Ἰησοῦ Χριστοῦ Treg NIV RP

17 Εἰ δὲ WH Treg NA28] Ἴδε RP
17 Εἰ δὲ WH Treg NA28] Ἴδε RP
- **νόμῳ** WH Treg NA28] τῷ νόμῳ RP

26 οὐχ WH Treg NA28] οὐχὶ RP

ROMANS 3

New Vocabulary by Frequency [Chapter, Book, SBLGNT Occurrences]

ἀδικία, ας, ἡ, *unrighteousness, injustice* [1, 7, 25]
ἄδικος, ον, *unjust* [1, 1, 12]
ἀκροβυστία, ας, ἡ, *uncircumcision* [1, 11, 20]
ἀληθής, ές, *true, honest* [1, 1, 26]
ἅμα, *at the same time, together* [1, 1, 10]
ἁμαρτάνω, *I sin, do wrong* [1, 7, 43]
ἁμάρτημα, ατος, τό, *sin, wrongdoing* [1, 1, 5]
ἁμαρτωλός, ον, *sinful* [1, 4, 47]
ἀνοχή, ῆς, ἡ, *forbearance, tolerance* [1, 2, 2]
ἀπέναντι, *before, opposite* [1, 1, 5]
ἀπιστέω, *I disbelieve, distrust* [1, 1, 8]
ἀπιστία, ας, ἡ, *unbelief, distrust* [1, 4, 11]
ἀπολύτρωσις, εως, ἡ, *redemption* [1, 2, 10]
ἀρά, ᾶς, ἡ, *curse* [1, 1, 1]
ἀσπίς, ίδος, ἡ, *asp* [1, 1, 1]
ἀχρειόω, *I make useless, become depraved* [1, 1, 1]
βλασφημέω, *I slander, revile* [1, 3, 34]
γέμω, *I am full* [1, 1, 11]
διαστολή, ῆς, ἡ, *distinction, difference* [1, 2, 3]
δικαιόω, *I justify, declare righteous* [6, 15, 39]
διότι, *because, for* [1, 4, 23]
δολιόω, *I deceive* [1, 1, 1]
δωρεάν, *as a gift* [1, 1, 9]
εἴπερ, *if really, if after all, since* [1, 3, 6]
ἐκζητέω, *I seek out* [1, 1, 7]
ἐκκλείω, *I shut out, exclude* [1, 1, 2]
ἐκκλίνω, *I avoid, turn away* [1, 2, 3]
ἐκχέω, *I pour out* [1, 2, 27]
Ἕλλην, ηνος, ὁ, *Greek, civilized* [1, 6, 25]
ἔνδειξις, εως, ἡ, *sign, demonstration* [2, 2, 4]
ἔνδικος, ον, *just* [1, 1, 2]
ἐπεί, *because, since* [1, 3, 26]
ἐπίγνωσις, εως, ἡ, *knowledge, recognition* [1, 3, 20]
ἐπιφέρω, *I bring on, inflict* [1, 1, 2]
ἱλαστήριον, ου, τό, *mercy seat* [1, 1, 2]
ἰός, ου, ὁ, *poison, venom, corrosion* [1, 1, 3]

καταργέω, *I invalidate, abolish* [2, 6, 27]
καύχησις, εως, ἡ, *boasting* [1, 2, 11]
κρίμα, ατος, τό, *judgment* [1, 6, 27]
λάρυγξ, ος, ὁ, *throat* [1, 1, 1]
λογίζομαι, *I regard, consider* [1, 19, 40]
λόγιον, ου, τό, *oracle, saying* [1, 1, 4]
ναί, *yes, certainly, indeed* [1, 1, 33]
νικάω, *I conquer, overcome* [1, 3, 28]
νυνί, *now* [1, 6, 20]
ὀξύς, εῖα, ύ, *sharp* [1, 1, 8]
ὀργή, ῆς, ἡ, *wrath* [1, 12, 36]
πάντως, *certainly, totally* [1, 1, 8]
πάρεσις, εως, ἡ, *passing over* [1, 1, 1]
περισσεύω, *I abound, overflow* [1, 3, 39]
περισσός, ή, όν, *abundant, extraordinary* [1, 1, 6]
περιτομή, ῆς, ἡ, *circumcision* [2, 15, 36]
πικρία, ας, ἡ, *bitterness* [1, 1, 4]
ποῖος, α, ον, *of what kind, which* [1, 1, 33]
ποῦ, *where* [1, 1, 45]
προαιτιάομαι, *I accuse beforehand* [1, 1, 1]
προγίνομαι, *I happen before, am born earlier* [1, 1, 1]
προέχω, *I excel, have an advantage* [1, 1, 1]
προτίθημι, *I intend, plan* [1, 2, 3]
συνίημι, *I understand* [1, 2, 26]
συνίστημι, *I bring together* [1, 3, 16]
σύντριμμα, ατος, τό, *destruction* [1, 1, 1]
ταλαιπωρία, ας, ἡ, *misery, trouble* [1, 1, 2]
τάφος, ου, ὁ, *grave, tomb* [1, 1, 7]
τρόπος, ου, ὁ, *way, manner* [1, 1, 13]
ὑπόδικος, ον, *answerable* [1, 1, 1]
ὑστερέω, *I fail, come short of* [1, 1, 16]
φανερόω, *I reveal, make known* [1, 2, 48]
φόβος, ου, ὁ, *fear, reverence* [1, 5, 47]
φράσσω, *I shut, bar* [1, 1, 3]
χεῖλος, ους, τό, *lip, shore* [1, 1, 7]
χρηστότης, ητος, ἡ, *kindness, generosity* [1, 5, 10]
χωρίς, *without, apart* [2, 6, 42]
ψεῦσμα, ατος, τό, *lying, untruthfulness* [1, 1, 1]
ψεύστης, ου, ὁ, *liar* [1, 1, 10]
ὠφέλεια, ας, ἡ, *help, use* [1, 1, 2]

3.1 Τί [1] οὖν τὸ περισσὸν [2] τοῦ Ἰουδαίου, ἢ τίς [3]
ἡ ὠφέλεια[4] τῆς περιτομῆς;[5] **2** πολὺ κατὰ πάντα τρόπον.[6]
πρῶτον μὲν ⸀γὰρ ὅτι ἐπιστεύθησαν τὰ λόγια[7] τοῦ θεοῦ.
3 τί γάρ; εἰ ἠπίστησάν[8] τινες, μὴ ἡ ἀπιστία[9] αὐτῶν τὴν
πίστιν τοῦ θεοῦ καταργήσει;[10] **4** μὴ γένοιτο·[11] γινέσθω δὲ
ὁ θεὸς ἀληθής,[12] πᾶς δὲ ἄνθρωπος[13] ψεύστης,[14] ⸀καθὼς
γέγραπται· Ὅπως ἂν δικαιωθῇς[15] ἐν τοῖς λόγοις σου καὶ
⸀νικήσεις[16] ἐν τῷ κρίνεσθαί[17] σε.[18] **5** εἰ δὲ ἡ ἀδικία[19] ἡμῶν
θεοῦ δικαιοσύνην συνίστησιν,[20] τί ἐροῦμεν;[21] μὴ ἄδικος[22]
ὁ θεὸς ὁ ἐπιφέρων[23] τὴν ὀργήν;[24] κατὰ ἄνθρωπον λέγω.

---

[1] TH: "is" should be supplied after Τί.

[2] περισσός, ή, όν, *abundant, extraordinary,* ***advantage***.

[3] TH: "is" should be supplied after τίς.

[4] ὠφέλεια, ας, ἡ, *help, use,* ***value***.

[5] περιτομή, ῆς, ἡ, *circumcision.*

[6] τρόπος, ου, ὁ, *way, manner.* TH: πολὺ κατὰ πάντα τρόπον, *there is much in every way.*

[7] λόγιον, ου, τό, *oracle, saying.*

[8] ἀπιστέω, *I disbelieve, distrust.* MH: the ε lengthens to η before the tense formative.

[9] ἀπιστία, ας, ἡ, *unbelief, distrust.*

[10] καταργέω, *I invalidate, abolish,* ***nullify***. MH: the ε lengthens to η before the tense formative.

[11] MH: aor. mid. opt. 3rd sg. TH: μὴ γένοιτο conveys strong denial; *May it not be!*

[12] ἀληθής, ές, *true, honest.*

[13] TH: the verb γινέσθω is implied here from the previous clause.

[14] ψεύστης, ου, ὁ, *liar.*

[15] δικαιόω, *I justify, declare righteous.* MH: the ο lengthens to ω before the tense formative.

[16] νικάω, *I conquer, overcome.* MH: the α lengthens to η before the tense formative.

[17] TH: ἐν τῷ + inf. indicates contemporaneous time; *when you are judged.*

[18] TH: acc. subject of the inf. κρίνεσθαί.

[19] ἀδικία, ας, ἡ, *unrighteousness, injustice.*

[20] συνίστημι, *I bring together,* ***demonstrate***.

[21] MH: fut. act. indic. 1st pl. of λέγω.

[22] ἄδικος, ον, *unjust.* TH: ἄδικος is a pred. adj. to the subject ὁ θεὸς.

[23] ἐπιφέρω, *I bring on, inflict.*

[24] ὀργή, ῆς, ἡ, *wrath.*

6 μὴ γένοιτο·[1] ἐπεὶ[2] πῶς κρινεῖ[3] ὁ θεὸς τὸν κόσμον; **7** εἰ δὲ
ἡ ἀλήθεια τοῦ θεοῦ ἐν[4] τῷ ἐμῷ ψεύσματι[5] ἐπερίσσευσεν[6]
εἰς τὴν δόξαν αὐτοῦ, τί ἔτι κἀγὼ ὡς ἁμαρτωλὸς[7]
κρίνομαι, **8** καὶ μὴ[8] καθὼς βλασφημούμεθα[9] καὶ καθώς
φασίν[10] τινες ἡμᾶς[11] λέγειν ὅτι Ποιήσωμεν[12] τὰ κακὰ ἵνα
ἔλθῃ[13] τὰ ἀγαθά; ὧν[14] τὸ κρίμα[15] ἔνδικόν[16] ἐστιν.
9 Τί οὖν; προεχόμεθα;[17] οὐ πάντως,[18] προῃτιασάμεθα[19]
γὰρ Ἰουδαίους τε καὶ[20] Ἕλληνας[21] πάντας[22] ὑφ᾽ ἁμαρτίαν
εἶναι, **10** καθὼς γέγραπται ὅτι Οὐκ ἔστιν δίκαιος[23] οὐδὲ

---

[1] MH: aor. mid. opt. 3rd sg. TH: μὴ γένοιτο conveys strong denial; *May it not be!*

[2] ἐπεί, *because, since,* ***otherwise***.

[3] MH: since the root (κριν) ends in ν, the fut. tense formative is εσ. κριν + εσ + ε (3rd sg. ending) = κρινεε (intervocalic σ drops out) › κρινει (ε + ε = ει).

[4] TH: ἐν is instrumental; *by*.

[5] ψεῦσμα, ατος, τό, *lying, untruthfulness*.

[6] περισσεύω, *I abound, overflow*.

[7] ἁμαρτωλός, ον, *sinful*.

[8] TH: here, καὶ μὴ introduces a rhetorical question; *and (why) not (say)*.

[9] βλασφημέω, *I slander, blaspheme*. MH: the root (βλασφημε) ends in a vowel, so the connecting vowel contracts (ε + ο = ου).

[10] MH: pres. act. indic. 3rd pl. of φημί.

[11] TH: the acc. is the subject of the inf.; φασίν τινες ἡμᾶς λέγειν, *some affirm we say*.

[12] MH: the ε in ποιέω lengthens to η before the tense formative.

[13] MH: aor. act. subj. 3rd sg. of ἔρχομαι. 2nd aor.; aor. tense stem is ἐλθ.

[14] TH: rel. pron. refers to τινες and modifies τὸ κρίμα.

[15] κρίμα, ατος, τό, *judgment*.

[16] ἔνδικος, ον, *just,* ***deserved***.

[17] προέχω, *I excel, have an advantage*.

[18] πάντως, *certainly, totally*. TH: with οὐ; *not at all*.

[19] προαιτιάομαι, *I accuse beforehand*. MH: verbs with roots beginning with vowels aug. by lengthening the initial vowel. προ (prep.) + aug. + αιτια (root) › προῃτια (ι subscripts when immediately following η) + σα (aor. tense formative) + μεθα (1st pl. ending) › προῃτιασάμεθα (in some contract verbs, the vowel before the tense formative does not length.).

[20] TH: τε καὶ, *both … and*.

[21] Ἕλλην, ηνος, ὁ, *Greek; civilized*.

[22] TH: πάντας is subst. and is the subject of the inf.; πάντας ὑφ᾽ ἁμαρτίαν εἶναι, *all are under sin*.

[23] TH: δίκαιος is a pred. adj. to the subject of ἔστιν.

εἷς, **11** οὐκ ἔστιν ⸀ὁ συνίων,[1] οὐκ ἔστιν ⸀ὁ ἐκζητῶν[2] τὸν
θεόν· **12** πάντες ἐξέκλιναν,[3] ἅμα[4] ἠχρεώθησαν·[5] οὐκ ⸀ἔστιν
ποιῶν[6] χρηστότητα,[7] οὐκ ἔστιν ἕως ἑνός. **13** τάφος[8]
ἀνεῳγμένος[9] ὁ λάρυγξ[10] αὐτῶν, ταῖς γλώσσαις[11] αὐτῶν
ἐδολιοῦσαν,[12] ἰὸς[13] ἀσπίδων[14] ὑπὸ τὰ χείλη[15] αὐτῶν, **14** ὧν[16]
τὸ στόμα ἀρᾶς[17] καὶ πικρίας[18] γέμει·[19] **15** ὀξεῖς[20] οἱ πόδες
αὐτῶν ἐκχέαι[21] αἷμα, **16** σύντριμμα[22] καὶ ταλαιπωρία[23] ἐν

---

[1] συνίημι, *I understand.* TH: subst. prtc.

[2] ἐκζητέω, *I seek out.* MH: the root (εκζητε) ends in a vowel, so the connecting vowel contracts (ε + ω = ω). TH: subst. prtc.

[3] ἐκκλίνω, *I avoid, turn away.* MH: εκ (prep.) + ε (augment) + κλιν (aor. tense stem) + σαν (3rd pl. ending) › ἐξέκλιναν (κ changes to ξ when followed by a vowel; σ drops out of the ending when preceded by a λ, μ, ν, or ρ).

[4] ἅμα, *at the same time, together.*

[5] ἀχρειόω, *I make useless, become depraved.* MH: the ο lengthens to ω before the tense formative; ι is absent from the aor. pass. form.

[6] MH: the root (ποιε) ends in a vowel, so the connecting vowel contracts (ε + ω = ω). TH: subst. prtc. NA has ὁ ποιῶν.

[7] χρηστότης, ητος, ἡ, *kindness, generosity.*

[8] τάφος, ου, ὁ, *grave, tomb.* TH: pred. nom. to the subject ὁ λάρυγξ.

[9] MH: pf. pass. prtc. nom. sg. masc. of ἀνοίγω. This belongs to a small category of words that seem to double augment in the pf. tense (after the prep., ε is added and ο length. to ω; ι subscripts after ω). TH: ἀνεῳγμένος is attrib. to τάφος.

[10] λάρυγξ, ος, ὁ, *throat.*

[11] TH: dat. of mean; *with.*

[12] δολιόω, *I deceive.* MH: impf. act. indic. 3rd pl. This verb uses the alternate secondary ending σαν for the 3rd pl.; the root (δολιο) ends in a vowel, so the connecting vowel contracts (ο + ο = ου).

[13] ἰός, ου, ὁ, *poison, venom, corrosion.*

[14] ἀσπίς, ίδος, ἡ, *asp.*

[15] χεῖλος, ους, τό, *lip, shore.*

[16] TH: rel. pron. refers to πάντες in v. 12.

[17] ἀρά, ᾶς, ἡ, *curse.* TH: gen. dir. obj. of γέμει.

[18] πικρία, ας, ἡ, *bitterness.* TH: gen. dir. obj. of γέμει.

[19] γέμω, *I am full.*

[20] ὀξύς, εῖα, ύ, *sharp, **swift**.* TH: pred. adj. to the subject οἱ πόδες.

[21] ἐκχέω, *I pour out, **shed**.* MH: intervocalic σ (between ε and α) dropped out.

[22] σύντριμμα, ατος, τό, *destruction.*

[23] ταλαιπωρία, ας, ἡ, *misery, trouble.*

ταῖς ὁδοῖς αὐτῶν, **17** καὶ ὁδὸν εἰρήνης οὐκ ἔγνωσαν.[1]
18 οὐκ ἔστιν φόβος[2] θεοῦ ἀπέναντι[3] τῶν ὀφθαλμῶν αὐτῶν.
19 Οἴδαμεν δὲ ὅτι ὅσα ὁ νόμος λέγει τοῖς[4] ἐν τῷ νόμῳ
λαλεῖ, ἵνα πᾶν στόμα φραγῇ[5] καὶ ὑπόδικος[6] γένηται[7] πᾶς
ὁ κόσμος τῷ θεῷ· **20** διότι [8] ἐξ [9] ἔργων νόμου οὐ
δικαιωθήσεται [10] πᾶσα σὰρξ ἐνώπιον αὐτοῦ, διὰ γὰρ
νόμου[11] ἐπίγνωσις[12] ἁμαρτίας.
21 Νυνὶ [13] δὲ χωρὶς [14] νόμου δικαιοσύνη θεοῦ
πεφανέρωται,[15] μαρτυρουμένη ὑπὸ τοῦ νόμου καὶ τῶν
προφητῶν, **22** δικαιοσύνη δὲ[16] θεοῦ διὰ πίστεως Ἰησοῦ
Χριστοῦ, εἰς ⸀πάντας τοὺς πιστεύοντας, οὐ γάρ ἐστιν
διαστολή.[17] **23** πάντες γὰρ ἥμαρτον[18] καὶ ὑστεροῦνται[19]

---

[1] MH: aor. act. indic. 3rd pl of γινώσκω. The root is γνο, and the ο lengthens to ω before the tense formative.

[2] φόβος, ου, ὁ, *fear, reverence.*

[3] ἀπέναντι, *before, opposite.*

[4] TH: τοῖς substantivizes the prep. phrase ἐν τῷ νόμῳ; *to those in the law.*

[5] φράσσω, *I shut, bar.* MH: aor. pass. subj. 3rd sg.; the root ends in γ.

[6] ὑπόδικος, ον, *answerable.*

[7] MH: 2nd aor. of γίνομαι; root is γεν.

[8] διότι, *because, for.*

[9] TH: ἐξ is indicating means; *by.*

[10] δικαιόω, *I justify, declare righteous.* MH: the ο lengthens to ω before the tense formative.

[11] TH: this is a verbless clause, so a verb needs to be supplied; *comes.*

[12] ἐπίγνωσις, εως, ἡ, *knowledge, recognition.*

[13] νυνί, *now.*

[14] χωρίς, *without, apart.*

[15] φανερόω, *I reveal, make known.* MH: the ο lengthens to a ω before the tense formative.

[16] TH: δὲ is explanatory, connecting δικαιοσύνη θεοῦ in 3:21 and 3:22; *namely.*

[17] διαστολή, ῆς, ἡ, *distinction, difference.* TH: διαστολή is a pred. nom. to subject of the implied subject of ἐστιν.

[18] ἁμαρτάνω, *I sin, do wrong.* MH: 2nd aor.; root is ἁμαρτ.

[19] ὑστερέω, *I fail, come short of.* MH: the root (ὑστερε) ends in a vowel, so the connecting vowel contracts (ε + ο = ου).

τῆς δόξης τοῦ θεοῦ, **24** δικαιούμενοι[1] δωρεὰν[2] τῇ αὐτοῦ
χάριτι[3] διὰ τῆς ἀπολυτρώσεως[4] τῆς[5] ἐν Χριστῷ Ἰησοῦ·
25 ὃν[6] προέθετο[7] ὁ θεὸς ἱλαστήριον[8] ⸀διὰ πίστεως[9] ἐν τῷ
αὐτοῦ αἵματι εἰς ἔνδειξιν[10] τῆς δικαιοσύνης αὐτοῦ διὰ
τὴν πάρεσιν[11] τῶν προγεγονότων[12] ἁμαρτημάτων[13] **26** ἐν τῇ
ἀνοχῇ[14] τοῦ θεοῦ, πρὸς ⸀τὴν ἔνδειξιν[15] τῆς δικαιοσύνης
αὐτοῦ ἐν τῷ νῦν καιρῷ, εἰς τὸ εἶναι[16] αὐτὸν[17] δίκαιον καὶ
δικαιοῦντα[18] τὸν[19] ἐκ πίστεως Ἰησοῦ.

---

[1] δικαιόω, *I justify, declare righteous*. MH: the root (δικαιο) ends in a vowel, so the connecting vowel contracts (ο + ο = ου).

[2] δωρεάν, *as a gift,* ***freely***.

[3] TH: dat. of means; *by his grace*.

[4] ἀπολύτρωσις, εως, ἡ, *redemption*.

[5] TH: τῆς substantivizes the prep. phrase ἐν Χριστῷ Ἰησοῦ, allowing it to function as an attrib. adj. to τῆς ἀπολυτρώσεως; *the redemption in Christ Jesus*.

[6] TH: rel. pron. refers to Χριστῷ Ἰησοῦ in the previous verse.

[7] προτίθημι, *I intend, plan*. MH: aor. mid. indic. 3rd sg. The root of τίθημι and its compound forms is θε; προ (prep.) + ε (augment) + θε (aor. tense stem) + το (3rd sg. ending) › προέθετο.

[8] ἱλαστήριον, ου, τό, *mercy seat,* ***means of atonement***.

[9] NA has τῆς πίστεως, though τῆς is in brackets, indicating the questionable nature of its inclusion.

[10] ἔνδειξις, εως, ἡ, *sign, demonstration*.

[11] πάρεσις, εως, ἡ, *passing over*.

[12] προγίνομαι, *I happen before, am born earlier*. MH: perf. act. prtc. gen. pl. neut. The ε in the root (γεν) becomes ο due to ablaut. As a 2nd pf., there is no κ in the tense formative. TH: with ἁμαρτημάτων, *the sins committed previously*.

[13] ἁμάρτημα, ατος, τό, *sin, wrongdoing*.

[14] ἀνοχή, ῆς, ἡ, *forbearance, tolerance*.

[15] ἔνδειξις, εως, ἡ, *sign, demonstration*.

[16] TH: εἰς τὸ + inf. indicates purpose; *so that he would be*.

[17] TH: the acc. is the subject of the inf. εἶναι.

[18] δικαιόω, *I justify, declare righteous*. MH: the root (δικαιο) ends in a vowel, so the connecting vowel contracts (ο + ο = ου). TH: subst. prtc.; *the one justifying*.

[19] TH: τὸν substantivizes the prep. phrase ἐκ πίστεως Ἰησοῦ; *the one who is from the faithfulness of Jesus*.

27 Ποῦ[1] οὖν ἡ καύχησις;[2] ἐξεκλείσθη.[3] διὰ ποίου[4]
νόμου; τῶν ἔργων; οὐχί, ἀλλὰ διὰ νόμου πίστεως.
28 λογιζόμεθα[5] ⸂γὰρ ⸀δικαιοῦσθαι[6] πίστει[7]⸃ ἄνθρωπον[8]
χωρὶς[9] ἔργων νόμου. **29** ἢ Ἰουδαίων ὁ θεὸς μόνον;[10] ⸀οὐχὶ
καὶ[11] ἐθνῶν; ναὶ[12] καὶ[13] ἐθνῶν, **30** ⸀εἴπερ[14] εἷς[15] ὁ θεός, ὃς[16]
δικαιώσει[17] περιτομὴν[18] ἐκ πίστεως καὶ ἀκροβυστίαν[19]
διὰ τῆς πίστεως. **31** νόμον οὖν καταργοῦμεν[20] διὰ τῆς
πίστεως; μὴ γένοιτο,[21] ἀλλὰ νόμον ⸀ἱστάνομεν.[22]

---

[1] ποῦ, *where.*

[2] καύχησις, εως, ἡ, *boasting.*

[3] ἐκκλείω, *I shut out, exclude.* MH: κ of the prep. reverts to ξ when followed by a vowel; ἐκκλείω belongs to a group of words in which σ is inserted after the stem in aor. pass.

[4] ποῖος, α, ον, *of what kind, which*

[5] λογίζομαι, *I regard, consider.*

[6] δικαιόω, *I justify, declare righteous.* MH: the root (δικαιο) ends in a vowel, so the connecting vowel contracts (ο + ε = ου).

[7] TH: dat. of means; *by.*

[8] TH: the acc. is the subject of the inf. δικαιοῦσθαι.

[9] χωρίς, *without, apart.*

[10] TH: *Or is God only (God) of the Jews.*

[11] TH: καί is additive; *also.*

[12] ναί, *yes, certainly, indeed.*

[13] TH: καί is additive; *also.*

[14] εἴπερ, *if really, if after all, since.*

[15] TH: εἷς is a pred. adj. to the subject ὁ θεός.

[16] TH: rel. pron. refers to ὁ θεός.

[17] δικαιόω, *I justify, declare righteous.* MH: the ο lengthens to ω before the tense formative.

[18] περιτομή, ῆς, ἡ, *circumcision,* ***circumcised.***

[19] ἀκροβυστία, ας, ἡ, *uncircumcision,* ***uncircumcised.***

[20] καταργέω, *I invalidate, abolish,* ***nullify.*** MH: the root (καταργε) ends in a vowel, so the connecting vowel contracts (ε + ο = ου).

[21] MH: aor. mid. opt. 3rd sg. TH: μὴ γένοιτο conveys strong denial; *May it not be!*

[22] MH: pres. act. indic. 1st pl. of ἵστημι.

3:2 γὰρ WH NA28 RP] – Treg
4 καθὼς NA28 RP] καθάπερ WH Treg
- **νικήσεις** WH NA28] νικήσῃς Treg RP

7 δὲ WH NA28] γὰρ Treg RP
11 ⸢**ὁ** Treg NA28 RP] – WH
- ⸢**ὁ** Treg NA28 RP] – WH

12 ἔστιν WH Treg RP] + ὁ NA28
22 πάντας WH Treg NA28] καὶ ἐπὶ πάντας RP
25 διὰ WH Treg] + τῆς NA28 RP
26 τὴν WH Treg NA28] – RP
28 γὰρ WH Treg NA28] οὖν RP
- **δικαιοῦσθαι πίστει** WH Treg NA28] πίστει δικαιοῦσθαι RP
- **δικαιοῦσθαι πίστει** WH Treg NA28] πίστει δικαιοῦσθαι RP

29 οὐχὶ WH Treg NA28] + δὲ RP
30 εἴπερ WH Treg NA28] ἐπείπερ RP
31 ἱστάνομεν WH Treg NA28] ἱστῶμεν RP

ROMANS 4

New Vocabulary by Frequency [Chapter, Book, SBLGNT Occurrences]

ἀκροβυστία, ας, ἡ, *uncircumcision* [6, 11, 20]
ἀνομία, ας, ἡ, *lawlessness, lawless conduct* [1, 3, 15]
ἀπιστία, ας, ἡ, *unbelief, distrust* [1, 4, 11]
ἀσεβής, ές, *ungodly, profane* [1, 2, 10]
ἀσθενέω, *I am weak, sick* [1, 5, 34]
βέβαιος, α, ον, *firm, reliable, valid* [1, 1, 8]
διακρίνω, *I separate, evaluate* [1, 2, 19]
δικαιόω, *I justify, declare righteous* [2, 15, 39]
δικαίωσις, εως, ἡ, *justification, setting right* [1, 2, 2]
δυνατός, ή, όν, *able, capable* [1, 5, 32]
ἑκατονταετής, ές, *a hundred years old* [1, 1, 1]
ἐνδυναμόω, *I strengthen, become strong* [1, 1, 7]
ἐπικαλύπτω, *I cover up* [1, 1, 1]
ἐργάζομαι, *I work, labor, do* [2, 4, 41]
ζῳοποιέω, *I make alive, give life* [1, 2, 11]
ἴχνος, ους, τό, *footprint* [1, 1, 3]
καθάπερ, *just as* [1, 2, 13]
κατανοέω, *I consider, contemplate* [1, 1, 14]
καταργέω, *I invalidate, abolish* [1, 6, 27]
κατέναντι, *before, in the sight of* [1, 1, 8]
κατεργάζομαι, *I do, commit, bring about* [1, 11, 22]
καύχημα, ατος, τό, *(a reason to) boast* [1, 1, 11]
κενόω, *I empty, render void* [1, 1, 5]
κληρονόμος, ου, ὁ, *heir* [2, 4, 15]
λογίζομαι, *I regard, consider* [11, 19, 40]
μακαρισμός, οῦ, ὁ, *blessing* [2, 2, 3]
μήτρα, ας, ἡ, *womb* [1, 1, 2]
μισθός, οῦ, ὁ, *pay, wages* [1, 1, 29]
νεκρόω, *I put to death* [1, 1, 3]
νέκρωσις, εως, ἡ, *deadness, death* [1, 1, 2]
ὀργή, ῆς, ἡ, *wrath* [1, 12, 36]
οὗ, *where* [1, 3, 25]
ὀφείλημα, ατος, τό, *debt, what is due* [1, 1, 2]
παράπτωμα, ατος, τό, *wrongdoing, sin* [1, 9, 19]
περιτομή, ῆς, ἡ, *circumcision* [6, 15, 36]
πληροφορέω, *I fulfill, fully convince* [1, 2, 6]

πού, *somewhere, approximately* [1, 1, 7]
προπάτωρ, ορος, ὁ, *ancestor* [1, 1, 1]
Σάρρα, ας, ἡ, *Sarah* [1, 2, 4]
σπέρμα, ατος, τό, *seed, offspring, descendant* [3, 9, 43]
στοιχέω, *I hold to, conform, follow* [1, 1, 5]
σφραγίς, ῖδος, ἡ, *seal, signet* [1, 1, 16]
χωρίς, *without, apart* [1, 6, 42]

4.1 Τί οὖν ἐροῦμεν[1] ⸀εὑρηκέναι[2] Ἀβραὰμ[3] τὸν ⸀προ-
πάτορα[4] ⸀ἡμῶν κατὰ σάρκα; **2** εἰ γὰρ Ἀβραὰμ ἐξ[5] ἔργων
ἐδικαιώθη,[6] ἔχει καύχημα·[7] ἀλλ᾽ οὐ ⸀πρὸς[8] θεόν,
3 τί γὰρ ἡ γραφὴ λέγει; Ἐπίστευσεν δὲ Ἀβραὰμ τῷ θεῷ[9]
καὶ ἐλογίσθη[10] αὐτῷ εἰς δικαιοσύνην. **4** τῷ δὲ
ἐργαζομένῳ[11] ὁ μισθὸς[12] οὐ λογίζεται[13] κατὰ χάριν ἀλλὰ
κατὰ ὀφείλημα·[14] **5** τῷ δὲ μὴ ἐργαζομένῳ,[15] πιστεύοντι δὲ
ἐπὶ τὸν δικαιοῦντα[16] τὸν ἀσεβῆ,[17] λογίζεται[18] ἡ πίστις
αὐτοῦ εἰς δικαιοσύνην, **6** καθάπερ[19] καὶ[20] Δαυὶδ λέγει τὸν
μακαρισμὸν[21] τοῦ ἀνθρώπου ᾧ[22] ὁ θεὸς λογίζεται[23]
δικαιοσύνην χωρὶς[24] ἔργων· **7** Μακάριοι[25] ὧν ἀφέθησαν[26]

---

[1] MH: fut. act. indic. 1st pl. of λέγω.
[2] MH: pf. act. inf. of εὑρίσκω. An η is added after the root (εὑρ) before -κέναι.
[3] TH: Ἀβραὰμ is in app. to τὸν προπάτορα. The acc. functions as the subject of the inf. εὑρηκέναι.
[4] προπάτωρ, ορος, ὁ, *ancestor*.
[5] TH: ἐξ is indicating means; *by*.
[6] δικαιόω, *I justify, declare righteous*.
[7] καύχημα, ατος, τό, *(a reason to) boast*.
[8] TH: πρός is indicating orientation; *before*.
[9] TH: dat. dir. obj. of ἐπίστευσεν.
[10] λογίζομαι, *I regard, consider,* ***credit***. MH: the stem ends in δ; δ + θ = σθ.
[11] ἐργάζομαι, *I work, labor, do*.
[12] μισθός, οῦ, ὁ, *pay, wages*.
[13] λογίζομαι, *I regard, consider,* ***credit***.
[14] ὀφείλημα, ατος, τό, *debt, what is due*.
[15] ἐργάζομαι, *I work, labor, do*.
[16] δικαιόω, *I justify, declare righteous*. MH: the root (δικαιο) ends in a vowel, so the connecting vowel contracts (ο + ο = ου).
[17] ἀσεβής, ές, *ungodly, profane*.
[18] λογίζομαι, *I regard, consider,* ***credit***.
[19] καθάπερ, *just as*.
[20] TH: καὶ is ascensive; *even*.
[21] μακαρισμός, οῦ, ὁ, *blessing*.
[22] TH: rel. pron. refers to τοῦ ἀνθρώπου.
[23] λογίζομαι, *I regard, consider,* ***credit***.
[24] χωρίς, *without, apart*.
[25] TH: "are" should be supplied after Μακάριοι.
[26] MH: aor. pass. indic. 3rd pl. of ἀφίημι.

αἱ ἀνομίαι [1] καὶ ὧν ἐπεκαλύφθησαν [2] αἱ ἁμαρτίαι,
8 μακάριος[3] ἀνὴρ ⸀οὗ οὐ μὴ λογίσηται[4] κύριος ἁμαρτίαν.
9 Ὁ μακαρισμὸς[5] οὖν οὗτος ἐπὶ τὴν περιτομὴν[6] ἢ καὶ[7]
ἐπὶ τὴν ἀκροβυστίαν;[8] λέγομεν ⸀γάρ· Ἐλογίσθη[9] τῷ
Ἀβραὰμ ἡ πίστις εἰς δικαιοσύνην. **10** πῶς οὖν ἐλογίσθη;[10]
ἐν περιτομῇ[11] ὄντι[12] ἢ ἐν ἀκροβυστίᾳ;[13] οὐκ[14] ἐν
περιτομῇ[15] ἀλλ᾽ ἐν ἀκροβυστίᾳ·[16] **11** καὶ σημεῖον ἔλαβεν
περιτομῆς,[17] σφραγῖδα[18] τῆς δικαιοσύνης τῆς πίστεως
τῆς[19] ἐν τῇ ἀκροβυστίᾳ,[20] εἰς τὸ εἶναι[21] αὐτὸν[22] πατέρα
πάντων τῶν πιστευόντων δι᾽ ἀκροβυστίας,[23] εἰς τὸ
⸀λογισθῆναι[24] αὐτοῖς[25] τὴν δικαιοσύνην, **12** καὶ πατέρα

---

[1] ἀνομία, ας, ἡ, *lawlessness, lawless conduct.*

[2] ἐπικαλύπτω, *I cover up*. MH: ἐπικαλυβ; when the aug. is added, ι of the prep. drops out; β + θ = φθ.

[3] TH: "is" should be supplied after μακάριος.

[4] λογίζομαι, *I regard, consider,* ***credit***. MH: the stem ends in δ; δ + σ = σ.

[5] μακαρισμός, οῦ, ὁ, *blessing.*

[6] περιτομή, ῆς, ἡ, *circumcision,* ***circumcised***.

[7] TH: καί is additive; *also.*

[8] ἀκροβυστία, ας, ἡ, *uncircumcision,* ***uncircumcised.***

[9] λογίζομαι, *I regard, consider,* ***credit***. MH: the stem ends in δ; δ + θ = σθ.

[10] λογίζομαι, *I regard, consider,* ***credit***. MH: the stem ends in δ; δ + θ = σθ.

[11] περιτομή, ῆς, ἡ, *circumcision*. TH: ἐν περιτομῇ, *circumcised.*

[12] MH: pres. act. prtc. dat. sg. masc. of εἰμί. TH: ὄντι is temporal; *while he was.*

[13] ἀκροβυστία, ας, ἡ, *uncircumcision*. TH: ἐν ἀκροβυστίᾳ, *uncircumcised.*

[14] TH: *he was not.*

[15] περιτομή, ῆς, ἡ, *circumcision*. TH: ἐν περιτομῇ, *circumcised.*

[16] ἀκροβυστία, ας, ἡ, *uncircumcision*. TH: ἐν ἀκροβυστίᾳ, *uncircumcised.*

[17] περιτομή, ῆς, ἡ, *circumcision.*

[18] σφραγίς, ῖδος, ἡ, *seal, signet.*

[19] TH: τῆς substantivizes the prep. phrase ἐν τῇ ἀκροβυστίᾳ.

[20] ἀκροβυστία, ας, ἡ, *uncircumcision,* ***uncircumcised***.

[21] TH: εἰς τὸ + inf. here indicates result; *so that he would be.*

[22] TH: acc. is the subject of the inf. εἶναι.

[23] ἀκροβυστία, ας, ἡ, *uncircumcision.*

[24] λογίζομαι, *I regard, consider,* ***credit***. MH: the stem ends in δ; δ + θ = σθ. TH: εἰς τὸ + inf. indicates result; *so that righteousness would be credited.*

[25] NA has καὶ αὐτοῖς, though καὶ is in brackets, indicating the questionable nature of its inclusion.

περιτομῆς[1] τοῖς[2] οὐκ ἐκ περιτομῆς[3] μόνον ἀλλὰ καὶ[4] τοῖς
στοιχοῦσιν[5] τοῖς ἴχνεσιν[6] τῆς ˹ἐν ἀκροβυστίᾳ[7] πίστεως˺
τοῦ πατρὸς ἡμῶν Ἀβραάμ.
13 Οὐ γὰρ διὰ νόμου[8] ἡ ἐπαγγελία τῷ Ἀβραὰμ ἢ τῷ
σπέρματι[9] αὐτοῦ, τὸ κληρονόμον[10] αὐτὸν[11] ˹εἶναι κόσμου,
ἀλλὰ διὰ δικαιοσύνης πίστεως· **14** εἰ γὰρ οἱ ἐκ νόμου
κληρονόμοι,[12] κεκένωται[13] ἡ πίστις καὶ κατήργηται[14]
ἡ ἐπαγγελία· **15** ὁ γὰρ νόμος ὀργὴν[15] κατεργάζεται,[16] οὗ[17]
˹δὲ οὐκ ἔστιν νόμος, οὐδὲ[18] παράβασις.[19]

---

[1] περιτομή, ῆς, ἡ, *circumcision*, ***circumcised***.

[2] TH: τοῖς substantivizes the prep. phrase ἐκ περιτομῆς; with οὐκ, *to the ones who are not from circumcision.*

[3] περιτομή, ῆς, ἡ, *circumcision*, ***circumcised***.

[4] TH: καί is additive; *also.*

[5] στοιχέω, *I hold to, conform, follow*. MH: the root (στοιχε) ends in a vowel, so the connecting vowel contracts (ε + ου = ου).

[6] ἴχνος, ους, τό, *footprint*, ***footstep***.

[7] ἀκροβυστία, ας, ἡ, *uncircumcision*. TH: ἐν ἀκροβυστίᾳ, *uncircumcised.*

[8] TH: Οὐ … διὰ νόμου could be translated after κόσμου; *was not through the law.*

[9] σπέρμα, ατος, τό, *seed, offspring, descendant.*

[10] κληρονόμος, ου, ὁ, *heir.*

[11] TH: acc. functions as the subject of the inf. εἶναι. This inf. clause is the content of the promise to Abraham; *namely, that he would be the heir of the world.*

[12] κληρονόμος, ου, ὁ, *heir.*

[13] κενόω, *I empty, render void*. MH: the ο lengthens to ω before the ending in pf. mid./pass. forms.

[14] καταργέω, *I invalidate, abolish*, ***nullify***. MH: the ε lengthens to η before the ending in pf. mid./pass. forms.

[15] ὀργή, ῆς, ἡ, *wrath.*

[16] κατεργάζομαι, *I do, commit, bring about.*

[17] οὗ, *where.*

[18] TH: ἔστιν is implied from the previous clause.

[19] παράβασις, εως, ἡ, *transgression.*

16 Διὰ τοῦτο ἐκ πίστεως, [1] ἵνα [2] κατὰ χάριν,
εἰς τὸ εἶναι [3] βεβαίαν [4] τὴν ἐπαγγελίαν [5] παντὶ τῷ
σπέρματι,[6] οὐ τῷ[7] ἐκ τοῦ νόμου μόνον ἀλλὰ καὶ[8] τῷ[9] ἐκ
πίστεως Ἀβραάμ (ὅς [10] ἐστιν πατὴρ πάντων ἡμῶν,
17 καθὼς γέγραπται ὅτι Πατέρα πολλῶν ἐθνῶν τέθεικά[11]
σε), κατέναντι[12] οὗ ἐπίστευσεν θεοῦ[13] τοῦ ζῳοποιοῦντος[14]
τοὺς νεκροὺς καὶ καλοῦντος[15] τὰ μὴ ὄντα[16] ὡς ὄντα·[17]
18 ὅς [18] παρ' ἐλπίδα ἐπ' ἐλπίδι ἐπίστευσεν εἰς τὸ
γενέσθαι [19] αὐτὸν [20] πατέρα πολλῶν ἐθνῶν κατὰ τὸ
εἰρημένον· [21] Οὕτως ἔσται τὸ σπέρμα [22] σου·

---

[1] TH: the subject and verb of this verbless clause can be supplied from context; *the promise is from faith.*

[2] TH: ἵνα anticipates a subj. verb; *in order that it might be.*

[3] TH: εἰς τὸ + inf. here indicates result; *so that the promise can be.*

[4] βέβαιος, α, ον, *firm, reliable, valid.*

[5] TH: acc. is the subject of the inf. εἶναι.

[6] σπέρμα, ατος, το, *seed, offspring, descendant.*

[7] TH: τῷ substantivizes the prep. phrase ἐκ τοῦ νόμου; *to the one under the law.*

[8] TH: καί is additive; *also.*

[9] TH: τῷ substantivizes the prep. phrase ἐκ πίστεως Ἀβραάμ; *to the one (who is) from the faith of Abraham.*

[10] TH: rel. pron. refers to Ἀβραάμ.

[11] MH: pf. act. indic. 1st sg. of τίθημι.

[12] κατέναντι, *before, in the sight of.*

[13] TH: θεοῦ is in app. to the rel. pron. οὗ.

[14] ζῳοποιέω, *I make alive, give life.* MH: the root (ζῳοποιε) ends in a vowel, so the connecting vowel contracts (ε + ο = ου). TH: subst. prtc. in app. to θεοῦ.

[15] MH: the root (καλε) ends in a vowel, so the connecting vowel contracts (ε + ο = ου). TH: subst. prtc. in app. to θεοῦ.

[16] MH: pres. act. prtc. acc. pl. neut. of εἰμί.

[17] MH: pres. act. prtc. acc. pl. neut. of εἰμί.

[18] TH: rel. pron. refers to Ἀβραάμ.

[19] TH: εἰς τὸ + inf. here indicates result; *so that he became.*

[20] TH: acc. is the subject of the inf. γενέσθαι.

[21] MH: pf. pass. prtc. acc. sg. neut. of λέγω. TH: *that which has been spoken.*

[22] σπέρμα, ατος, τό, *seed, offspring, descendant.*

19 καὶ μὴ ἀσθενήσας[1] τῇ ⸀πίστει κατενόησεν[2] τὸ ἑαυτοῦ
⸀σῶμα νενεκρωμένον,[3] ἑκατονταετής[4] που[5] ὑπάρχων, καὶ
τὴν νέκρωσιν[6] τῆς μήτρας[7] Σάρρας,[8] **20** εἰς[9] δὲ τὴν
ἐπαγγελίαν τοῦ θεοῦ οὐ διεκρίθη[10] τῇ ἀπιστίᾳ[11] ἀλλὰ
ἐνεδυναμώθη[12] τῇ πίστει, δοὺς[13] δόξαν τῷ θεῷ **21** καὶ
πληροφορηθεὶς[14] ὅτι ὃ ἐπήγγελται[15] δυνατός[16] ἐστιν καὶ[17]
ποιῆσαι.[18] **22** ⸀διὸ ἐλογίσθη[19] αὐτῷ εἰς δικαιοσύνην. **23** Οὐκ
ἐγράφη[20] δὲ δι᾽ αὐτὸν μόνον ὅτι ἐλογίσθη[21] αὐτῷ,

---

[1] ἀσθενέω, *I am weak, sick*. MH: the ε lengthens to η before the tense formative.

[2] κατανοέω, *I consider, contemplate*. MH: κατανοε; the ε lengthens to η before the tense formative.

[3] νεκρόω, *I put to death*. MH: the ο lengthens to ω before the ending in pf. mid./pass. forms. NA has ἤδη νενεκρωμένον, though ἤδη is in brackets, indicating the questionable nature of its inclusion.

[4] ἑκατονταετής, ές, *a hundred years old*.

[5] πού, *somewhere, approximately*.

[6] νέκρωσις, εως, ἡ, *deadness, death*.

[7] μήτρα, ας, ἡ, *womb*.

[8] Σάρρα, ας, ἡ, *Sarah*.

[9] TH: εἰς is indicating reference; *with reference to*.

[10] διακρίνω, *I separate, evaluate,* ***waver***. MH: in a few liquid verbs, the ν drops out in the aor. pass.

[11] ἀπιστία, ας, ἡ, *unbelief, distrust*.

[12] ἐνδυναμόω, *I strengthen, become strong*. MH: the ο lengthens to ω before the tense formative.

[13] MH: aor. act. prtc. nom. sg. masc. of δίδωμι.

[14] πληροφορέω, *I fulfill, fully convince*. MH: the ε lengthens to η before the tense formative.

[15] ἐπαγγέλλομαι, *I promise, profess*. MH: perf. mid./pass. indic. 3rd sg.

[16] δυνατός, ή, όν, *able, capable*. TH: pred. adj. to the implied subject of ἐστιν.

[17] TH: καί is additive´ *also*.

[18] MH: the ε lengthens to η before the tense formative.

[19] λογίζομαι, *I regard, consider,* ***credit***. MH: the stem ends in δ; δ + θ = σθ. NA has καὶ ἐλογίσθη, though καὶ is in brackets, indicating the questionable nature of its inclusion.

[20] MH: 2nd aor. pass. does not include θ in the tense formative.

[21] λογίζομαι, *I regard, consider,* ***credit***. MH: the stem ends in δ; δ + θ = σθ.

24 ἀλλὰ καὶ [1] δι᾽ ἡμᾶς οἷς [2] μέλλει λογίζεσθαι, [3] τοῖς
πιστεύουσιν [4] ἐπὶ τὸν ἐγείραντα [5] Ἰησοῦν τὸν κύριον [6]
ἡμῶν ἐκ νεκρῶν, 25 ὃς [7] παρεδόθη [8] διὰ τὰ παραπτώματα [9]
ἡμῶν καὶ ἠγέρθη [10] διὰ τὴν δικαίωσιν [11] ἡμῶν.

⸀ **4:1 εὑρηκέναι** Treg NA28] – WH RP
⸀ • **προπάτορα** WH Treg NA28] πατέρα RP
⸀ • **ἡμῶν** WH Treg NA28] + εὑρηκέναι RP
⸀ **2 πρὸς** WH Treg NA28] + τὸν RP
⸀ **8 οὗ** WH Treg NA28] ᾧ RP
⸀ **9 γάρ** WH Treg NA28] + ὅτι RP
⸀ **11 λογισθῆναι** WH Treg NIV] + καὶ RP NA28
⸂ **12 ἐν ἀκροβυστίᾳ πίστεως** WH Treg NA28] πίστεως τῆς ἐν τῇ ἀκροβυστίᾳ RP
⸃ **12 ἐν ἀκροβυστίᾳ πίστεως** WH Treg NA28] πίστεως τῆς ἐν τῇ ἀκροβυστίᾳ RP
⸀ **13 εἶναι** WH Treg NA28] + τοῦ RP
⸀ **15 δὲ** WH Treg NA28] γὰρ RP
⸀ **19 πίστει** WH Treg NA28] + οὐ RP
⸀ • **σῶμα** Holmes WH^marg] + ἤδη WH Treg NA28 RP
⸀ **22 διὸ** Holmes WH^marg] + καὶ WH Treg NA28 RP

---

[1] TH: καί is additive; *also.*
[2] TH: rel. pron. refers to ἡμᾶς.
[3] λογίζομαι, *I regard, consider,* ***credit***. MH: the stem ends in δ; δ + θ = σθ. TH: complementary inf. with μέλλει.
[4] TH: τοῖς πιστεύουσιν is in app. to οἷς.
[5] TH: subst. prtc.; *the one who raised.*
[6] TH: τὸν κύριον is in app. to Ἰησοῦν.
[7] TH: rel. pron. refers to Ἰησοῦν.
[8] MH: aor. pass. indic. 3rd sg. of παραδίδωμι. The root is παραδο. The ο does not lengthen here.
[9] παράπτωμα, ατος, τό, *wrongdoing, sin.*
[10] MH: aor. pass. indic. 3rd sg. of ἐγείρω. The root is ἐγερ.
[11] δικαίωσις, εως, ἡ, *justification, setting right.*

ROMANS 5

New Vocabulary by Frequency [Chapter, Book, SBLGNT Occurrences]

Ἀδάμ, ὁ, *Adam* [2, 2, 9]
ἁμαρτάνω, *I sin, do wrong* [3, 7, 43]
ἁμαρτωλός, όν, *sinful* [2, 4, 47]
ἆρα, *consequently* [1, 11, 52]
ἀσεβής, ές, *ungodly, profane* [1, 2, 10]
ἀσθενής, ές, *sick, weak* [1, 1, 26]
ἄχρι, *until* [1, 4, 49]
βασιλεύω, *I rule, am king* [5, 6, 21]
διέρχομαι, *I go through, pass through* [1, 1, 41]
δικαιόω, *I justify, declare righteous* [2, 15, 39]
δικαίωμα, ατος, τό, *requirement, righteous deed* [2, 5, 10]
δικαίωσις, εως, ἡ, *justification, setting right* [1, 2, 2]
δοκιμή, ῆς, ἡ, *test* [2, 2, 7]
δωρεά, ᾶς, ἡ, *gift* [2, 2, 11]
δώρημα, ατος, τὸ, *gift* [1, 1, 2]
ἐκχέω, *I pour out* [1, 2, 27]
ἐλλογέω, *I count, take into account* [1, 1, 2]
ἐχθρός, ά, όν, *hostile, enemy* [1, 3, 32]
θλῖψις, εως, ἡ, *affliction, tribulation* [2, 5, 45]
καθίστημι, *I appoint, cause* [2, 2, 21]
καταισχύνω, *I dishonor, put to shame* [1, 3, 13]
κατάκριμα, ατος, τό, *judgement, condemnation* [2, 3, 3]
καταλλαγή, ῆς, ἡ, *reconciliation* [1, 2, 4]
καταλλάσσω, *I reconcile* [2, 2, 6]
κατεργάζομαι, *I do, commit, bring about* [1, 11, 22]
καυχάομαι, *I boast* [3, 5, 36]
κρίμα, ατος, τό, *judgment* [1, 6, 27]
μέχρι, *until, as far as* [1, 2, 18]
μόλις, *rarely, scarcely* [1, 1, 6]
ὁμοίωμα, ατος, τό, *likeness* [1, 4, 6]
ὀργή, ῆς, ἡ, *wrath* [1, 12, 36]
οὗ, *where* [1, 3, 25]
παράβασις, εως, ἡ, *transgression* [1, 3, 7]
παρακοή, ῆς, ἡ, *disobedience* [1, 1, 3]
παράπτωμα, ατος, τό, *wrongdoing, sin* [6, 9, 19]
παρεισέρχομαι, *I slip in, come in* [1, 1, 2]

περισσεία, ας, ἡ, *surplus, abundance* [1, 1, 4]
περισσεύω, *I abound, overflow* [1, 3, 39]
πλεονάζω, *I grow, increase* [2, 3, 9]
προσαγωγή, ῆς, ἡ, *access* [1, 1, 3]
συνίστημι, *I bring together* [1, 3, 16]
τάχα, *perhaps, maybe* [1, 1, 2]
τολμάω, *I dare, show courage* [1, 2, 16]
τύπος, ου, ὁ, *pattern, type* [1, 2, 15]
ὑπακοή, ῆς, ἡ, *obedience* [1, 6, 14]
ὑπερπερισσεύω, *I abound more* [1, 1, 2]
ὑπομονή, ῆς, ἡ, *endurance, perseverance* [2, 6, 32]
χάρισμα, ατος, τὸ, *gift* [2, 6, 17]
ὥσπερ, *just as, even as* [3, 6, 36]

5.1 Δικαιωθέντες[1] οὖν ἐκ[2] πίστεως εἰρήνην ⸀ἔχομεν
πρὸς τὸν θεὸν διὰ τοῦ κυρίου ἡμῶν Ἰησοῦ Χριστοῦ,[3]
2 δι' οὗ[4] καὶ[5] τὴν προσαγωγὴν[6] ἐσχήκαμεν[7] τῇ πίστει
εἰς τὴν χάριν ταύτην ἐν ᾗ[8] ἑστήκαμεν,[9] καὶ καυχώμεθα[10]
ἐπ' ἐλπίδι τῆς δόξης τοῦ θεοῦ· **3** οὐ μόνον δέ, ἀλλὰ καὶ[11]
⸀καυχώμεθα[12] ἐν ταῖς θλίψεσιν,[13] εἰδότες[14] ὅτι ἡ θλῖψις[15]
ὑπομονὴν[16] κατεργάζεται,[17] **4** ἡ δὲ ὑπομονὴ[18] δοκιμήν,[19]
ἡ δὲ δοκιμὴ[20] ἐλπίδα. **5** ἡ δὲ ἐλπὶς οὐ καταισχύνει·[21]

---

[1] δικαιόω, *I justify, declare righteous*. MH: the ο lengthens to an ω before the tense formative.

[2] TH: ἐκ is indicating means; *by*.

[3] TH: Ἰησοῦ Χριστοῦ is in app. to τοῦ κυρίου.

[4] TH: rel. pron. refers to Ἰησοῦ Χριστοῦ.

[5] TH: καί is additive; *also*.

[6] προσαγωγή, ῆς, ἡ, *access*.

[7] MH: pf. act. indic. 1st pl. of ἔχω = σεχ (root) › ἑσχη (redupl. of initial σ dissimilates to a rough breathing mark; ε and χ exchange places, known as metathesis; ε lengthens to η) › ἐσχη (rough breathing mark deaspirates due to χ) + κα (tense formative) + μεν (1st pl. ending) › ἐσχήκαμεν.

[8] TH: rel. pron. refers to τὴν χάριν.

[9] MH: pf. act. indic. 1st pl. of ἵστημι = στα (root) › ἑστη (redupl. of initial σ dissimilates to a rough breathing mark; α lengthens to η) + κα (tense formative) + μεν (1st pl. ending) › ἑστήκαμεν.

[10] καυχάομαι, *I boast*. MH: the root (καυχα) ends in a vowel, so the connecting vowel contracts (α + ο = ω).

[11] TH: καί is additive; *also*.

[12] καυχάομαι, *I boast*. MH: the root (καυχα) ends in a vowel, so the connecting vowel contracts (α + ο = ω).

[13] θλῖψις, εως, ἡ, *affliction, tribulation*.

[14] MH: pf. act. prtc. nom. pl. masc. of οἶδα.

[15] θλῖψις, εως, ἡ, *affliction, tribulation*.

[16] ὑπομονή, ῆς, ἡ, *endurance, perseverance*.

[17] κατεργάζομαι, *I do, commit, bring about*.

[18] ὑπομονή, ῆς, ἡ, *endurance, perseverance*. TH: κατεργάζεται should be supplied from the previous verse.

[19] δοκιμή, ῆς, ἡ, *test, **character***.

[20] δοκιμή, ῆς, ἡ, *test, **character***. TH: κατεργάζεται should be supplied from the previous verse.

[21] καταισχύνω, *I dishonor, put to shame, **disappoint***.

ὅτι ἡ ἀγάπη τοῦ θεοῦ ἐκκέχυται[1] ἐν ταῖς καρδίαις ἡμῶν
διὰ πνεύματος ἁγίου τοῦ δοθέντος[2] ἡμῖν.

6 ⸂Ἔτι γὰρ⸃ Χριστὸς ὄντων[3] ἡμῶν ἀσθενῶν[4] ⸀ἔτι κατὰ
καιρὸν[5] ὑπὲρ ἀσεβῶν[6] ἀπέθανεν.[7] **7** μόλις[8] γὰρ ὑπὲρ
δικαίου τις ἀποθανεῖται·[9] ὑπὲρ γὰρ τοῦ ἀγαθοῦ τάχα[10]
τις καὶ[11] τολμᾷ[12] ἀποθανεῖν·[13] **8** συνίστησιν[14] δὲ τὴν
ἑαυτοῦ ἀγάπην εἰς ἡμᾶς ὁ θεὸς ὅτι ἔτι ἁμαρτωλῶν[15]
ὄντων[16] ἡμῶν Χριστὸς ὑπὲρ ἡμῶν ἀπέθανεν[17]. **9** πολλῷ οὖν
μᾶλλον δικαιωθέντες[18] νῦν ἐν[19] τῷ αἵματι αὐτοῦ
σωθησόμεθα[20] δι᾽ αὐτοῦ ἀπὸ τῆς ὀργῆς.[21] **10** εἰ γὰρ ἐχθροὶ[22]

---

[1] ἐκχέω, *I pour out*. MH: when χ reduplicates, it deaspirates to κ.

[2] MH: aor. pass. prtc. gen. sg. neut. of δίδωμι. The root is δο.

[3] MH: pres. act. prtc. gen. pl. masc. of εἰμί. TH: with ἡμῶν ἀσθενῶν, *while we were helpless*.

[4] ἀσθενής, ές, *sick, weak,* ***helpless***.

[5] TH: ἔτι κατὰ καιρὸν, *at the right time*.

[6] ἀσεβής, ές, *ungodly, profane*.

[7] MH: 2nd aor. of ἀποθνῄσκω; the root is ἀποθαν.

[8] μόλις, *rarely, scarcely*.

[9] MH: fut. mid. indic. 3rd sg. of ἀποθνῄσκω = ἀποθαν (root) + εσ (tense formative) + ε (connecting vowel) › ἀποθανει (intervocalic σ drops out; ε + ε = ει) + ται (3rd sg. ending) › ἀποθανεῖται.

[10] τάχα, *perhaps, maybe*.

[11] TH: καὶ is ascensive; *even*.

[12] τολμάω, *I dare, show courage*. MH: the root (τολμα) ends in a vowel, so the connecting vowel contracts (α + ε = α; ι subscripts).

[13] MH: 2nd aor. of ἀποθνῄσκω; the root is ἀποθαν. TH: complementary inf. with τολμᾷ.

[14] συνίστημι, *I bring together,* ***demonstrate***. MH: pres. act. indic. 3rd sg. of συνίστημι.

[15] ἁμαρτωλός, όν, *sinful*.

[16] MH: pres. act. prtc. gen. pl. masc. of εἰμί. TH: ἔτι ἁμαρτωλῶν ὄντων ἡμῶν, *while we were still sinners*.

[17] MH: 2nd aor. of ἀποθνῄσκω; the root is ἀποθαν.

[18] δικαιόω, *I justify, declare righteous*. MH: the ο lengthens to an ω before the tense formative.

[19] TH: ἐν is instrumental; *by*.

[20] MH: fut. tense stem of σῴζω is σω.

[21] ὀργή, ῆς, ἡ, *wrath*.

[22] ἐχθρός, ά, όν, *hostile, enemy*.

ὄντες[1] κατηλλάγημεν[2] τῷ θεῷ διὰ τοῦ θανάτου τοῦ υἱοῦ
αὐτοῦ, πολλῷ μᾶλλον καταλλαγέντες[3] σωθησόμεθα[4] ἐν[5]
τῇ ζωῇ αὐτοῦ· **11** οὐ μόνον δέ, ἀλλὰ καὶ[6] καυχώμενοι[7] ἐν τῷ
θεῷ διὰ τοῦ κυρίου ἡμῶν Ἰησοῦ Χριστοῦ,[8] δι᾽ οὗ[9] νῦν τὴν
καταλλαγὴν[10] ἐλάβομεν.[11]

12 Διὰ τοῦτο ὥσπερ[12] δι᾽ ἑνὸς ἀνθρώπου ἡ ἁμαρτία εἰς
τὸν κόσμον εἰσῆλθεν[13] καὶ διὰ τῆς ἁμαρτίας ὁ θάνατος,[14]
καὶ οὕτως εἰς πάντας ἀνθρώπους ὁ θάνατος διῆλθεν[15] ἐφ᾽
ᾧ[16] πάντες ἥμαρτον—[17] **13** ἄχρι[18] γὰρ νόμου ἁμαρτία ἦν ἐν
κόσμῳ, ἁμαρτία δὲ οὐκ ἐλλογεῖται[19] μὴ ὄντος[20] νόμου,

---

[1] MH: pres. act. indic. nom. pl. masc. of εἰμί. TH: with ἐχθροὶ, *while we were enemies.*

[2] καταλλάσσω, *I reconcile.* MH: root is καταλλαγ; 2nd aor. pass. does not include θ in the tense formative.

[3] καταλλάσσω, *I reconcile.* MH: root is καταλλαγ; 2nd aor. pass. does not include θ in the tense formative.

[4] MH: fut. tense stem of σῴζω is σω.

[5] TH: ἐν is instrumental; *by.*

[6] TH: καί is additive; *also.*

[7] καυχάομαι, *I boast.* MH: the root (καυχα) ends in a vowel, so the connecting vowel contracts (α + ο = ω).

[8] TH: Ἰησοῦ Χριστοῦ is in app. to κυρίου.

[9] TH: rel. pron. refers to Ἰησοῦ Χριστοῦ.

[10] καταλλαγή, ῆς, ἡ, *reconciliation.*

[11] MH: 2nd aor.; root is λαβ.

[12] ὥσπερ, *just as, even as.*

[13] MH: 2nd aor. of εἰσέρχομαι; root is εἰσελθ.

[14] TH: εἰσῆλθεν is implied here from the first clause; *death entered (the world) through sin.*

[15] διέρχομαι, *I go through, pass through.* MH: 2nd aor.; root is διελθ.

[16] TH: ἐφ᾽ ᾧ is functioning as a conjunction; *because.*

[17] ἁμαρτάνω, *I sin, do wrong.* MH: 2nd aor.; root is ἁμαρτ.

[18] ἄχρι, *until,* ***before.***

[19] ἐλλογέω, *I count, take into account.* MH: the root (ἐλλογε) ends in a vowel, so the connecting vowel contracts (ε + ε = ει).

[20] MH: pres. act. prtc. gen. sg. masc. of εἰμί. TH: μὴ ὄντος νόμου, *when there is no law.*

14 ἀλλὰ ἐβασίλευσεν [1] ὁ θάνατος ἀπὸ Ἀδὰμ [2] μέχρι [3]
Μωϋσέως καὶ [4] ἐπὶ τοὺς μὴ ἁμαρτήσαντας [5] ἐπὶ τῷ
ὁμοιώματι [6] τῆς παραβάσεως [7] Ἀδάμ, [8] ὅς [9] ἐστιν τύπος [10]
τοῦ μέλλοντος. [11]

15 Ἀλλʼ οὐχ ὡς τὸ παράπτωμα, [12] οὕτως καὶ [13] τὸ
χάρισμα· [14] εἰ γὰρ τῷ τοῦ ἑνὸς παραπτώματι [15] οἱ πολλοὶ
ἀπέθανον, [16] πολλῷ μᾶλλον ἡ χάρις τοῦ θεοῦ καὶ ἡ δωρεὰ [17]
ἐν χάριτι τῇ [18] τοῦ ἑνὸς ἀνθρώπου Ἰησοῦ Χριστοῦ [19]
εἰς τοὺς πολλοὺς ἐπερίσσευσεν. [20] **16** καὶ οὐχ ὡς διʼ ἑνὸς
ἁμαρτήσαντος [21] τὸ δώρημα· [22] τὸ μὲν [23] γὰρ κρίμα [24]

---

[1] βασιλεύω, *I rule, am king.*
[2] Ἀδάμ, ὁ, *Adam.*
[3] μέχρι, *until, as far as.*
[4] TH: καὶ is ascensive; *even.*
[5] ἁμαρτάνω, *I sin, do wrong.* MH: root is ἁμαρτ; non-indic. aor. forms insert η after the tense stem.
[6] ὁμοίωμα, ατος, τό, *likeness.* TH: ἐπὶ τῷ ὁμοιώματι, *like.*
[7] παράβασις, εως, ἡ, *transgression.*
[8] Ἀδάμ, ὁ, *Adam.*
[9] TH: rel. pron. refers to Ἀδάμ.
[10] τύπος, ου, ὁ, *pattern, type.* TH: pred. nom. to the subject ὅς.
[11] TH: *the coming one.*
[12] παράπτωμα, ατος, τό, *wrongdoing, sin.*
[13] TH: καί is additive; *also.*
[14] χάρισμα, ατος, τὸ, *gift.*
[15] παράπτωμα, ατος, τό, *wrongdoing, sin.*
[16] MH: 2nd aor. of ἀποθνῄσκω; the root is ἀποθαν.
[17] δωρεά, ᾶς, ἡ, *gift.*
[18] TH: τῇ substantivizes τοῦ ἑνὸς ἀνθρώπου, which modifies χάριτι.
[19] TH: Ἰησοῦ Χριστοῦ is in app. to ἀνθρώπου.
[20] περισσεύω, *I abound, overflow.*
[21] ἁμαρτάνω, *I sin, do wrong.* MH: root is ἁμαρτ; non-indic. aor. forms insert η after the tense stem.
[22] δώρημα, ατος, τὸ, *gift.* TH: subject of a verbless class; καὶ οὐχ … τὸ δώρημα, *and the gift is not.*
[23] TH: μὲν … δὲ, *on the one hand … on the other hand.*
[24] κρίμα, ατος, τό, *judgment.*

ἐξ ἑνὸς[1] εἰς κατάκριμα,[2] τὸ δὲ χάρισμα[3] ἐκ πολλῶν
παραπτωμάτων[4] εἰς δικαίωμα.[5] **17** εἰ γὰρ τῷ τοῦ ἑνὸς
παραπτώματι[6] ὁ θάνατος ἐβασίλευσεν[7] διὰ τοῦ ἑνός,
πολλῷ μᾶλλον οἱ[8] τὴν περισσείαν[9] τῆς χάριτος καὶ τῆς
δωρεᾶς[10] τῆς δικαιοσύνης λαμβάνοντες ἐν ζωῇ
βασιλεύσουσιν[11] διὰ τοῦ ἑνὸς Ἰησοῦ Χριστοῦ.[12]

18 Ἄρα[13] οὖν ὡς δι᾽ ἑνὸς[14] παραπτώματος[15] εἰς[16] πάντας
ἀνθρώπους εἰς[17] κατάκριμα,[18] οὕτως καὶ[19] δι᾽ ἑνὸς[20] δικαι-
ώματος[21] εἰς[22] πάντας ἀνθρώπους εἰς[23] δικαίωσιν[24] ζωῆς·

---

[1] TH: "leads" should be supplied after ἑνὸς.

[2] κατάκριμα, ατος, τό, *condemnation*.

[3] χάρισμα, ατος, τὸ, *gift*.

[4] παράπτωμα, ατος, τό, *wrongdoing, sin*. TH: "leads" should be supplied after παραπτωμάτων.

[5] δικαίωμα, ατος, τό, *requirement, righteous deed,* ***justification***.

[6] παράπτωμα, ατος, τό, *wrongdoing, sin*.

[7] βασιλεύω, *I rule, am king*.

[8] TH: οἱ is the art. for the prtc. λαμβάνοντες later in the verse.

[9] περισσεία, ας, ἡ, *surplus, abundance*.

[10] δωρεά, ᾶς, ἡ, *gift*.

[11] βασιλεύω, *I rule, am king*.

[12] TH: Ἰησοῦ Χριστοῦ is in app. to ἑνός.

[13] ἆρα, *consequently*.

[14] TH: ἑνὸς is masc. and embedded between the prep. and its obj.; δι᾽ ἑνὸς παραπτώματος, *the sin of the one (man)*.

[15] παράπτωμα, ατος, τό, *wrongdoing, sin*.

[16] TH: εἰς is indicating advantage; *for*.

[17] TH: εἰς is indicating result; in this verbless clause: εἰς κατάκριμα, *there is judgment*.

[18] κατάκριμα, ατος, τό, *judgment, condemnation*.

[19] TH: καί is additive; *also*.

[20] TH: ἑνὸς is masc. and embedded between the prep. and its obj.; δι᾽ ἑνὸς δικαιώματος, *through the righteous deed of the one (man)*.

[21] δικαίωμα, ατος, τό, *requirement, righteous deed*.

[22] TH: εἰς is indicating advantage; *for*.

[23] TH: εἰς indicates result; εἰς δικαίωσιν, *there is justification*.

[24] δικαίωσις, εως, ἡ, *justification, setting right*.

19 ὥσπερ[1] γὰρ διὰ τῆς παρακοῆς[2] τοῦ ἑνὸς ἀνθρώπου
ἁμαρτωλοὶ[3] κατεστάθησαν[4] οἱ πολλοί,[5] οὕτως καὶ[6] διὰ
τῆς ὑπακοῆς[7] τοῦ ἑνὸς δίκαιοι κατασταθήσονται[8]
οἱ πολλοί.[9] 20 νόμος δὲ παρεισῆλθεν[10] ἵνα πλεονάσῃ[11]
τὸ παράπτωμα· [12] οὗ[13] δὲ ἐπλεόνασεν[14] ἡ ἁμαρτία,
ὑπερεπερίσσευσεν[15] ἡ χάρις, 21 ἵνα ὥσπερ[16] ἐβασίλευσεν[17]
ἡ ἁμαρτία ἐν τῷ θανάτῳ, οὕτως καὶ[18] ἡ χάρις βασιλεύσῃ[19]
διὰ δικαιοσύνης εἰς ζωὴν αἰώνιον διὰ Ἰησοῦ Χριστοῦ
τοῦ κυρίου ἡμῶν.

5:1 ἔχομεν NA28 RP] ἔχωμεν WH Treg

3 καυχώμεθα WH NA28 RP] καυχώμενοι Treg

6 Ἔτι γὰρ Treg NA28 RP] Εἴ γε WH

6 Ἔτι γὰρ Treg NA28 RP] Εἴ γε WH

- **ἔτι** WH Treg NA28] – RP

---

[1] ὥσπερ, *just as, even as.*

[2] παρακοή, ῆς, ἡ, *disobedience.*

[3] ἁμαρτωλός, ον, *sinful.*

[4] καθίστημι, *I appoint, cause,* ***declare***. MH: the root is κατάστα.

[5] TH: ἁμαρτωλοὶ κατεστάθησαν οἱ πολλοί, *the many were declared sinful.*

[6] TH: καί is additive; *also.*

[7] ὑπακοή, ῆς, ἡ, *obedience.*

[8] καθίστημι, *I appoint, cause,* ***declare***. MH: the root is καταστα.

[9] TH: δίκαιοι κατασταθήσονται οἱ πολλοί, *the many will be declared righteous.*

[10] παρεισέρχομαι, *I slip in, come in.* MH: 2nd aor.; aor. tense stem is παρεισελθ.

[11] πλεονάζω, *I grow, increase.* MH: the root ends in δ; δ + σ = σ. Subj. mood has length. connecting vowel (ε › η).

[12] παράπτωμα, ατος, τό, *wrongdoing, sin.*

[13] οὗ, *where.*

[14] πλεονάζω, *I grow, increase.* MH: the root ends in δ; δ + σ = σ.

[15] ὑπερπερισσεύω, *I abound more.*

[16] ὥσπερ, *just as, even as.*

[17] βασιλεύω, *I rule, am king.*

[18] TH: καί is additive; *also.*

[19] βασιλεύω, *I rule, am king.* MH: subj. mood has length. connecting vowel (ε › η).

ROMANS 6

New Vocabulary by Frequency [Chapter, Book, SBLGNT Occurrences]

ἁγιασμός, οῦ, ὁ, *sanctification* [2, 2, 10]
ἀγνοέω, *I am unaware, ignorant (of)* [1, 6, 22]
ἀδικία, ας, ἡ, *unrighteousness, injustice* [1, 7, 25]
ἀκαθαρσία, ας, ἡ, *impurity, immorality* [1, 2, 10]
ἁμαρτάνω, *I sin, do wrong* [1, 7, 43]
ἀνάστασις, εως, ἡ, *resurrection* [1, 2, 42]
ἀνθρώπινος, η, ον, *human* [1, 1, 7]
ἀνομία, ας, ἡ, *lawlessness, lawless conduct* [2, 3, 15]
ἀσθένεια, ας, ἡ, *weakness* [1, 2, 24]
βάπτισμα, ατος, τό, *washing, baptism* [1, 1, 19]
βασιλεύω, *I rule, am king* [1, 6, 21]
διδαχή, ῆς, ἡ, *teaching* [1, 2, 30]
δικαιόω, *I justify, declare righteous* [1, 15, 39]
δουλεύω, *I serve* [1, 7, 25]
δουλόω, *I enslave* [2, 2, 8]
ἐλεύθερος, α, ον, *free* [1, 2, 23]
ἐλευθερόω, *I set free* [2, 4, 7]
ἐπαισχύνομαι, *I am ashamed (of)* [1, 2, 11]
ἐπιθυμία, ας, ἡ, *desire, lust* [1, 5, 38]
ἐπιμένω, *I remain, continue* [1, 3, 16]
ἐφάπαξ, *once, once for all* [1, 1, 5]
ἤτοι, *whether* [1, 1, 1]
θνητός, ή, όν, *mortal* [1, 2, 6]
καινότης, ητος, ἡ, *newness* [1, 2, 2]
καταργέω, *I invalidate, abolish* [1, 6, 27]
κυριεύω, *I rule, am master of* [2, 4, 7]
λογίζομαι, *I regard, consider* [1, 19, 40]
μέλος, ους, τό, *member, part* [4, 10, 34]
μηκέτι, *no longer* [1, 3, 22]
νυνί, *now* [1, 6, 20]
ὁμοίωμα, ατος, τό, *likeness* [1, 4, 6]
ὅπλον, ου, τό, *tool, weapon* [2, 3, 6]
οὐκέτι, *no longer* [2, 7, 47]
ὀψώνιον, ου, τό, *wage, pay* [1, 1, 4]
παλαιός, ά, όν, *old* [1, 1, 19]
παρίστημι, *I present, demonstrate* [5, 8, 41]

πλεονάζω, *I grow, increase* [1, 3, 9]
συζάω, *I live with* [1, 1, 3]
σύμφυτος, ον, *identified with* [1, 1, 1]
συνθάπτω, *I bury with* [1, 1, 2]
συσταυρόω, *I crucify with* [1, 1, 5]
τέλος, ους, τό, *end* [2, 5, 40]
τύπος, ου, ὁ, *pattern, type* [1, 2, 15]
ὑπακοή, ῆς, ἡ, *obedience* [2, 6, 14]
ὑπακούω, *I obey, listen* [3, 4, 21]
χάρισμα, ατος, τό, *gift* [1, 6, 17]
ὡσεί, as, *like* [1, 1, 20]
ὥσπερ, *just as, even as.* [2, 6, 36]

6.1 Τί οὖν ἐροῦμεν;[1] ⸀ἐπιμένωμεν[2] τῇ ἁμαρτίᾳ, ἵνα ἡ
χάρις πλεονάσῃ;[3] **2** μὴ γένοιτο·[4] οἵτινες ἀπεθάνομεν[5] τῇ
ἁμαρτίᾳ, πῶς ἔτι ζήσομεν ἐν αὐτῇ; **3** ἢ ἀγνοεῖτε[6] ὅτι ὅσοι
ἐβαπτίσθημεν[7] εἰς Χριστὸν Ἰησοῦν εἰς τὸν θάνατον
αὐτοῦ ἐβαπτίσθημεν;[8] **4** συνετάφημεν[9] οὖν αὐτῷ[10] διὰ τοῦ
βαπτίσματος[11] εἰς τὸν θάνατον, ἵνα ὥσπερ[12] ἠγέρθη[13]
Χριστὸς ἐκ νεκρῶν διὰ τῆς δόξης τοῦ πατρός, οὕτως καὶ[14]
ἡμεῖς ἐν καινότητι[15] ζωῆς περιπατήσωμεν.[16]

5 Εἰ γὰρ σύμφυτοι[17] γεγόναμεν[18] τῷ ὁμοιώματι[19] τοῦ
θανάτου αὐτοῦ, ἀλλὰ[20] καὶ[21] τῆς ἀναστάσεως[22] ἐσόμεθα·

---

[1] MH: fut. act. indic. 1st pl. of λέγω.

[2] ἐπιμένω, *I remain, continue*. MH: subj. mood has a lengthened connecting vowel (ο › ω).

[3] πλεονάζω, *I grow, increase*. MH: the stem ends in δ; δ + σ = σ. Subj. mood has a lengthened connecting vowel (ε › η).

[4] MH: aor. mid. opt. 3rd sg. TH: μὴ γένοιτο conveys strong denial; *May it not be!*

[5] MH: 2nd aor. of ἀποθνήσκω; the root is ἀποθαν. TH: οἵτινες ἀπεθάνομεν, *we who died.*

[6] ἀγνοέω, *I am unaware, ignorant (of)*. MH: the root (ἀγνοε) ends in a vowel, so the connecting vowel contracts (ε + ε = ει).

[7] MH: the root ends in δ; δ + θ = σθ.

[8] MH: the root ends in δ; δ + θ = σθ.

[9] συνθάπτω, *I bury with*. MH: 2nd aor. pass. does not have θ in the tense formative; συν + θαπ › συν + ταφ (aspiration transfer; θ deaspirates and π aspirates).

[10] TH: dat. of association; *with.*

[11] βάπτισμα, ατος, τό, *washing, baptism.*

[12] ὥσπερ, *just as, even as.*

[13] MH: aor. pass. indic. 3rd sg. of ἐγείρω. The root is ἐγερ.

[14] TH: καί is additive; *also.*

[15] καινότης, ητος, ἡ, *newness.*

[16] MH: the ε lengthens to η before the tense formative; subj. mood has a lengthened connecting vowel (ο › ω).

[17] σύμφυτος, ον, *identified with*. TH: pred. nom. to the subj. of γεγόναμεν.

[18] MH: 2nd pf. of γίνομαι. The root (γεν) becomes γον due to ablaut.

[19] ὁμοίωμα, ατος, τό, *likeness.*

[20] TH: ἀλλά is emphatic; *certainly.*

[21] TH: καί is additive; *also.*

[22] ἀνάστασις, εως, ἡ, *resurrection*. TH: the gen. here implies σύμφυτοι … τῷ ὁμοιώματι from the previous clause.

6 τοῦτο γινώσκοντες ὅτι ὁ παλαιὸς[1] ἡμῶν ἄνθρωπος
συνεσταυρώθη,[2] ἵνα καταργηθῇ[3] τὸ σῶμα τῆς ἁμαρτίας,
τοῦ μηκέτι[4] δουλεύειν[5] ἡμᾶς[6] τῇ ἁμαρτίᾳ,[7] **7** ὁ γὰρ
ἀποθανὼν[8] δεδικαίωται[9] ἀπὸ τῆς ἁμαρτίας. **8** εἰ δὲ ἀπε-
θάνομεν[10] σὺν Χριστῷ, πιστεύομεν ὅτι καὶ[11] συζήσομεν[12]
αὐτῷ· **9** εἰδότες[13] ὅτι Χριστὸς ἐγερθεὶς[14] ἐκ νεκρῶν
οὐκέτι[15] ἀποθνῄσκει, θάνατος αὐτοῦ[16] οὐκέτι[17] κυριεύει·[18]
10 ὃ[19] γὰρ ἀπέθανεν,[20] τῇ ἁμαρτίᾳ ἀπέθανεν[21] ἐφάπαξ·[22]

---

[1] παλαιός, ά, όν, *old*.

[2] συσταυρόω, *I crucify with*. MH: when the aug. is added, the ν of the prep. reappears; the ο lengthens to an ω before the tense formative. TH: *was crucified with him*.

[3] καταργέω, *I invalidate, abolish,* ***nullify***. MH: the ε lengthens to η before the tense formative.

[4] μηκέτι, *no longer*.

[5] δουλεύω, *I serve*. TH: τοῦ + inf. here indicates result; τοῦ μηκέτι δουλεύειν ἡμᾶς, *so that we no longer serve*.

[6] TH: the acc. is the subject of the inf.

[7] TH: dat. dir. obj. of δουλεύειν.

[8] MH: 2nd aor. of ἀποθνήσκω; the root is ἀποθαν.

[9] δικαιόω, *I justify, declare righteous,* ***make free***. MH: the ο lengthens to ω before the ending in pf. mid./pass. forms.

[10] MH: 2nd aor. of ἀποθνήσκω; the root is ἀποθαν.

[11] TH: καί is additive; *also*.

[12] συζάω, *I live with*. MH: the α lengthens to η before the tense formative.

[13] MH: pf. act. prtc. nom. pl. masc. of οἶδα.

[14] MH: aor. pass. prtc. nom. sg. masc. of ἐγείρω. The root is ἐγερ.

[15] οὐκέτι, *no longer*.

[16] TH: gen. dir. obj. of κυριεύω.

[17] οὐκέτι, *no longer*.

[18] κυριεύω, *I rule, am master of*.

[19] TH: rel. pron. is neut., but likely refers to θάνατος; *the death which*.

[20] MH: 2nd aor. of ἀποθνήσκω; the root is ἀποθαν.

[21] MH: 2nd aor. of ἀποθνήσκω; the root is ἀποθαν.

[22] ἐφάπαξ, *once, once for all*.

ὃ[1] δὲ ζῇ,[2] ζῇ[3] τῷ θεῷ. **11** οὕτως καὶ[4] ὑμεῖς λογίζεσθε[5]
ἑαυτοὺς ⸂εἶναι νεκροὺς μὲν⸃ τῇ ἁμαρτίᾳ ζῶντας δὲ τῷ θεῷ
ἐν Χριστῷ ⸆Ἰησοῦ.

12 Μὴ οὖν βασιλευέτω[6] ἡ ἁμαρτία ἐν τῷ θνητῷ[7] ὑμῶν
σώματι εἰς τὸ ⸀ὑπακούειν[8] ταῖς ἐπιθυμίαις[9] αὐτοῦ,
13 μηδὲ παριστάνετε[10] τὰ μέλη[11] ὑμῶν ὅπλα[12] ἀδικίας[13] τῇ
ἁμαρτίᾳ, ἀλλὰ παραστήσατε[14] ἑαυτοὺς τῷ θεῷ ⸀ὡσεὶ[15] ἐκ
νεκρῶν ζῶντας καὶ τὰ μέλη[16] ὑμῶν ὅπλα[17] δικαιοσύνης τῷ
θεῷ. **14** ἁμαρτία γὰρ ὑμῶν[18] οὐ κυριεύσει,[19] οὐ γάρ ἐστε
ὑπὸ νόμον ἀλλὰ ὑπὸ χάριν.

---

[1] TH: rel. pron. is neut., but likely refers to ζωή; *the life which.*

[2] MH: from ζάω; in Classical Greek, the root was ζη, which is retained in some forms in Koine (η + ει = ῃ).

[3] MH: from ζάω; in Classical Greek, the root was ζη, which is retained in some forms in Koine (η + ει = ῃ).

[4] TH: καί is additive; *also.*

[5] λογίζομαι, *I regard, consider.*

[6] βασιλεύω, *I rule, am king.*

[7] θνητός, ή, όν, *mortal.*

[8] ὑπακούω, *I obey, listen.* TH: εἰς τὸ + inf. indicates result; *so that you obey.*

[9] ἐπιθυμία, ας, ἡ, *desire, lust.*

[10] παρίστημι, *I present, demonstrate.* MH: root is παραστα.

[11] μέλος, ους, τό, *member, part.*

[12] ὅπλον, ου, τό, *tool, weapon.* TH: *as tools.*

[13] ἀδικία, ας, ἡ, *unrighteousness, injustice.*

[14] παρίστημι, *I present, demonstrate.* MH: root is παραστα; the α lengthens to η before the tense formative.

[15] ὡσεί, *as, like.*

[16] μέλος, ους, τό, *member, part.*

[17] ὅπλον, ου, τό, *tool, weapon.* TH: *as tools.*

[18] TH: gen. dir. obj. of κυριεύω.

[19] κυριεύω, *I rule, am master of.*

15 Τί οὖν; ἁμαρτήσωμεν[1] ὅτι οὐκ ἐσμὲν ὑπὸ νόμον
ἀλλὰ ὑπὸ χάριν; μὴ γένοιτο·[2] **16** οὐκ οἴδατε ὅτι
ᾧ παριστάνετε[3] ἑαυτοὺς δούλους εἰς ὑπακοήν,[4] δοῦλοί[5]
ἐστε ᾧ ὑπακούετε,[6] ἤτοι[7] ἁμαρτίας εἰς θάνατον ἢ
ὑπακοῆς[8] εἰς δικαιοσύνην; **17** χάρις[9] δὲ τῷ θεῷ ὅτι ἦτε
δοῦλοι[10] τῆς ἁμαρτίας ὑπηκούσατε[11] δὲ ἐκ καρδίας εἰς ὃν
παρεδόθητε[12] τύπον[13] διδαχῆς,[14] **18** ἐλευθερωθέντες[15] δὲ
ἀπὸ τῆς ἁμαρτίας ἐδουλώθητε[16] τῇ δικαιοσύνῃ·
19 ἀνθρώπινον[17] λέγω διὰ τὴν ἀσθένειαν[18] τῆς σαρκὸς
ὑμῶν· ὥσπερ[19] γὰρ παρεστήσατε[20] τὰ μέλη[21] ὑμῶν δοῦλα[22]

---

[1] ἁμαρτάνω, *I sin, do wrong*. MH: root is ἁμαρτ; non-indic. aor. forms insert η after the tense stem. Subj. mood has a length. connecting vowel (ο › ω).

[2] MH: aor. mid. opt. 3rd sg. TH: μὴ γένοιτο conveys strong denial; *May it not be!*

[3] παρίστημι, *I present, demonstrate*. MH: root is παραστα. TH: This verb takes a double dir. obj.; *to whom you present yourselves (as) slaves ….*

[4] ὑπακοή, ῆς, ἡ, *obedience*.

[5] TH: pred. nom. to the subject of ἐστε.

[6] ὑπακούω, *I obey, listen*.

[7] ἤτοι, *whether*.

[8] ὑπακοή, ῆς, ἡ, *obedience*.

[9] TH: *thanks*.

[10] TH: pred. nom. to the subject of ἦτε.

[11] ὑπακούω, *I obey, listen*.

[12] MH: root is παραδο.

[13] τύπος, ου, ὁ, *pattern, type*.

[14] διδαχή, ῆς, ἡ, *teaching*. TH: εἰς ὃν παρεδόθητε τύπον διδαχῆς, *the type of teaching to which you were entrusted*.

[15] ἐλευθερόω, *I set free*. MH: the ο lengthens to an ω before the tense formative.

[16] δουλόω, *I enslave*. MH: the ο lengthens to an ω before the tense formative.

[17] ἀνθρώπινος, η, ον, *human*, ***in human terms***.

[18] ἀσθένεια, ας, ἡ, *weakness*.

[19] ὥσπερ, *just as, even as*.

[20] παρίστημι, *I present, demonstrate*. MH: root is παραστα; the α lengthens to η before the tense formative.

[21] μέλος, ους, τό, *member, part*.

[22] TH: *as slaves*.

τῇ ἀκαθαρσίᾳ [1] καὶ τῇ ἀνομίᾳ [2] εἰς [3] τὴν ἀνομίαν, [4]
οὕτως νῦν παραστήσατε [5] τὰ μέλη [6] ὑμῶν δοῦλα [7] τῇ
δικαιοσύνῃ εἰς[8] ἁγιασμόν.[9]
20 Ὅτε γὰρ δοῦλοι[10] ἦτε τῆς ἁμαρτίας, ἐλεύθεροι[11] ἦτε
τῇ δικαιοσύνῃ. **21** τίνα οὖν καρπὸν εἴχετε τότε ἐφ᾽ οἷς νῦν
ἐπαισχύνεσθε; [12] τὸ γὰρ τέλος [13] ἐκείνων θάνατος· [14] **22**
νυνὶ [15] δέ, ἐλευθερωθέντες [16] ἀπὸ τῆς ἁμαρτίας
δουλωθέντες [17] δὲ τῷ θεῷ, ἔχετε τὸν καρπὸν ὑμῶν εἰς
ἁγιασμόν,[18] τὸ δὲ τέλος[19] ζωὴν αἰώνιον. **23** τὰ γὰρ ὀψώνια[20]
τῆς ἁμαρτίας θάνατος,[21] τὸ δὲ χάρισμα[22] τοῦ θεοῦ ζωὴ[23]
αἰώνιος ἐν Χριστῷ Ἰησοῦ τῷ κυρίῳ[24] ἡμῶν.

---

[1] ἀκαθαρσία, ας, ἡ, *impurity, immorality.*
[2] ἀνομία, ας, ἡ, *lawlessness, lawless conduct.*
[3] TH: *leading to.*
[4] ἀνομία, ας, ἡ, *lawlessness, lawless conduct.*
[5] παρίστημι, *I present, demonstrate.* MH: root is παραστα; the α lengthens to η before the tense formative.
[6] μέλος, ους, τό, *member, part.*
[7] TH: *as slaves.*
[8] TH: *leading to.*
[9] ἁγιασμός, οῦ, ὁ, *sanctification.*
[10] TH: pred. nom. to the subject of ἦτε.
[11] ἐλεύθερος, α, ον, *free.* TH: pred. nom. to the subject of ἦτε.
[12] ἐπαισχύνομαι, *I am ashamed (of).*
[13] τέλος, ους, τό, *end.*
[14] TH: pred. nom. to τέλος.
[15] νυνί, *now.*
[16] ἐλευθερόω, *I set free.* MH: the ο lengthens to an ω before the tense formative.
[17] δουλόω, *I enslave.* MH: the ο lengthens to an ω before the tense formative.
[18] ἁγιασμός, οῦ, ὁ, *sanctification.*
[19] τέλος, ους, τό, *end.*
[20] ὀψώνιον, ου, τό, *wage, pay.*
[21] TH: pred. nom to ὀψώνια.
[22] χάρισμα, ατος, τό, *gift.*
[23] TH: pred. nom. to χάρισμα.
[24] TH: τῷ κυρίῳ is in app. to Χριστῷ Ἰησοῦ.

6:1 **ἐπιμένωμεν** WH Treg NA28] Ἐπιμένομεν RP
11 **εἶναι νεκροὺς μὲν** WH Treg NA28] νεκροὺς μὲν εἶναι RP; νεκροὺς μὲν NIV
11 **εἶναι νεκροὺς μὲν** WH Treg NA28] νεκροὺς μὲν εἶναι RP; νεκροὺς μὲν NIV
• **Ἰησοῦ** WH Treg NA28] + τῷ κυρίῳ ἡμῶν RP
12 **ὑπακούειν** WH Treg NA28] + αὐτῇ ἐν RP
13 **ὡσεὶ** WH Treg NA28] ὡς RP
15 **ἁμαρτήσωμεν** WH Treg NA28] Ἁμαρτήσομεν RP

ROMANS 7

New Vocabulary by Frequency [Chapter, Book, SBLGNT Occurrences]

ἀγνοέω, *I am unaware, ignorant (of)* [1, 6, 22]
αἰχμαλωτίζω, *I take captive* [1, 1, 4]
ἁμαρτωλός, ον, *sinful* [1, 4, 47]
ἀναζάω, *I come to life, return to life* [1, 1, 2]
ἀντιστρατεύομαι, *I am at war with* [1, 1, 1]
ἆρα, *consequently* [3, 11, 52]
ἀφορμή, ῆς, ἡ, *occasion, opportunity* [2, 2, 7]
γράμμα, ατος, τό, *letter* [1, 3, 14]
δέω, *I bind, tie* [1, 1, 43]
δουλεύω, *I serve* [2, 7, 25]
ἐλεύθερος, α, ον, *free* [1, 2, 23]
ἐνεργέω, *I am active, at work* [1, 1, 21]
ἐξαπατάω, *I deceive* [1, 2, 6]
ἐπιθυμέω, *I covet, desire* [1, 2, 16]
ἐπιθυμία, ας, ἡ, *desire, lust* [2, 5, 38]
ἔσω, *inner, inside* [1, 1, 9]
θανατόω, *I kill, put to death* [1, 3, 11]
καινότης, ητος, ἡ, *newness* [1, 2, 2]
καρποφορέω, *I bear fruit* [2, 2, 8]
καταργέω, *I invalidate, abolish* [2, 6, 27]
κατεργάζομαι, *I do, commit, bring about* [6, 11, 22]
κατέχω, I *restrain, hold back* [1, 2, 17]
κυριεύω, *I rule, am master of* [1, 4, 7]
μέλος, ους, τό, *member, part* [3, 10, 34]
μισέω, *I hate* [1, 2, 40]
μοιχαλίς, ίδος, ἡ, *adulteress* [2, 2, 7]
νοῦς, ός, ὁ, *mind, way of thinking* [2, 6, 24]
νυνί, *now* [2, 6, 20]
οἰκέω, *I live, dwell* [3, 5, 9]
οὐκέτι, *no longer* [2, 7, 47]
πάθημα, ατος, τό, *suffering, feeling* [1, 2, 16]
παλαιότης, ητος, ἡ, *oldness* [1, 1, 1]
παράκειμαι, *I am present, ready* [2, 2, 2]
πιπράσκω, *I sell* [1, 1, 9]
πνευματικός, ή, όν, *spiritual* [1, 3, 26]
ποτέ, *once* [1, 3, 29]

πράσσω, *I do, engage in* [2, 10, 38]
ῥύομαι, *I save, rescue, deliver* [1, 3, 17]
σάρκινος, η, ον, *fleshly* [1, 1, 4]
σύμφημι, *I concur, agree with* [1, 1, 1]
συνήδομαι, *I delight in* [1, 1, 1]
ταλαίπωρος, ον, *wretched, miserable* [1, 1, 2]
ὕπανδρος, ον, *married* [1, 1, 1]
ὑπερβολή, ῆς, ἡ, *excess, exceeding* [1, 1, 8]
φαίνω, *I appear, shine* [1, 1, 31]
χρηματίζω, *I call, warn* [1, 1, 9]
χωρίς, *without, apart* [2, 6, 42]

7.1 Ἢ ἀγνοεῖτε,[1] ἀδελφοί, γινώσκουσιν[2] γὰρ νόμον
λαλῶ, ὅτι ὁ νόμος κυριεύει[3] τοῦ ἀνθρώπου ἐφ' ὅσον
χρόνον[4] ζῇ;[5] **2** ἡ γὰρ ὕπανδρος[6] γυνὴ τῷ ζῶντι ἀνδρὶ
δέδεται[7] νόμῳ· ἐὰν δὲ ἀποθάνῃ[8] ὁ ἀνήρ, κατήργηται[9] ἀπὸ
τοῦ νόμου τοῦ ἀνδρός. **3** ἄρα[10] οὖν ζῶντος τοῦ ἀνδρὸς[11]
μοιχαλὶς[12] χρηματίσει[13] ἐὰν γένηται[14] ἀνδρὶ ἑτέρῳ· ἐὰν δὲ
ἀποθάνῃ[15] ὁ ἀνήρ, ἐλευθέρα[16] ἐστὶν ἀπὸ τοῦ νόμου, τοῦ
μὴ εἶναι[17] αὐτὴν[18] μοιχαλίδα[19] γενομένην[20] ἀνδρὶ ἑτέρῳ.
4 Ὥστε, ἀδελφοί μου, καὶ[21] ὑμεῖς ἐθανατώθητε[22] τῷ
νόμῳ διὰ τοῦ σώματος τοῦ Χριστοῦ, εἰς τὸ γενέσθαι[23]

---

[1] ἀγνοέω, *I am unaware, ignorant (of).* MH: the root (ἀγνοε) ends in a vowel, so the connecting vowel contracts (ε + ε = ει).

[2] TH: subst. prtc.; *to those who know.*

[3] κυριεύω, *I rule, am master of.*

[4] TH: ἐφ' ὅσον χρόνον, *for however long.*

[5] MH: from ζάω; in Classical Greek, the root was ζη, which is retained in some forms in Koine (η + ει = ῃ).

[6] ὕπανδρος, ον, *married.*

[7] δέω, *I bind, tie.*

[8] MH: 2nd aor. of ἀποθνῄσκω; the root is ἀποθαν.

[9] καταργέω, *I invalidate, abolish,* ***release.*** MH: the ε lengthens to η before the tense formative.

[10] ἄρα, *consequently.*

[11] TH: ζῶντος τοῦ ἀνδρὸς, *while the husband lives.*

[12] μοιχαλίς, ιδος, ἡ, *adulteress.* TH: pred. nom. to the subject of χρηματίσει.

[13] χρηματίζω, *I call, warn.*

[14] MH: 2nd aor. of γίνομαι; root is γεν. TH: *she is joined.*

[15] MH: 2nd aor. of ἀποθνῄσκω; the root is ἀποθαν.

[16] ἐλεύθερος, α, ον, *free.* TH: pred. nom. to the subject of ἐστὶν.

[17] TH: τοῦ + inf. here indicates result; τοῦ μὴ εἶναι αὐτήν, *so that she would not be.*

[18] TH: acc. is the subject of the inf.

[19] μοιχαλίς, ίδος, ἡ, *adulteress.*

[20] MH: 2nd aor. of γίνομαι; root is γεν. TH: prtc. of condition; *if she is joined.*

[21] TH: καί is additive; *also.*

[22] θανατόω, *I kill, put to death.* MH: the ο lengthens to ω before the tense formative.

[23] TH: εἰς τὸ + inf. here indicates result; *so that you are joined.*

ὑμᾶς[1] ἑτέρῳ, τῷ ἐκ νεκρῶν ἐγερθέντι[2] ἵνα καρποφορή-
σωμεν[3] τῷ θεῷ. **5** ὅτε γὰρ ἦμεν ἐν τῇ σαρκί, τὰ παθήματα[4]
τῶν ἁμαρτιῶν τὰ[5] διὰ τοῦ νόμου ἐνηργεῖτο[6] ἐν τοῖς
μέλεσιν[7] ἡμῶν εἰς τὸ καρποφορῆσαι[8] τῷ θανάτῳ· **6** νυνὶ[9]
δὲ κατηργήθημεν[10] ἀπὸ τοῦ νόμου, ἀποθανόντες[11] ἐν ᾧ[12]
κατειχόμεθα,[13] ὥστε δουλεύειν[14] ἡμᾶς[15] ἐν καινότητι[16]
πνεύματος καὶ οὐ παλαιότητι[17] γράμματος.[18]

7 Τί οὖν ἐροῦμεν;[19] ὁ νόμος ἁμαρτία; μὴ γένοιτο· ἀλλὰ
τὴν ἁμαρτίαν οὐκ ἔγνων[20] εἰ μὴ διὰ νόμου, τήν τε γὰρ
ἐπιθυμίαν[21] οὐκ ᾔδειν[22] εἰ μὴ ὁ νόμος ἔλεγεν·

---

[1] TH: acc. is the subject of the inf. γενέσθαι.

[2] MH: aor. pass. prtc. dat. sg. masc. of ἐγείρω. The root is ἐγερ. TH: τῷ ἐκ νεκρῶν ἐγερθέντι is in app. to ἑτέρῳ.

[3] καρποφορέω, *I bear fruit*. MH: the ε lengthens to η before the tense formative; subj. mood has lengthened connecting vowel (ο › ω).

[4] πάθημα, ατος, τό, *suffering, feeling*, ***desire***.

[5] TH: τὰ substantivizes the prep. phrase διὰ τοῦ νόμου; τὰ παθήματα τῶν ἁμαρτιῶν τὰ διὰ τοῦ νόμου, *the desires of sin through the law*.

[6] ἐνεργέω, *I am active, at work*. MH: the root (ἐνεργε) ends in a vowel, so the connecting vowel contracts (ε + ε = ει).

[7] μέλος, ους, τό, *member, part*.

[8] καρποφορέω, *I bear fruit*. MH: the ε lengthens to η before the tense formative. TH: εἰς τὸ + inf. here indicates purpose; *to bear fruit*.

[9] νυνί, *now*.

[10] καταργέω, *I invalidate, abolish*, ***release***. MH: the ε lengthens to η before the tense formative.

[11] MH: 2nd aor. of ἀποθνήσκω; the root is ἀποθαν.

[12] TH: rel. pron. refers to τοῦ νόμου; ἐν ᾧ, *by which*.

[13] κατέχω, I *restrain, hold back*. MH: κατα (prep.) + ε (aug.) + σεχ (root) › κατεσεχ › κατειχ (intervocalic σ drops out; ε + ε = ει). TH: ἀποθανόντες ἐν ᾧ κατειχόμεθα, *having died (to the thing) by which we were restrained*.

[14] δουλεύω, *I serve*. TH: ὥστε + inf. indicates result; *so that we serve*.

[15] TH: acc. is the subject of the inf. δουλεύειν.

[16] καινότης, ητος, ἡ, *newness*.

[17] παλαιότης, ητος, ἡ, *oldness*.

[18] γράμμα, ατος, τό, *letter*.

[19] MH: fut. act. indic. 1st pl. of λέγω.

[20] MH: 2nd aor. from γινώσκω; root is γνο.

[21] ἐπιθυμία, ας, ἡ, *desire, lust*.

[22] MH: plpf. act. indic. 1st sg. of οἶδα.

Οὐκ ἐπιθυμήσεις·[1] **8** ἀφορμὴν[2] δὲ λαβοῦσα[3] ἡ ἁμαρτία διὰ
τῆς ἐντολῆς κατειργάσατο[4] ἐν ἐμοὶ πᾶσαν ἐπιθυμίαν,[5]
χωρὶς[6] γὰρ νόμου ἁμαρτία νεκρά.[7] **9** ἐγὼ δὲ ἔζων[8] χωρὶς[9]
νόμου ποτέ·[10] ἐλθούσης[11] δὲ τῆς ἐντολῆς ἡ ἁμαρτία
ἀνέζησεν,[12] **10** ἐγὼ δὲ ἀπέθανον,[13] καὶ εὑρέθη[14] μοι ἡ
ἐντολὴ ἡ[15] εἰς ζωὴν αὕτη[16] εἰς θάνατον· **11** ἡ γὰρ ἁμαρτία
ἀφορμὴν[17] λαβοῦσα[18] διὰ τῆς ἐντολῆς ἐξηπάτησέν[19] με
καὶ δι' αὐτῆς[20] ἀπέκτεινεν.[21] **12** ὥστε ὁ μὲν νόμος ἅγιος,[22]
καὶ ἡ ἐντολὴ ἁγία καὶ δικαία καὶ ἀγαθή.[23]

---

[1] ἐπιθυμέω, *I covet, desire*. MH: the ε lengthens to η before the tense formative.

[2] ἀφορμή, ῆς, ἡ, *occasion, opportunity*.

[3] MH: 2nd aor.; root is λαβ.

[4] κατεργάζομαι, *I do, commit, bring about*. MH: the root is κατα + Ϝεργαδ; κατα (prep.) + ε (aug.) + Ϝεργαδ (root) › κατειργαδ (intervocalic Ϝ drops out; ε + ε = ει) + σα (tense formative) + το (aor. mid. indic. 3rd sg. ending) › κατειργάσατο.

[5] ἐπιθυμία, ας, ἡ, *desire, lust*.

[6] χωρίς, *without, apart*.

[7] TH: pred. adj. to ἁμαρτία.

[8] MH: the root (ζα) ends in a vowel, so the connecting vowel contracts (α + ο = ω).

[9] χωρίς, *without, apart*.

[10] ποτέ, *once*.

[11] MH: aor. tense stem of ἔρχομαι is ἐλθ. TH: gen. abs.; with τῆς ἐντολῆς, *with the coming of the commandment*.

[12] ἀναζάω, *I come to life, return to life*. MH: root is ἀναζα; the α lengthens to η before the tense formative.

[13] MH: 2nd aor. of ἀποθνῄσκω; the root is ἀποθαν.

[14] MH: 2nd aor. of εὑρίσκω; the root is εὑρ, and here ε is added after the tense stem.

[15] TH: ἡ substantivizes the prep. phrase εἰς ζωήν; ἡ ἐντολὴ ἡ εἰς ζωήν, *the commandment for life*.

[16] TH: "is" should be inserted after αὕτη.

[17] ἀφορμή, ῆς, ἡ, *occasion, opportunity*.

[18] MH: 2nd aor.; root is λαβ.

[19] ἐξαπατάω, *I deceive*. MH: the α lengthens to η before the tense formative.

[20] TH: rel. pron. refers to ἐντολῆς.

[21] MH: since the root ends in ν, the aor. tense formative is just α, which shifts to ε and can add ν in the 3rd sg. TH: με is implied after ἀπέκτεινεν.

[22] TH: pred. adj. to νόμος.

[23] TH: ἁγία, δικαία, and ἀγαθή are pred. adj. to ἐντολή.

13 Τὸ οὖν ἀγαθὸν[1] ἐμοὶ ⸀ἐγένετο[2] θάνατος; μὴ γένοιτο·
ἀλλὰ ἡ ἁμαρτία, ἵνα φανῇ[3] ἁμαρτία διὰ τοῦ ἀγαθοῦ[4] μοι
κατεργαζομένη[5] θάνατον· ἵνα γένηται[6] καθ' ὑπερβολὴν[7]
ἁμαρτωλὸς[8] ἡ ἁμαρτία διὰ τῆς ἐντολῆς.
14 Οἴδαμεν γὰρ ὅτι ὁ νόμος πνευματικός[9] ἐστιν· ἐγὼ
δὲ ⸀σάρκινός[10] εἰμι, πεπραμένος[11] ὑπὸ τὴν ἁμαρτίαν. **15** ὃ[12]
γὰρ κατεργάζομαι[13] οὐ γινώσκω· οὐ[14] γὰρ ὃ θέλω τοῦτο[15]
πράσσω,[16] ἀλλ' ὃ μισῶ[17] τοῦτο ποιῶ. **16** εἰ δὲ ὃ οὐ[18] θέλω
τοῦτο ποιῶ, σύμφημι[19] τῷ νόμῳ[20] ὅτι καλός.[21] **17** νυνὶ[22] δὲ
οὐκέτι[23] ἐγὼ κατεργάζομαι[24] αὐτὸ ἀλλὰ ἡ ⸀οἰκοῦσα[25] ἐν

---

[1] TH: subst. adj.; *what is good.*

[2] MH: 2nd aor. of γίνομαι; root is γεν.

[3] φαίνω, *I appear, shine.* MH: 2nd aor.; root is φαν. Since the root ends in ν, the σ does not appear in the tense formative. Subj. mood has a lengthened connecting vowel (ε › η).

[4] TH: subst. adj.; *what is good.*

[5] κατεργάζομαι, *I do, commit, bring about.*

[6] MH: 2nd aor. of γίνομαι; root is γεν.

[7] ὑπερβολή, ῆς, ἡ, *excess, exceeding.*

[8] ἁμαρτωλός, ον, *sinful.* TH: καθ' ὑπερβολὴν ἁμαρτωλὸς, *exceedingly sinful.*

[9] πνευματικός, ή, όν, *spiritual.*

[10] σάρκινος, η, ον, *fleshly.*

[11] πιπράσκω, *I sell.* MH: root is πρα.

[12] TH: acc. neut. rel. pron. occurs 7 times in Rom 7; *what* or *that.*

[13] κατεργάζομαι, *I do, commit, bring about.*

[14] TH: negates πράσσω.

[15] TH: in 7:15-20, τοῦτο refers to the combination of ὃ + verb.

[16] πράσσω, *I do, engage in.*

[17] μισέω, *I hate.*

[18] TH: negates θέλω.

[19] σύμφημι, *I concur, agree with.*

[20] TH: dat. dir. obj. of σύμφημι.

[21] TH: pred. adj. to the implied 3rd sg. subject of the verbless clause; ὅτι καλός, *that it is good.*

[22] νυνί, *now.*

[23] οὐκέτι, *no longer.*

[24] κατεργάζομαι, *I do, commit, bring about.*

[25] οἰκέω, *I live, dwell.* MH: the root (οἰκε) ends in a vowel, so the connecting vowel contracts (ε + ου = ου).

ἐμοὶ ἁμαρτία. **18** οἶδα γὰρ ὅτι οὐκ οἰκεῖ[1] ἐν ἐμοί, τοῦτ’
ἔστιν ἐν τῇ σαρκί μου, ἀγαθόν·[2] τὸ γὰρ θέλειν[3]
παράκειταί[4] μοι, τὸ δὲ κατεργάζεσθαι[5] τὸ καλὸν ⸀οὔ·
19 οὐ[6] γὰρ ὃ θέλω ποιῶ ἀγαθόν,[7] ἀλλὰ ὃ οὐ[8] θέλω κακὸν
τοῦτο[9] πράσσω.[10] **20** εἰ δὲ ὃ οὐ[11] ⸀θέλω τοῦτο[12] ποιῶ,
οὐκέτι[13] ἐγὼ κατεργάζομαι[14] αὐτὸ ἀλλὰ ἡ οἰκοῦσα[15] ἐν
ἐμοὶ ἁμαρτία.

21 Εὑρίσκω ἄρα[16] τὸν νόμον τῷ θέλοντι ἐμοὶ[17] ποιεῖν
τὸ καλὸν ὅτι ἐμοὶ τὸ κακὸν παράκειται·[18] **22** συνήδομαι[19]
γὰρ τῷ νόμῳ[20] τοῦ θεοῦ κατὰ τὸν ἔσω[21] ἄνθρωπον, **23**
βλέπω δὲ ἕτερον νόμον ἐν τοῖς μέλεσίν[22] μου
ἀντιστρατευόμενον[23] τῷ νόμῳ τοῦ νοός[24] μου καὶ

---

[1] οἰκέω, *I live, dwell.*
[2] TH: subst. adj. is the subject of οἰκεῖ.
[3] TH: articular inf. functions as the subject of the verb παράκειταί; *the desire.*
[4] παράκειμαι, *I am present, ready.*
[5] κατεργάζομαι, *I do, commit, bring about.* TH: articular inf. functions as the subject of the implied verb παράκειται; *the work.*
[6] TH: negates ποιῶ.
[7] TH: οὐ γὰρ ὃ θέλω ποιῶ ἀγαθόν, *I do not do the good that I want to do.*
[8] TH: negates θέλω.
[9] TH: κακὸν τοῦτο is the obj. of πράσσω.
[10] πράσσω, *I do, engage in.*
[11] TH: negates θέλω.
[12] NA has ἐγὼ τοῦτο, though ἐγὼ is in brackets, indicating the questionable nature of its inclusion.
[13] οὐκέτι, *no longer.*
[14] κατεργάζομαι, *I do, commit, bring about.*
[15] οἰκέω, *I live, dwell.* MH: the root (οἰκε) ends in a vowel, so the connecting vowel contracts (ε + ου = ου).
[16] ἆρα, *consequently.*
[17] TH: τῷ θέλοντι ἐμοὶ, *in my desire.*
[18] παράκειμαι, *I am present, ready.*
[19] συνήδομαι, *I delight in.*
[20] TH: dat. dir. obj. of συνήδομαι.
[21] ἔσω, *inner, inside.*
[22] μέλος, ους, τό, *member, part.*
[23] ἀντιστρατεύομαι, *I am at war with.* TH: attrib. prtc. modifying νόμον.
[24] νοῦς, ός, ὁ, *mind, way of thinking.*

αἰχμαλωτίζοντά[1] με ⸀ἐν τῷ νόμῳ τῆς ἁμαρτίας τῷ ὄντι[2] ἐν
τοῖς μέλεσίν[3] μου. **24** ταλαίπωρος[4] ἐγὼ ἄνθρωπος·[5] τίς με
ῥύσεται[6] ἐκ τοῦ σώματος τοῦ θανάτου τούτου;

25 ⸀χάρις[7] τῷ θεῷ διὰ Ἰησοῦ Χριστοῦ τοῦ κυρίου[8] ἡμῶν.

Ἄρα[9] οὖν αὐτὸς[10] ἐγὼ τῷ μὲν[11] νοῒ[12] δουλεύω[13] νόμῳ[14]
θεοῦ, τῇ δὲ σαρκὶ νόμῳ[15] ἁμαρτίας.

⸀ **7:13 ἐγένετο** WH Treg NA28] γέγονεν RP
⸀ **14 σάρκινός** WH Treg NA28] σαρκικός RP
⸀ **17 οἰκοῦσα** Treg NA28 RP] ἐνοικοῦσα WH
⸀ **18 οὔ** WH Treg NA28] + οὐχ εὑρίσκω RP
⸀ **20 θέλω** WH Treg] + ἐγώ NA28 RP
⸀ **23 ἐν** WH Treg NA28] – RP
⸀ **25 χάρις** Treg] χάρις δὲ WH NA28; εὐχαριστῶ RP

---

[1] αἰχμαλωτίζω, *I take captive*. TH: attrib. prtc. modifying νόμον.
[2] MH: pres. act. prtc. dat. sg. masc. of εἰμί. TH: *which is*.
[3] μέλος, ους, τό, *member, part*.
[4] ταλαίπωρος, ον, *wretched, miserable*. TH: attrib. adj. to ἄνθρωπος.
[5] TH: pred. nom. to ἐγὼ.
[6] ῥύομαι, *I save, rescue, deliver*.
[7] TH: *thanks be*. NA has χάρις δὲ.
[8] TH: τοῦ κυρίου is in app. to Ἰησοῦ Χριστοῦ.
[9] ἄρα, *consequently*.
[10] TH: αὐτὸς is emphatic; *myself*.
[11] TH: μὲν … δὲ, *on the one hand … on the other hand*.
[12] νοῦς, ός, ὁ, *mind, way of thinking*.
[13] δουλεύω, *I serve*.
[14] TH: dat. dir. obj. of δουλεύω.
[15] TH: dat. dir. obj. of δουλεύω.

ROMANS 8

New Vocabulary by Frequency [Chapter, Book, SBLGNT Occurrences]

ἀββα, *abba, father* [1, 1, 3]
ἀδύνατος, ον, *powerless, impossible* [1, 2, 10]
ἀλάλητος, *inexpressible, wordless* [1, 1, 1]
ἄξιος, ία, ον, *deserving, worthy* [1, 2, 41]
ἀπαρχή, ῆς, ἡ, *first fruit* [1, 3, 9]
ἀπεκδέχομαι, *I await eagerly* [3, 3, 8]
ἀποκαλύπτω, *I reveal, make fully known* [1, 3, 26]
ἀποκάλυψις, εως, ἡ, *revelation* [1, 2, 17]
ἀποκαραδοκία, ας, ἡ, *eager expectation* [1, 1, 2]
ἀπολύτρωσις, εως, ἡ, *redemption* [1, 2, 10]
ἆρα, *consequently* [2, 11, 52]
ἀρέσκω, *I please* [1, 4, 17]
ἀσθένεια, ας, ἡ, *weakness* [1, 2, 24]
ἀσθενέω, *I am weak, sick* [1, 5, 34]
ἄχρι, *until* [1, 4, 49]
βάθος, ους, τό, *depth* [1, 2, 8]
γέ, *indeed* [1, 1, 20]
γυμνότης, ητος, ἡ, *nakedness* [1, 1, 3]
δικαιόω, *I justify, declare righteous* [3, 15, 39]
δικαίωμα, ατος, τό, *requirement, righteous deed* [1, 5, 10]
διότι, *because, for* [1, 4, 23]
διωγμός, οῦ, ὁ, *persecution* [1, 1, 10]
δουλεία, ας, ἡ, *slavery, bondage* [2, 2, 5]
ἐγκαλέω, *I bring a charge, accuse* [1, 1, 7]
εἰκών, όνος, ἡ, *image* [1, 2, 23]
εἴπερ, *if really, if after all, since* [2, 3, 6]
ἐκλεκτός, ή, όν, *chosen* [1, 2, 23]
ἑκών, οῦσα, όν, *willingly* [1, 1, 2]
ἐλευθερία, ας, ἡ, *freedom* [1, 1, 11]
ἐλευθερόω, *I set free* [2, 4, 7]
ἐλπίζω, *I hope for* [2, 4, 31]
ἕνεκα, *on account of, for the sake of* [1, 2, 26]
ἐνίστημι, *I am present* [1, 1, 7]
ἐνοικέω, *I live in, inhabit* [1, 1, 5]
ἐντυγχάνω, *I intercede, appeal* [2, 3, 5]
ἐραυνάω, *I search, examine* [1, 1, 6]

ἔχθρα, ας, ἡ, *enmity, hatred* [1, 1, 6]
ζῳοποιέω, *I make alive, give life* [1, 2, 11]
θανατόω, *I kill, put to death* [2, 3, 11]
θλῖψις, εως, ἡ, *affliction, trouble* [1, 5, 45]
θνητός, ή, όν, *mortal* [1, 2, 6]
καθό, *just as* [1, 1, 4]
κατάκριμα, ατος, τό, *judgement, condemnation* [1, 3, 3]
κατακρίνω, *I pronounce a sentence on* [2, 4, 17]
κίνδυνος, ου, ὁ, *danger* [1, 1, 9]
κληρονόμος, ου, ὁ, *heir* [2, 4, 15]
κλητός, ή, όν, *called* [1, 4, 10]
κτίσις, εως, ἡ, *creation* [5, 7, 19]
λιμός, οῦ, ὁ, *famine, hunger* [1, 1, 12]
λογίζομαι, *I regard, consider* [2, 19, 40]
ματαιότης, ητος, ἡ, *futility* [1, 1, 3]
μάχαιρα, ης, ἡ, *sword* [1, 2, 29]
οἰκέω, *I live, dwell* [2, 5, 9]
ὁμοίωμα, ατος, τό, *likeness* [1, 4, 6]
ὀφειλέτης, ου, ὁ, *debtor, one who is under obligation* [1, 3, 7]
πάθημα, ατος, τό, *suffering, feeling* [1, 2, 16]
πρᾶξις, εως, ἡ, *act, deed* [1, 2, 6]
πρόβατον, ου, τό, *sheep* [1, 1, 39]
προγινώσκω, *I foreknow* [1, 2, 5]
πρόθεσις, εως, ἡ, *purpose, plan* [1, 2, 12]
προορίζω, *I predetermine, decide beforehand* [2, 2, 6]
πρωτότοκος, ον, *firstborn* [1, 1, 8]
στεναγμός, *groan* [1, 1, 2]
στενάζω, *I groan* [1, 1, 6]
στενοχωρία, ας, ἡ, *distress, trouble* [1, 2, 4]
συγκληρονόμος, ον, *co-heir* [1, 1, 4]
συμμαρτυρέω, *I bear witness with* [1, 3, 3]
σύμμορφος, ον, *similar in form* [1, 1, 2]
συμπάσχω, *I suffer with* [1, 1, 2]
συναντιλαμβάνομαι, *I help, assist* [1, 1, 2]
συνδοξάζω, *I am glorified with* [1, 1, 1]
συνεργέω, *I work together* [1, 1, 5]
συνωδίνω, *I suffer together* [1, 1, 1]
συστενάζω, *I groan together* [1, 1, 1]
σφαγή, ῆς, ἡ, *slaughter* [1, 1, 3]
υἱοθεσία, ας, ἡ, *adoption* [2, 3, 5]
ὑπερεντυγχάνω, *I intercede* [1, 1, 1]

ὑπερνικάω, *I prevail completely* [1, 1, 1]
ὑπομονή, ῆς, ἡ, *endurance, perseverance* [1, 6, 32]
ὑποτάσσω, *I subject, subordinate* [3, 6, 38]
ὕψωμα, ατος, τό, *height* [1, 1, 2]
φείδομαι, *I spare* [1, 3, 10]
φθορά, ᾶς, ἡ, *decay, corruption* [1, 1, 9]
φόβος, ου, ὁ, *fear, reverence* [1, 5, 47]
φρονέω, *I think, am intent on* [1, 9, 26]
φρόνημα, ατος, τό, *way of thinking, mind* [4, 4, 4]
χαρίζομαι, *I give, grant* [1, 1, 23]
χωρίζω, *I separate* [2, 2, 13]
ὡσαύτως, *likewise, in the same way* [1, 1, 17]

8.1 Οὐδὲν[1] ἄρα[2] νῦν κατάκριμα[3] τοῖς[4] ἐν Χριστῷ
⸀Ἰησοῦ· **2** ὁ γὰρ νόμος τοῦ πνεύματος τῆς ζωῆς ἐν Χριστῷ
Ἰησοῦ ἠλευθέρωσέν[5] ⸀σε ἀπὸ τοῦ νόμου τῆς ἁμαρτίας καὶ
τοῦ θανάτου. **3** τὸ γὰρ ἀδύνατον[6] τοῦ νόμου, ἐν ᾧ[7] ἠσθένει[8]
διὰ τῆς σαρκός, ὁ θεὸς τὸν ἑαυτοῦ υἱὸν πέμψας[9] ἐν
ὁμοιώματι[10] σαρκὸς ἁμαρτίας[11] καὶ περὶ ἁμαρτίας
κατέκρινε[12] τὴν ἁμαρτίαν ἐν τῇ σαρκί, **4** ἵνα τὸ
δικαίωμα[13] τοῦ νόμου πληρωθῇ[14] ἐν ἡμῖν τοῖς μὴ κατὰ
σάρκα περιπατοῦσιν ἀλλὰ κατὰ πνεῦμα· **5** οἱ γὰρ κατὰ
σάρκα ὄντες[15] τὰ[16] τῆς σαρκὸς φρονοῦσιν,[17] οἱ δὲ κατὰ
πνεῦμα[18] τὰ[19] τοῦ πνεύματος.[20] **6** τὸ γὰρ φρόνημα[21] τῆς
σαρκὸς θάνατος,[22] τὸ δὲ φρόνημα[23] τοῦ πνεύματος ζωὴ

---

[1] TH: *there is no.*

[2] ἄρα, *consequently.*

[3] κατάκριμα, ατος, τό, *judgment, condemnation.*

[4] TH: τοῖς substantivizes the prep. phrase Χριστῷ Ἰησοῦ, *for the ones (who are) in Christ Jesus.*

[5] ἐλευθερόω, *I set free.* MH: the ο lengthens to an ω before the tense formative.

[6] ἀδύνατος, ον, *powerless, impossible.* TH: τὸ ἀδύνατον, *what was impossible.*

[7] TH: ἐν ᾧ indicates cause; *because.*

[8] ἀσθενέω, *I am weak, sick.* MH: the root (ἀσθενε) ends in a vowel, so the connecting vowel contracts (ε + ε = ει).

[9] MH: root ends in π; π + σ = ψ.

[10] ὁμοίωμα, ατος, τό, *likeness.*

[11] TH: σαρκὸς ἁμαρτίας, *sinful flesh.*

[12] κατακρίνω, *I pronounce a sentence on,* ***condemn.*** MH: since the root ends in ν, the aor. tense formative is just α, which shifts to ε in the 3rd sg.

[13] δικαίωμα, ατος, τό, *requirement, righteous deed.*

[14] MH: the ο lengthens to ω before the tense formative.

[15] MH: pres. act. indic. nom. pl. masc. of εἰμί, *the ones who live.*

[16] TH: τὰ substantivizes τῆς σαρκὸς; *the things of the flesh.*

[17] φρονέω, *I think, am intent on.*

[18] TH: οἱ … κατὰ πνεῦμα mirrors the first half of the verse and implies ὄντες.

[19] TH: τὰ substantivizes τοῦ πνεύματος; *the things of the spirit.*

[20] TH: τὰ τοῦ πνεύματος mirrors the first half of the verse and implies φρονοῦσιν.

[21] φρόνημα, ατος, τό, *way of thinking, mind.*

[22] TH: pred. nom. to φρόνημα.

[23] φρόνημα, ατος, τό, *way of thinking, mind.*

καὶ εἰρήνη·[1] **7** διότι[2] τὸ φρόνημα[3] τῆς σαρκὸς ἔχθρα[4] εἰς
θεόν, τῷ γὰρ νόμῳ τοῦ θεοῦ οὐχ ὑποτάσσεται,[5] οὐδὲ γὰρ
δύναται· **8** οἱ δὲ ἐν σαρκὶ ὄντες[6] θεῷ ἀρέσαι[7] οὐ δύνανται.

9 Ὑμεῖς δὲ οὐκ ἐστὲ ἐν σαρκὶ ἀλλὰ ἐν πνεύματι,
εἴπερ[8] πνεῦμα θεοῦ οἰκεῖ[9] ἐν ὑμῖν. εἰ δέ τις πνεῦμα
Χριστοῦ οὐκ ἔχει, οὗτος οὐκ ἔστιν αὐτοῦ. **10** εἰ δὲ
Χριστὸς[10] ἐν ὑμῖν, τὸ μὲν σῶμα νεκρὸν[11] διὰ ἁμαρτίαν, τὸ
δὲ πνεῦμα ζωὴ[12] διὰ δικαιοσύνην. **11** εἰ δὲ τὸ πνεῦμα τοῦ
ἐγείραντος ⸀τὸν Ἰησοῦν ἐκ νεκρῶν οἰκεῖ[13] ἐν ὑμῖν,
ὁ ἐγείρας ⸂ἐκ νεκρῶν Χριστὸν Ἰησοῦν[14]⸃ ζῳοποιήσει[15]
καὶ[16] τὰ θνητὰ[17] σώματα ὑμῶν διὰ ⸂τὸ ἐνοικοῦν[18] αὐτοῦ
πνεῦμα[19]⸃ ἐν ὑμῖν.

---

[1] TH: ζωή and εἰρήνη are pred. nom. to φρόνημα.

[2] διότι, *because, for.*

[3] φρόνημα, ατος, τό, *way of thinking, mind.*

[4] ἔχθρα, ας, ἡ, *enmity, hatred.* TH: pred. nom. to φρόνημα.

[5] ὑποτάσσω, *I subject, subordinate.*

[6] MH: pres. act. indic. nom. pl. masc. of εἰμί. TH: *the ones who live.*

[7] ἀρέσκω, *I please.* MH: root is αρε. TH: complementary inf. with δύνανται; regularly takes a dat. obj.

[8] εἴπερ, *if really, if after all, since.*

[9] οἰκέω, *I live, dwell.*

[10] TH: "is" should be supplied after Χριστὸς.

[11] TH: pred. adj. to σῶμα.

[12] TH: pred. nom. to πνεῦμα.

[13] οἰκέω, *I live, dwell.*

[14] NA has Χριστὸν ἐκ νεκρῶν instead of ἐκ νεκρῶν Χριστὸν Ἰησοῦν.

[15] ζῳοποιέω, *I make alive, give life.* MH: the ε lengthens to η before the tense formative.

[16] TH: καί is additive; *also.*

[17] θνητός, ή, όν, *mortal.*

[18] ἐνοικέω, *I live in, inhabit.* MH: the root (ἐνοικε) ends in a vowel, so the connecting vowel contracts (ε + ο = ου). TH: ἐνοικοῦν is attrib. to πνεῦμα.

[19] NA here has τοῦ ἐνοικοῦντος αὐτοῦ πνεύματος.

12 Ἄρα[1] οὖν, ἀδελφοί, ὀφειλέται[2] ἐσμέν, οὐ τῇ σαρκὶ
τοῦ[3] κατὰ σάρκα ζῆν,[4] **13** εἰ γὰρ κατὰ σάρκα ζῆτε[5]
μέλλετε ἀποθνῄσκειν, εἰ δὲ πνεύματι[6] τὰς πράξεις[7] τοῦ
σώματος θανατοῦτε,[8] ζήσεσθε.[9] **14** ὅσοι γὰρ πνεύματι
θεοῦ ἄγονται, οὗτοι ʽυἱοί[10] εἰσιν θεοῦ[11]ʼ. **15** οὐ γὰρ
ἐλάβετε[12] πνεῦμα δουλείας[13] πάλιν εἰς φόβον,[14] ἀλλὰ
ἐλάβετε πνεῦμα υἱοθεσίας[15] ἐν ᾧ κράζομεν· Αββα[16] ὁ
πατήρ· **16** αὐτὸ[17] τὸ πνεῦμα συμμαρτυρεῖ[18] τῷ πνεύματι
ἡμῶν ὅτι ἐσμὲν τέκνα θεοῦ.

17 εἰ δὲ τέκνα,[19] καὶ[20] κληρονόμοι·[21] κληρονόμοι μὲν
θεοῦ, συγκληρονόμοι[22] δὲ Χριστοῦ, εἴπερ[23] συμπάσχ-
ομεν[24] ἵνα καὶ συνδοξασθῶμεν.[25]

---

[1] ἄρα, *consequently.*

[2] ὀφειλέτης, ου, ὁ, *debtor, one who is under obligation.*

[3] TH: τοῦ + inf. ζῆν works with ὀφειλέται; *obligators not to the flesh to live according to the flesh.*

[4] MH: pres. act. inf. from ζάω; α + ε(ε)ν = ην.

[5] MH: pres. act. indic. 2nd pl. from ζάω; ά + ετε = ῆτε.

[6] TH: dat. of means, *by the spirit.*

[7] πρᾶξις, εως, ἡ, *act, deed.*

[8] θανατόω, *I kill, put to death.* MH: a contraction occurs (ό + ετε = οῦτε).

[9] MH: pres. act. indic. 2nd pl. from ζάω; ά + ετε = ῆτε.

[10] TH: pred. nom. to οὗτοι.

[11] NA has υἱοὶ θεοῦ εἰσιν instead of υἱοί εἰσιν θεοῦ.

[12] MH: from λαμβάνω. 2nd aor.; root is λαβ.

[13] δουλεία, ας, ἡ, *slavery, bondage.*

[14] φόβος, ου, ὁ, *fear, reverence.*

[15] υἱοθεσία, ας, ἡ, *adoption.*

[16] ἀββα, *abba, father.*

[17] TH: αὐτὸ is intensive; with τὸ πνεῦμα, *the Spirit itself.*

[18] συμμαρτυρέω, *I bear witness with.* MH: a contraction occurs (έ+ ει = εῖ).

[19] TH: ἐσμὲν is implied from the previous verse.

[20] TH: καί is additive; *also.*

[21] κληρονόμος, ου, ὁ, *heir.* TH: ἐσμὲν is implied from the previous verse.

[22] συγκληρονόμος, ον, *co-heir.*

[23] εἴπερ, *if really, if after all, since.*

[24] συμπάσχω, *I suffer with.*

[25] συνδοξάζω, *I am glorified with.* MH: the stem ends in δ; δ + θ = σθ. Subj. mood has a lengthened connecting vowel (ο › ω). TH: the prior καί is additive; *also.*

18 Λογίζομαι[1] γὰρ ὅτι οὐκ ἄξια[2] τὰ παθήματα[3] τοῦ νῦν
καιροῦ πρὸς τὴν μέλλουσαν[4] δόξαν ἀποκαλυφθῆναι[5] εἰς
ἡμᾶς. **19** ἡ γὰρ ἀποκαραδοκία[6] τῆς κτίσεως[7] τὴν
ἀποκάλυψιν[8] τῶν υἱῶν τοῦ θεοῦ ἀπεκδέχεται·[9] **20** τῇ γὰρ
ματαιότητι[10] ἡ κτίσις[11] ὑπετάγη,[12] οὐχ ἑκοῦσα[13] ἀλλὰ διὰ
τὸν ὑποτάξαντα,[14] ⸀ἐφ' ἐλπίδι **21** ὅτι καὶ[15] αὐτὴ[16] ἡ κτίσις[17]
ἐλευθερωθήσεται[18] ἀπὸ τῆς δουλείας[19] τῆς φθορᾶς[20] εἰς
τὴν ἐλευθερίαν[21] τῆς δόξης τῶν τέκνων τοῦ θεοῦ.
22 οἴδαμεν γὰρ ὅτι πᾶσα ἡ κτίσις[22] συστενάζει[23] καὶ
συνωδίνει[24] ἄχρι[25] τοῦ νῦν· **23** οὐ μόνον δέ, ἀλλὰ ⸆καὶ

---

[1] λογίζομαι, *I regard, consider.*

[2] ἄξιος, ία, ον, *deserving, worthy.* TH: pred. adj. to παθήματα; *the sufferings … are not worthy (of comparison).*

[3] πάθημα, ατος, τό, *suffering, feeling.*

[4] TH: adj. prtc. attrib. to δόξαν; *the glory that will.*

[5] ἀποκαλύπτω, *I reveal, make fully known.* MH: the root is ἀποκαλυπ; π + θ = φθ.

[6] ἀποκαραδοκία, ας, ἡ, *eager expectation.*

[7] κτίσις, εως, ἡ, *creation.*

[8] ἀποκάλυψις, εως, ἡ, *revelation.*

[9] ἀπεκδέχομαι, *I await eagerly.*

[10] ματαιότης, ητος, ἡ, *futility.*

[11] κτίσις, εως, ἡ, *creation.*

[12] ὑποτάσσω, *I subject, subordinate.* MH: the root is ὑποταγ; 2nd aor. pass. does not include θ in tense formative.

[13] ἑκών, οῦσα, όν, *willingly.*

[14] ὑποτάσσω, *I subject, subordinate.* MH: the root is ὑποταγ; γ + σ = ξ. TH: subst. prtc.; *the one who subjected (it).*

[15] TH: καί is additive; *also.*

[16] TH: αὐτὴ is intensive; with ἡ κτίσις, *creation itself.*

[17] κτίσις, εως, ἡ, *creation.*

[18] ἐλευθερόω, *I set free.* MH: the ο lengthens to ω before the tense formative.

[19] δουλεία, ας, ἡ, *slavery, bondage.*

[20] φθορά, ᾶς, ἡ, *decay, corruption.*

[21] ἐλευθερία, ας, ἡ, *freedom.*

[22] κτίσις, εως, ἡ, *creation.*

[23] συστενάζω, *I groan together.*

[24] συνωδίνω, *I suffer together.*

[25] ἄχρι, *until.*

αὐτοὶ[1]⸆ τὴν ἀπαρχὴν[2] τοῦ πνεύματος ἔχοντες ⸂ἡμεῖς καὶ⸃
αὐτοὶ[3] ἐν ἑαυτοῖς στενάζομεν,[4] υἱοθεσίαν[5] ἀπεκδεχ-
όμενοι[6] τὴν ἀπολύτρωσιν[7] τοῦ σώματος ἡμῶν. **24** τῇ γὰρ
ἐλπίδι ἐσώθημεν·[8] ἐλπὶς δὲ βλεπομένη οὐκ ἔστιν ἐλπίς,
ὃ γὰρ βλέπει ⸀τίς[9] ἐλπίζει;[10] **25** εἰ δὲ ὃ οὐ βλέπομεν
ἐλπίζομεν,[11] δι᾽ ὑπομονῆς[12] ἀπεκδεχόμεθα.[13]

26 Ὡσαύτως[14] δὲ καὶ[15] τὸ πνεῦμα συναντιλαμβάνεται[16]
⸀τῇ ἀσθενείᾳ[17] ἡμῶν· τὸ[18] γὰρ τί ⸀προσευξώμεθα[19] καθὸ[20]
δεῖ οὐκ οἴδαμεν, ἀλλὰ αὐτὸ[21] τὸ πνεῦμα ⸀ὑπερεν-
τυγχάνει[22] στεναγμοῖς[23] ἀλαλήτοις,[24] **27** ὁ δὲ ἐραυνῶν[25] τὰς
καρδίας οἶδεν τί τὸ φρόνημα[26] τοῦ πνεύματος,[27] ὅτι κατὰ
θεὸν ἐντυγχάνει[28] ὑπὲρ ἁγίων.

---

[1] TH: αὐτοὶ is intensive; with ἡμεῖς later in the verse, *we ourselves.*

[2] ἀπαρχή, ῆς, ἡ, *first fruit.*

[3] TH: αὐτοὶ is intensive; with ἐν ἑαυτοῖς, *we within ourselves.*

[4] στενάζω, *I groan.*

[5] υἱοθεσία, ας, ἡ, *adoption.*

[6] ἀπεκδέχομαι, *I await eagerly.*

[7] ἀπολύτρωσις, εως, ἡ, *redemption.* TH: ἀπολύτρωσιν is in app. to υἱοθεσίαν.

[8] MH: aor. tense stem of σῴζω is σω.

[9] TH: τίς is the subject of ἐλπίζει.

[10] ἐλπίζω, *I hope for.*

[11] ἐλπίζω, *I hope for.*

[12] ὑπομονή, ῆς, ἡ, *endurance, perseverance.*

[13] ἀπεκδέχομαι, *I await eagerly.*

[14] ὡσαύτως, *likewise, in the same way.*

[15] TH: καί is additive; *also.*

[16] συναντιλαμβάνομαι, *I help, assist.*

[17] ἀσθένεια, ας, ἡ, *weakness.*

[18] TH: τὸ frames τί προσευξώμεθα καθὸ δεῖ as the the object of οἴδαμεν.

[19] MH: root ends in χ; χ + σ = ξ. Subj. mood has lengthened connecting vowel (ο › ω).

[20] καθό, *just as.*

[21] TH: αὐτὸ is intensive; with τὸ πνεῦμα, *the Spirit itself.*

[22] ὑπερεντυγχάνω, *I intercede.*

[23] στεναγμός, οῦ, ὁ, *groan.*

[24] ἀλάλητος, ον, *inexpressible, wordless.*

[25] ἐραυνάω, *I search, examine.*

[26] φρόνημα, ατος, τό, *way of thinking, mind.*

[27] TH: subjective gen.; τί τὸ φρόνημα τοῦ πνεύματος, *what the spirit thinks.*

[28] ἐντυγχάνω, *I intercede, appeal.*

28 Οἴδαμεν δὲ ὅτι τοῖς ἀγαπῶσι τὸν θεὸν πάντα
⸀συνεργεῖ[1] εἰς ἀγαθόν, τοῖς[2] κατὰ πρόθεσιν[3] κλητοῖς[4]
οὖσιν.[5] **29** ὅτι οὓς προέγνω,[6] καὶ[7] προώρισεν[8] συμμόρφους[9]
τῆς εἰκόνος[10] τοῦ υἱοῦ αὐτοῦ, εἰς τὸ[11] εἶναι αὐτὸν[12]
πρωτότοκον[13] ἐν πολλοῖς ἀδελφοῖς· **30** οὓς δὲ προώρισεν,[14]
τούτους καὶ[15] ἐκάλεσεν· καὶ οὓς ἐκάλεσεν, τούτους καὶ[16]
ἐδικαίωσεν·[17] οὓς δὲ ἐδικαίωσεν,[18] τούτους καὶ[19]
ἐδόξασεν.[20]

31 Τί οὖν ἐροῦμεν[21] πρὸς ταῦτα; εἰ ὁ θεὸς[22] ὑπὲρ[23]
ἡμῶν, τίς[24] καθ' ἡμῶν; **32** ὅς γε[25] τοῦ ἰδίου υἱοῦ[26] οὐκ

---

[1] συνεργέω, *I work together.*
[2] TH: τοῖς is the art. for the prtc. οὖσιν.
[3] πρόθεσις, εως, ἡ, *purpose, plan.*
[4] κλητός, ή, όν, *called.*
[5] MH: pres. act. indic. dat. pl. masc. of εἰμί; τοῖς … κλητοῖς οὖσιν, *to the ones who are called.*
[6] προγινώσκω, *I foreknow.* MH: 2nd aor.; root is προγνο. aor. act. indic. 3rd sg.
[7] TH: καί is additive; *also.*
[8] προορίζω, *I predetermine, decide beforehand.* MH: the root ends with δ; δ + σ = σ.
[9] σύμμορφος, ον, *similar in form,* ***conformed.*** TH: *to be conformed.*
[10] εἰκών, όνος, ἡ, *image.*
[11] TH: εἰς τὸ + inf. here indicates result; *so that he is.*
[12] TH: acc. is the subject of the inf. εἶναι.
[13] πρωτότοκος, ον, *firstborn.*
[14] προορίζω, *I predetermine, decide beforehand.* MH: the root ends with δ; δ + σ = σ.
[15] TH: καί is additive; *also.*
[16] TH: καί is additive; *also.*
[17] δικαιόω, *I justify, declare righteous.* MH: the ο lengthens to ω before the tense formative.
[18] δικαιόω, *I justify, declare righteous.* MH: the ο lengthens to ω before the tense formative.
[19] TH: καί is additive; *also.*
[20] MH: root ends with δ; δ + σ = σ.
[21] MH: fut. act. indic. 1st pl. of λέγω.
[22] TH: "is" should be inserted after θεός.
[23] TH: ὑπὲρ indicates advantage; *for.*
[24] TH: "is" should be inserted after τίς.
[25] γέ, *indeed.*
[26] TH: gen. dir. obj. of ἐφείσατο.

ἐφείσατο[1], ἀλλὰ ὑπὲρ[2] ἡμῶν πάντων παρέδωκεν[3] αὐτόν,
πῶς οὐχὶ καὶ[4] σὺν αὐτῷ τὰ πάντα[5] ἡμῖν χαρίσεται;[6] **33** τίς
ἐγκαλέσει[7] κατὰ ἐκλεκτῶν[8] θεοῦ; θεὸς ὁ δικαιῶν·[9] **34** τίς ὁ
⸀κατακρινῶν;[10] ⸀Χριστὸς[11] ὁ ἀποθανών,[12] μᾶλλον ⸀δὲ
⸀ἐγερθείς,[13] ὅς ⸀καί[14] ἐστιν ἐν[15] δεξιᾷ τοῦ θεοῦ, ὃς καὶ[16]
ἐντυγχάνει[17] ὑπὲρ[18] ἡμῶν· **35** τίς ἡμᾶς χωρίσει[19] ἀπὸ τῆς
ἀγάπης τοῦ Χριστοῦ; θλῖψις[20] ἢ στενοχωρία[21] ἢ διωγμὸς[22]
ἢ λιμὸς[23] ἢ γυμνότης[24] ἢ κίνδυνος[25] ἢ μάχαιρα;[26]

---

[1] φείδομαι, *I spare*. MH: δ + σ = σ.
[2] TH: ὑπὲρ indicates advantage; *for*.
[3] MH: aor. act. indic. 3rd sg. of παραδίδωμι. The root is παραδο. The ο lengthens to ω before tense formative. δίδωμι and cognates belong to a small group of verbs called "*kappa* aorists."
[4] TH: καί is additive; *also*.
[5] TH: τὰ πάντα, *all things*.
[6] χαρίζομαι, *I give, grant*. MH: root ends with δ; δ + σ = σ.
[7] ἐγκαλέω, *I bring a charge, accuse*.
[8] ἐκλεκτός, ή, όν, *chosen*. TH: subst. adj.; *chosen ones*.
[9] δικαιόω, *I justify, declare righteous*. TH: pred. adj. prtc. to the subject θεὸς.
[10] κατακρίνω, *I pronounce a sentence on*, ***condemn***. TH: pred. adj. prtc. to the subject τίς.
[11] NA has Χριστὸς Ἰησοῦς, though Ἰησοῦς is in brackets, indicating the questionable nature of its inclusion.
[12] MH: 2nd aor. of ἀποθνῄσκω; the root is ἀποθαν. TH: pred. adj. prtc. to the subject Χριστὸς.
[13] MH: aor. pass. prtc. nom. sg. masc. of ἐγείρω. The root is ἐγερ.
[14] TH: καί is additive; *also*.
[15] TH: ἐν is locative; *at*.
[16] TH: καί is additive; *also*.
[17] ἐντυγχάνω, *I intercede, appeal*.
[18] TH: ὑπὲρ indicates advantage; *for*.
[19] χωρίζω, *I separate*. MH: root ends with δ; δ + σ = σ.
[20] θλῖψις, εως, ἡ, *affliction, tribulation*.
[21] στενοχωρία, ας, ἡ, *distress, trouble*.
[22] διωγμός, οῦ, ὁ, *persecution*.
[23] λιμός, οῦ, ὁ, *famine, hunger*.
[24] γυμνότης, ητος, ἡ, *nakedness*.
[25] κίνδυνος, ου, ὁ, *danger*.
[26] μάχαιρα, ης, ἡ, *sword*.

36 καθὼς γέγραπται ὅτι Ἕνεκεν[1] σοῦ θανατούμεθα[2] ὅλην
τὴν ἡμέραν, ἐλογίσθημεν[3] ὡς πρόβατα[4] σφαγῆς.[5] **37** ἀλλ᾽
ἐν τούτοις πᾶσιν ὑπερνικῶμεν[6] διὰ τοῦ ἀγαπήσαντος[7]
ἡμᾶς. **38** πέπεισμαι[8] γὰρ ὅτι οὔτε θάνατος οὔτε ζωὴ οὔτε
ἄγγελοι οὔτε ἀρχαὶ οὔτε ἐνεστῶτα[9] οὔτε μέλλοντα[10] οὔτε
δυνάμεις **39** οὔτε ὕψωμα[11] οὔτε βάθος[12] οὔτε τις κτίσις[13]
ἑτέρα δυνήσεται[14] ἡμᾶς χωρίσαι[15] ἀπὸ τῆς ἀγάπης τοῦ
θεοῦ τῆς[16] ἐν Χριστῷ Ἰησοῦ τῷ κυρίῳ[17] ἡμῶν.

---

[1] ἕνεκα, *on account of, for the sake of.*

[2] θανατόω, *I kill, put to death.* MH: the root (θανατο) ends in a vowel, so the connecting vowel contracts (ο + ο = ου).

[3] λογίζομαι, *I regard, consider.* MH: root ends with δ; δ + θ = σθ.

[4] πρόβατον, ου, τό, *sheep.*

[5] σφαγή, ῆς, ἡ, *slaughter.*

[6] ὑπερνικάω, *I prevail completely,* ***am more than a conqueror.*** MH: the root (ὑπερνικα) ends in a vowel, so the connecting vowel contracts (α + ο = ω).

[7] MH: the α lengthens to η before the tense formative.

[8] MH: root ends with θ; θ + μ = σμ.

[9] ἐνίστημι, *I am present.* MH: pf. act. prtc. nom. pl. neut. TH: subst. prtc.; *present things.*

[10] TH: subst. prtc.; *future things.*

[11] ὕψωμα, ατος, τό, *height.*

[12] βάθος, ους, τό, *depth.*

[13] κτίσις, εως, ἡ, *creation.* TH: τις κτίσις ἑτέρα, *any other created thing.*

[14] MH: the α lengthens to η before the tense formative in δύναμαι as if it is a contract verb.

[15] χωρίζω, *I separate.* MH: root ends with δ; δ + σ = σ. TH: complementary inf. with δυνήσεται.

[16] TH: τῆς substantivizes the prep. phrase ἐν Χριστῷ Ἰησοῦ.

[17] TH: τῷ κυρίῳ is in app. to Χριστῷ Ἰησοῦ.

8:1 Ἰησοῦ WH Treg NA28] + μὴ κατὰ σάρκα περιπατοῦσιν ἀλλὰ κατὰ πνεῦμα RP

2 σε WH NA28] με Treg NIV RP

11 τὸν WH Treg NA28] – RP

- **ἐκ νεκρῶν Χριστὸν Ἰησοῦν** WH] χριστὸν ἐκ νεκρῶν Treg NA28; τὸν χριστὸν ἐκ νεκρῶν RP
- **ἐκ νεκρῶν Χριστὸν Ἰησοῦν** WH] χριστὸν ἐκ νεκρῶν Treg NA28; τὸν χριστὸν ἐκ νεκρῶν RP
- **τὸ ἐνοικοῦν αὐτοῦ πνεῦμα** Treg RP] τοῦ ἐνοικοῦντος αὐτοῦ πνεύματος WH NA28
- **τὸ ἐνοικοῦν αὐτοῦ πνεῦμα** Treg RP] τοῦ ἐνοικοῦντος αὐτοῦ πνεύματος WH NA28

14 υἱοί εἰσιν θεοῦ Treg] υἱοὶ θεοῦ εἰσιν WH NA28; εἰσιν υἱοὶ θεοῦ RP

14 υἱοί εἰσιν θεοῦ Treg] υἱοὶ θεοῦ εἰσιν WH NA28; εἰσιν υἱοὶ θεοῦ RP

20 ἐφ' WH NA28] ἐπ' RP Treg

23 καὶ αὐτοὶ WH Treg RP NA28] – NIV

23 καὶ αὐτοὶ WH Treg RP NA28] – NIV

- **ἡμεῖς καὶ** WH Treg NA28] καὶ ἡμεῖς RP
- **ἡμεῖς καὶ** WH Treg NA28] καὶ ἡμεῖς RP

24 τίς WH NA28] + τί Treg; + τί καὶ RP

26 τῇ ἀσθενείᾳ WH Treg NA28] ταῖς ἀσθενείαις RP

26 τῇ ἀσθενείᾳ WH Treg NA28] ταῖς ἀσθενείαις RP

- **προσευξώμεθα** WH Treg NA28] προσευξόμεθα RP
- **ὑπερεντυγχάνει** WH Treg NA28] + ὑπὲρ ἡμῶν RP

28 συνεργεῖ Treg NA28 RP] + ὁ θεὸς WH

34 κατακρινῶν WH NA28] κατακρίνων Treg RP

- **Χριστὸς** Treg RP] + Ἰησοῦς WH NA28
- **δὲ** WH Treg NA28] + καὶ RP
- **ἐγερθείς** Treg NA28 RP] + ἐκ νεκρῶν WH
- **καί** Treg NA28 RP] – WH

38 ἐνεστῶτα οὔτε μέλλοντα οὔτε δυνάμεις WH Treg NA28] δυνάμεις οὔτε ἐνεστῶτα οὔτε μέλλοντα RP

38 ἐνεστῶτα οὔτε μέλλοντα οὔτε δυνάμεις WH Treg NA28] δυνάμεις οὔτε ἐνεστῶτα οὔτε μέλλοντα RP

ROMANS 9

New Vocabulary by Frequency [Chapter, Book, SBLGNT Occurrences]

ἀδιάλειπτος, ον, *unceasing* [1, 1, 2]
ἀδικία, ας, ἡ, *unrighteousness, injustice* [1, 7, 25]
ἀνάθεμα, ατος, τό, *cursed* [1, 1, 6]
ἀνθίστημι, *I oppose, resist* [1, 3, 14]
ἀνταποκρίνομαι, *I answer back, argue against* [1, 1, 2]
ἀπώλεια, ας, ἡ, *destruction* [1, 1, 18]
ἆρα, *consequently* [2, 11, 52]
ἀριθμός, οῦ, ὁ, *number* [1, 1, 18]
ἀτιμία, ας, ἡ, *shame, dishonor, disgrace* [1, 2, 7]
βούλημα, ατος, τό, *purpose* [1, 1, 3]
γνωρίζω, *I make known* [2, 2, 24]
Γόμορρα, *Gomorrah* [1, 1, 4]
διαγγέλλω, *I proclaim* [1, 1, 3]
διαθήκη, ης, ἡ, *covenant* [1, 2, 33]
διώκω, *I pursue, chase* [2, 5, 45]
δουλεύω, *I serve* [1, 7, 25]
δυνατός, ή, όν, *able, capable* [1, 3, 32]
ἐγκαταλείπω, *I leave behind* [1, 1, 10]
ἐκλογή, ῆς, ἡ, *election, choice* [1, 4, 7]
ἐκπίπτω, *I fall* [1, 1, 10]
ἐλάσσων, *less* [1, 1, 4]
ἐλεέω, *I have mercy (on)* [3, 6, 28]
ἔλεος, ους, τό, *mercy, compassion* [1, 3, 27]
ἐνδείκνυμι, *I show, point out* [2, 3, 11]
ἐξεγείρω, *I raise up, awaken* [1, 1, 2]
εὐλογητός, ή, όν, *blessed, praised* [1, 2, 8]
εὔχομαι, *I pray, wish* [1, 1, 7]
Ἠσαΐας, ου, ὁ, *Isaiah* [2, 5, 22]
Ἠσαῦ, ὁ, *Esau* [1, 1, 3]
Ἰακώβ, *Jacob* [1, 2, 27]
Ἰσαάκ, *Isaac* [2, 2, 20]
Ἰσραηλίτης, ου, ὁ, *Israelite* [1, 2, 9]
καταισχύνω, *I dishonor, put to shame* [1, 3, 13]
καταλαμβάνω, *I attain, seize* [1, 1, 15]
καταρτίζω, *I prepare, put in order* [1, 1, 13]
κεραμεύς, έως, ὁ, *potter* [1, 1, 3]

κοίτη, ης, ἡ, *bed* [1, 2, 4]
λατρεία, ας, ἡ, *service, worship* [1, 2, 5]
λογίζομαι, *I regard, consider* [1, 19, 40]
λύπη, ης, ἡ, *grief, sorrow* [1, 1, 16]
μακροθυμία, ας, ἡ, *patience, steadfastness* [1, 2, 14]
μέμφομαι, *I blame, find fault* [1, 1, 2]
μενοῦνγε, *rather, on the contrary* [1, 2, 3]
μήπω, *not yet* [1, 1, 2]
μισέω, *I hate* [1, 2, 40]
νομοθεσία, ας, ἡ, *legislation, giving of the law* [1, 1, 1]
οἰκτίρω, *I have compassion (on)* [2, 2, 2]
οἷος, α, ον, *as, such as* [1, 1, 14]
ὁμοιόω, *I make alike, resemble* [1, 1, 15]
ὀργή, ῆς, ἡ, *wrath* [2, 12, 36]
οὗ, *where* [1, 3, 25]
πέτρα, ας, ἡ, *rock* [1, 1, 15]
πηλός, οῦ, ὁ, *clay* [1, 1, 6]
πλάσμα, ατος, τό, *a thing molded or formed* [1, 1, 1]
πλάσσω, *I mold, form* [1, 1, 2]
πλοῦτος, *wealth, riches* [1, 5, 22]
πράσσω, *I do, engage in* [1, 10, 38]
προετοιμάζω, *I prepare beforehand* [1, 1, 2]
πρόθεσις, εως, ἡ, *purpose, plan* [1, 2, 12]
προλέγω, *I foretell, predict* [1, 1, 15]
πρόσκομμα, ατος, τό, *hinderance, obstacle* [2, 4, 6]
προσκόπτω, *I stumble* [1, 2, 8]
Ῥεβέκκα, ας, ἡ, *Rebecca* [1, 1, 1]
Σαβαώθ, *hosts, armies* [1, 1, 2]
Σάρρα, ας, ἡ, *Sarah* [1, 2, 4]
Σιών, *Zion* [1, 2, 7]
σκάνδαλον, ου, τό, *trap, offense* [1, 4, 15]
σκεῦος, ους, τό, *vessel* [3, 3, 23]
σκληρύνω, *I harden* [1, 1, 6]
Σόδομα, *Sodom* [1, 1, 9]
σπέρμα, ατος, τό, *seed, offspring, descendant* [4, 9, 43]
συγγενής, ές, *related, of the same race* [1, 4, 11]
συμμαρτυρέω, *I bear witness with* [1, 3, 3]
συνείδησις, εως, ἡ, *conscience* [1, 3, 36]
συντελέω, *I complete, bring to an end* [1, 1, 6]
συντέμνω, *I cut short, limit, end* [1, 1, 1]
τιμή, ῆς, ἡ, *honor* [1, 6, 41]

τρέχω, *I run* [1, 1, 20]
υἱοθεσία, ας, ἡ, *adoption* [1, 3, 5]
ὑπόλειμμα, ατος, τό, *remnant* [1, 1, 1]
Φαραώ, *Pharaoh* [1, 1, 5]
φαῦλος, η, ον, *bad, evil* [1, 1, 6]
φθάνω, *I attain* [1, 1, 7]
φύραμα, ατος, τό, *dough* [1, 2, 5]
ψεύδομαι, *I lie* [1, 1, 12]
ὦ, *O!, Oh* [1, 4, 17]
Ὡσηέ, ὁ, *Hosea* [1, 1, 1]

9.1 Ἀλήθειαν λέγω ἐν Χριστῷ, οὐ ψεύδομαι,[1] συμ-
μαρτυρούσης[2] μοι τῆς συνειδήσεώς[3] μου ἐν πνεύματι
ἁγίῳ, 2 ὅτι λύπη[4] μοί ἐστιν[5] μεγάλη καὶ ἀδιάλειπτος[6]
ὀδύνη[7] τῇ καρδίᾳ μου· 3 ηὐχόμην[8] γὰρ ἀνάθεμα[9] εἶναι
αὐτὸς[10] ἐγὼ[11] ἀπὸ τοῦ Χριστοῦ ὑπὲρ[12] τῶν ἀδελφῶν μου
τῶν συγγενῶν[13] μου κατὰ σάρκα, 4 οἵτινές εἰσιν
Ἰσραηλῖται,[14] ὧν[15] ἡ υἱοθεσία[16] καὶ ἡ δόξα καὶ αἱ
διαθῆκαι[17] καὶ ἡ νομοθεσία[18] καὶ ἡ λατρεία[19] καὶ αἱ
ἐπαγγελίαι, 5 ὧν[20] οἱ πατέρες, καὶ ἐξ ὧν ὁ χριστὸς τὸ[21]
κατὰ σάρκα, ὁ ὢν[22] ἐπὶ πάντων, θεὸς[23] εὐλογητὸς[24] εἰς
τοὺς αἰῶνας· ἀμήν.

---

[1] ψεύδομαι, *I lie.*

[2] συμμαρτυρέω, *I bear witness with.* MH: the root (συμμαρτυρε) ends in a vowel, so the connecting vowel contracts (ε + ου = ου).

[3] συνείδησις, εως, ἡ, *conscience.*

[4] λύπη, ης, ἡ, *grief, sorrow.* TH: pred. nom. to the subject of ἐστιν.

[5] TH: with μοί, lit. *there is to me*; *I have.*

[6] ἀδιάλειπτος, ον, *unceasing.*

[7] ὀδύνη, ης, ἡ, *pain, distress.* TH: pred. nom. to the subject of ἐστιν.

[8] εὔχομαι, *I pray, wish.*

[9] ἀνάθεμα, ατος, τό, *cursed.*

[10] TH: αὐτὸς is intensive; with ἐγὼ, *I myself.*

[11] TH: here, nom. is the subject of the inf. εἶναι.

[12] TH: ὑπὲρ indicates advantage; *for.*

[13] συγγενής, ές, *related, of the same race,* ***compatriot.***

[14] Ἰσραηλίτης, ου, ὁ, *Israelite.*

[15] TH: this gen. rel. pron. introduces a list, implying possession; *who have.*

[16] υἱοθεσία, ας, ἡ, *adoption.*

[17] διαθήκη, ης, ἡ, *covenant.*

[18] νομοθεσία, ας, ἡ, *legislation, giving of the law.*

[19] λατρεία, ας, ἡ, *service, worship.*

[20] TH: this gen. rel. pron. introduces a list, implying possession; *who have.*

[21] TH: τὸ substantivizes the prep. phrase κατὰ σάρκα; with ὁ χριστὸς, *the messiah according to the flesh.*

[22] MH: pres. act. indic. nom. sg. masc. of εἰμί. TH: *the one who is.*

[23] TH: θεὸς is in app. to ὁ ὢν.

[24] εὐλογητός, ή, όν, *blessed, praised.*

6 Οὐχ οἷον[1] δὲ ὅτι ἐκπέπτωκεν[2] ὁ λόγος τοῦ θεοῦ. οὐ
γὰρ πάντες οἱ[3] ἐξ Ἰσραήλ, οὗτοι[4] Ἰσραήλ· **7** οὐδ᾽ ὅτι[5]
εἰσὶν σπέρμα[6] Ἀβραάμ, πάντες τέκνα, ἀλλ᾽· Ἐν Ἰσαὰκ[7]
κληθήσεταί[8] σοι σπέρμα.[9] **8** τοῦτ᾽ ἔστιν,[10] οὐ[11] τὰ τέκνα
τῆς σαρκὸς ταῦτα[12] τέκνα τοῦ θεοῦ, ἀλλὰ τὰ τέκνα τῆς
ἐπαγγελίας λογίζεται[13] εἰς σπέρμα·[14] **9** ἐπαγγελίας[15] γὰρ
ὁ λόγος[16] οὗτος· Κατὰ τὸν καιρὸν τοῦτον ἐλεύσομαι[17] καὶ
ἔσται τῇ Σάρρᾳ[18] υἱός. **10** οὐ μόνον δέ, ἀλλὰ καὶ Ῥεβέκκα[19]
ἐξ[20] ἑνὸς κοίτην[21] ἔχουσα, Ἰσαὰκ[22] τοῦ πατρὸς ἡμῶν·
11 μήπω[23] γὰρ γεννηθέντων[24] μηδὲ πραξάντων[25] τι ἀγαθὸν

---

[1] οἷος, α, ον, *as, such as*. TH: Οὐχ οἷον δὲ ὅτι, *It is not as if*.

[2] ἐκπίπτω, *I fall*, ***fail***. MH: the root is εκ + πτ; after redupl., adds ω before tense formative.

[3] TH: οἱ substantivizes the prep. phrase ἐξ Ἰσραήλ; *those (descended) from Israel*.

[4] TH: οὗτοι is redundant, but marks Ἰσραήλ as a pred. nom.

[5] TH: οὐδ᾽ ὅτι, *nor*.

[6] σπέρμα, ατος, τό, *seed, offspring, descendant*. TH: pred. nom. to πάντες τέκνα.

[7] Ἰσαάκ, ὁ, *Isaac*.

[8] MH: from καλέω; the root, καλ, becomes κλη in the fut. pass.

[9] σπέρμα, ατος, τό, *seed, offspring, descendant*.

[10] TH: τοῦτ᾽ ἔστιν continues the argument; *that is*.

[11] TH: *it is not*.

[12] TH: *that are*.

[13] λογίζομαι, *I regard, consider*.

[14] σπέρμα, ατος, τό, *seed, offspring, descendant*.

[15] TH: ἐπαγγελίας is fronted but should be translated after λόγος.

[16] TH: pred. nom. to οὗτος; *this is the word*.

[17] MH: from ἔρχομαι; fut. tense is built from the root ἐλευθ (θ + σ = σ).

[18] Σάρρα, ας, ἡ, *Sarah*.

[19] Ῥεβέκκα, ας, ἡ, *Rebecca*.

[20] TH: *with*.

[21] κοίτη, ης, ἡ, *bed*, ***sexual intercourse***.

[22] Ἰσαάκ, ὁ, *Isaac*. TH: Ἰσαὰκ is in app. to ἑνός.

[23] μήπω, *not yet*.

[24] MH: the α lengthens to η before the tense formative. TH: prtc. of concession; with μήπω, *though they had not yet been born*.

[25] πράσσω, *I do, engage in*. MH: the root is πραγ; γ + σ = ξ. TH: concession.

ἢ ⸀φαῦλον,[1] ἵνα ἡ κατ᾽ ἐκλογὴν[2] πρόθεσις[3] τοῦ θεοῦ μένῃ,[4]
12 οὐκ ἐξ ἔργων ἀλλ᾽ ἐκ τοῦ καλοῦντος,[5] ἐρρέθη[6] αὐτῇ ὅτι
Ὁ μείζων[7] δουλεύσει[8] τῷ ἐλάσσονι·[9] **13** ⸀καθὼς γέγραπται·
Τὸν Ἰακὼβ[10] ἠγάπησα,[11] τὸν δὲ Ἠσαῦ[12] ἐμίσησα.[13]
14 Τί οὖν ἐροῦμεν;[14] μὴ ἀδικία[15] παρὰ τῷ θεῷ;[16] μὴ
γένοιτο· **15** τῷ ⸀Μωϋσεῖ γὰρ⸀ λέγει· Ἐλεήσω[17] ὃν ἂν ἐλεῶ,[18]
καὶ οἰκτιρήσω[19] ὃν ἂν οἰκτίρω.[20] **16** ἄρα[21] οὖν οὐ[22] τοῦ
θέλοντος οὐδὲ τοῦ τρέχοντος[23] ἀλλὰ τοῦ ἐλεῶντος[24]
θεοῦ.[25] **17** λέγει γὰρ ἡ γραφὴ τῷ Φαραὼ[26] ὅτι Εἰς αὐτὸ

---

[1] φαῦλος, η, ον, *bad, evil.*

[2] ἐκλογή, ῆς, ἡ, *election, choice.*

[3] πρόθεσις, εως, ἡ, *purpose, plan.*

[4] MH: subj. mood has a lengthened connecting vowel (ε › η).

[5] MH: καλέω is an epsilon contract verb, so a contraction occurs here (ε + ου = ου).

[6] MH: aor. pass. indic. 3rd sg. of λέγω.

[7] TH: μείζων is comp. and subst.; *the older (one).*

[8] δουλεύω, *I serve.*

[9] ἐλάσσων, *less.* TH: dat. dir. obj. of δουλεύσει. ἐλάσσονι is comp. and subst.; *the younger (one).*

[10] Ἰακώβ, ὁ, *Jacob.*

[11] MH: the α lengthens to η before the tense formative.

[12] Ἠσαῦ, ὁ, *Esau.*

[13] μισέω, *I hate.* MH: the ε lengthens to η before the tense formative.

[14] MH: fut. act. indic. 1st pl. of λέγω.

[15] ἀδικία, ας, ἡ, *unrighteousness, injustice.*

[16] TH: μὴ ἀδικία παρὰ τῷ θεῷ, *is there unrighteousness with God?*

[17] ἐλεέω, *I have mercy (on).* MH: the ε lengthens to η before the tense formative.

[18] ἐλεέω, *I have mercy (on).*

[19] οἰκτίρω, *I have compassion (on).* MH: inserts η before the tense formative in the fut. tense.

[20] οἰκτίρω, *I have compassion (on).*

[21] ἆρα, *consequently.*

[22] TH: *it is not.*

[23] τρέχω, *I run,* ***exert.***

[24] ἐλεέω, *I have mercy (on).* MH: although the root ends in ε, ἐλεέω occasionally contracts as if it ends in α; α + ο = ω.

[25] TH: θεοῦ is in app. to τοῦ ἐλεῶντος; *of the one who has mercy—God.*

[26] Φαραώ, ὁ, *Pharaoh.*

τοῦτο[1] ἐξήγειρά[2] σε ὅπως ἐνδείξωμαι[3] ἐν σοὶ τὴν δύναμίν
μου, καὶ ὅπως διαγγελῇ[4] τὸ ὄνομά μου ἐν πάσῃ τῇ γῇ.
18 ἄρα[5] οὖν ὃν[6] θέλει ἐλεεῖ,[7] ὃν[8] δὲ θέλει σκληρύνει.[9]
19 Ἐρεῖς[10] μοι οὖν· Τί οὖν ἔτι μέμφεται;[11] τῷ γὰρ
βουλήματι[12] αὐτοῦ τίς ἀνθέστηκεν;[13] **20** ὦ[14] ἄνθρωπε,
μενοῦνγε[15] σὺ[16] τίς εἶ ὁ ἀνταποκρινόμενος[17] τῷ θεῷ; μὴ
ἐρεῖ[18] τὸ πλάσμα[19] τῷ πλάσαντι[20] Τί με ἐποίησας[21]
οὕτως;[22] **21** ἢ οὐκ ἔχει ἐξουσίαν ὁ κεραμεὺς[23] τοῦ πηλοῦ[24]
ἐκ τοῦ αὐτοῦ[25] φυράματος[26] ποιῆσαι ὃ μὲν[27] εἰς τιμὴν[28]

---

[1] TH: Εἰς αὐτὸ τοῦτο, *for this very reason.*

[2] ἐξεγείρω, *I raise up, awaken.* MH: since the root ends in ρ, the aor. tense formative is just α.

[3] ἐνδείκνυμι, *I show, point out,* ***demonstrate.*** MH: the root is ἐνδεικ; κ + σ = ξ.

[4] διαγγέλλω, *I proclaim.* MH: aor. pass. subj. 3rd sg.; 2nd aor. pass. does not include θ in the tense formative.

[5] ἆρα, *consequently.*

[6] TH: acc. rel. pron. is the obj. of ἐλεεῖ; *he has mercy on whom.*

[7] ἐλεέω, *I have mercy (on).*

[8] TH: acc. rel. pron. is the obj. of σκληρύνει; *he hardens whom.*

[9] σκληρύνω, *I harden.*

[10] MH: fut. act. indic. 2nd sg. of λέγω.

[11] μέμφομαι, *I blame, find fault.*

[12] βούλημα, ατος, τό, *purpose,* ***will.*** TH: dat. dir. obj. of ἀνθέστηκεν.

[13] ἀνθίστημι, *I oppose, resist.* MH: pf. act. indic. 3rd sg.

[14] ὦ, *O!, Oh.*

[15] μενοῦνγε, *rather, on the contrary.*

[16] TH: pred. nom. to τίς.

[17] ἀνταποκρίνομαι, *I answer back, argue against.* TH: ἀνταποκρινόμενος is in app. to σὺ; *you who are talking back.*

[18] MH: fut. act. indic. 3rd sg. of λέγω.

[19] πλάσμα, ατος, τό, *a thing molded or formed.*

[20] πλάσσω, *I mold, form.* MH: root is πλατ; τ drops when followed by σ.

[21] MH: the ε lengthens to η before the tense formative.

[22] TH: *this way.*

[23] κεραμεύς, έως, ὁ, *potter.*

[24] πηλός, οῦ, ὁ, *clay.*

[25] TH: τοῦ αὐτοῦ is intensive; with ἐκ … φυράματος, *from the same lump of clay.*

[26] φύραμα, ατος, τό, *dough,* ***lump of clay.***

[27] TH: ὃ μὲν … ὃ δὲ, *one … another.*

[28] τιμή, ῆς, ἡ, *honor.*

σκεῦος [1] ὃ δὲ εἰς ἀτιμίαν; [2] **22** εἰ δὲ θέλων [3] ὁ θεὸς
ἐνδείξασθαι[4] τὴν ὀργὴν[5] καὶ γνωρίσαι[6] τὸ δυνατὸν[7] αὐτοῦ
ἤνεγκεν [8] ἐν πολλῇ μακροθυμίᾳ [9] σκεύη [10] ὀργῆς [11]
κατηρτισμένα[12] εἰς ἀπώλειαν,[13] **23** ⸀καὶ ἵνα γνωρίσῃ[14] τὸν
πλοῦτον [15] τῆς δόξης αὐτοῦ ἐπὶ σκεύη [16] ἐλέους,[17] ἃ [18]
προητοίμασεν[19] εἰς δόξαν, **24** οὓς καὶ[20] ἐκάλεσεν ἡμᾶς[21] οὐ
μόνον ἐξ Ἰουδαίων ἀλλὰ καὶ ἐξ ἐθνῶν;— **25** ὡς καὶ[22] ἐν τῷ
Ὡσηὲ[23] λέγει· Καλέσω τὸν οὐ λαόν μου λαόν μου καὶ τὴν
οὐκ ἠγαπημένην[24] ἠγαπημένην· **26** καὶ ἔσται ἐν τῷ τόπῳ
οὗ [25] ἐρρέθη [26] ⸀αὐτοῖς· Οὐ λαός [27] μου ὑμεῖς, ἐκεῖ
κληθήσονται[28] υἱοὶ θεοῦ ζῶντος.

---

[1] σκεῦος, ους, τό, *vessel.*
[2] ἀτιμία, ας, ἡ, *shame, dishonor, disgrace.*
[3] TH: causal prtc.; *because he is willing.*
[4] ἐνδείκνυμι, *I show, point out,* ***demonstrate***. MH: root is ἐνδεικ; κ + σ = ξ.
[5] ὀργή, ῆς, ἡ, *wrath.*
[6] γνωρίζω, *I make known.*
[7] δυνατός, ή, όν, *able, capable,* ***power***.
[8] MH: aor. act. indic. 3rd sg of φέρω.
[9] μακροθυμία, ας, ἡ, *patience, steadfastness.*
[10] σκεῦος, ους, τό, *vessel.*
[11] ὀργή, ῆς, ἡ, *wrath.*
[12] καταρτίζω, *I prepare, put in order*. MH: root ends with δ; δ + μ = σμ.
[13] ἀπώλεια, ας, ἡ, *destruction.*
[14] γνωρίζω, *I make known*. MH: root ends with δ; δ + σ = σ.
[15] πλοῦτος, ου, ὁ, *wealth, riches.*
[16] σκεῦος, ους, τό, *vessel.*
[17] ἔλεος, ους, τό, *mercy, compassion.*
[18] TH: rel. pron. refers to σκεύη.
[19] προετοιμάζω, *I prepare beforehand*. MH: root ends with δ; δ + σ = σ.
[20] TH: καί is additive; *also.*
[21] TH: ἡμᾶς is in app. to οὓς.
[22] TH: καί is additive; *also.*
[23] Ὡσηέ, ὁ, *Hosea*. TH: τῷ marks Ὡσηὲ as dat.
[24] MH: the α lengthens to η before the tense formative.
[25] οὗ, *where.*
[26] MH: aor. pass. indic. 3rd sg. of λέγω.
[27] TH: pred. nom. to ὑμεῖς.
[28] MH: from καλέω; the root, καλ, becomes κλη in the fut. pass.

27 Ἠσαΐας[1] δὲ κράζει ὑπὲρ τοῦ Ἰσραήλ· Ἐὰν ᾖ[2]
ὁ ἀριθμὸς[3] τῶν υἱῶν Ἰσραὴλ ὡς ἡ ἄμμος[4] τῆς θαλάσσης,
τὸ ⸀ὑπόλειμμα[5] σωθήσεται·[6] **28** λόγον γὰρ συντελῶν[7] καὶ
⸀συντέμνων[8] ποιήσει[9] κύριος ἐπὶ τῆς γῆς. **29** καὶ καθὼς
προείρηκεν[10] Ἠσαΐας·[11] Εἰ μὴ[12] κύριος Σαβαὼθ[13]
ἐγκατέλιπεν[14] ἡμῖν σπέρμα,[15] ὡς Σόδομα[16] ἂν[17]
ἐγενήθημεν[18] καὶ ὡς Γόμορρα[19] ἂν[20] ὡμοιώθημεν.[21]

30 Τί οὖν ἐροῦμεν;[22] ὅτι ἔθνη τὰ[23] μὴ διώκοντα[24]
δικαιοσύνην κατέλαβεν[25] δικαιοσύνην, δικαιοσύνην δὲ
τὴν[26] ἐκ πίστεως· **31** Ἰσραὴλ δὲ διώκων[27] νόμον δικαιοσύνης

---

[1] Ἠσαΐας, ου, ὁ, *Isaiah.*
[2] MH: pres. subj. 3rd sg. of εἰμί.
[3] ἀριθμός, οῦ, ὁ, *number.*
[4] ἄμμος, ου, ἡ, *sand.*
[5] ὑπόλειμμα, ατος, τό, *remnant.*
[6] MH: fut. tense stem of σῴζω is σω.
[7] συντελέω, *I complete, bring to an end.* TH: συντελῶν καὶ συντέμνων are adv. prtcs. modifying ποιήσει; *he will do … completely and quickly.*
[8] συντέμνω, *I cut short, limit, end.* See TH immediately above.
[9] MH: the ε lengthens to η before the tense formative.
[10] προλέγω, *I foretell, predict.* MH: pf. act. indic. 3rd sg.
[11] Ἠσαΐας, ου, ὁ, *Isaiah.*
[12] TH: Εἰ μὴ marks the protasis of a conditional statement; *If … not,*
[13] Σαβαώθ, *hosts, armies.* TH: transliterated Hebrew term; with κύριος, *Lord of hosts.*
[14] ἐγκαταλείπω, *I leave behind.* MH: 2nd aor.; the diphthong ει becomes ι.
[15] σπέρμα, ατος, το, *seed, offspring, descendant.*
[16] Σόδομα, ων, τά, *Sodom.*
[17] TH: The ἂν here marks the apodosis of a past contrary-to-fact condition.
[18] MH: 2nd aor. of γίνομαι; root is γεν.
[19] Γόμορρα, ων, τά, *Gomorrah.*
[20] TH: The ἂν here marks the apodosis of a past contrary-to-fact condition.
[21] ὁμοιόω, *I make alike, resemble.* MH: ο lengthens to ω before the tense formative.
[22] MH: fut. act. indic. 1st pl. of λέγω.
[23] TH: τὰ substantivizes μὴ διώκοντα; with ἔθνη, *the nations who did not pursue.*
[24] διώκω, *I pursue, chase.*
[25] καταλαμβάνω, *I attain, seize.* MH: 2nd aor.; root is καταλαβ.
[26] TH: τὴν substantivizes the prep. phrase ἐκ πίστεως; with δικαιοσύνην, *righteousness that is from faith.*
[27] διώκω, *I pursue, chase.*

εἰς[1] ⸀νόμον οὐκ ἔφθασεν.[2] **32** διὰ τί; ὅτι[3] οὐκ ἐκ πίστεως
ἀλλ᾽ ὡς ἐξ ⸀ἔργων· ⸀προσέκοψαν [4] τῷ λίθῳ τοῦ
προσκόμματος,[5] **33** καθὼς γέγραπται· Ἰδοὺ τίθημι ἐν
Σιὼν[6] λίθον προσκόμματος[7] καὶ πέτραν[8] σκανδάλου,[9] ⸀καὶ
ὁ πιστεύων ἐπ᾽ αὐτῷ οὐ καταισχυνθήσεται.[10]

⸀**9:3 ἀνάθεμα εἶναι αὐτὸς ἐγὼ** WH Treg NA28] αὐτὸς ἐγὼ ἀνάθεμα εἶναι RP

⸃**9:3 ἀνάθεμα εἶναι αὐτὸς ἐγὼ** WH Treg NA28] αὐτὸς ἐγὼ ἀνάθεμα εἶναι RP

⸀**11 φαῦλον** WH Treg NA28] κακόν RP

⸀**13 καθὼς** Treg NA28 RP] καθάπερ WH

⸂**15 Μωϋσεῖ γὰρ** WH Treg NA28] γὰρ Μωϋσεῖ RP

⸃**15 Μωϋσεῖ γὰρ** WH Treg NA28] γὰρ Μωϋσεῖ RP

⸂**19 μοι οὖν** WH Treg NA28] οὖν μοι RP

⸃**19 μοι οὖν** WH Treg NA28] οὖν μοι RP

⸀ • **οὖν** NA28] – WH Treg RP

⸂**20 ὦ ἄνθρωπε μενοῦνγε** WH Treg NA28] Μενοῦνγε ὦ ἄνθρωπε RP

⸃**20 ὦ ἄνθρωπε μενοῦνγε** WH Treg NA28] Μενοῦνγε ὦ ἄνθρωπε RP

⸀**23 καὶ** Treg NA28 RP] – WH

⸀**26 αὐτοῖς** WH NA28 RP] – Treg

⸀**27 ὑπόλειμμα** WH Treg NA28] κατάλειμμα RP

⸀**28 συντέμνων** WH Treg NA28] + ἐν δικαιοσύνῃ ὅτι λόγον συντετμημένον RP

⸀**31 νόμον** WH Treg NA28] + δικαιοσύνης RP

⸀**32 ἔργων** WH Treg NA28] + νόμου RP

⸀ • **προσέκοψαν** WH Treg NA28] + γὰρ RP

⸀**33 καὶ** WH Treg NA28] + πᾶς RP

---

[1] TH: εἰς is spatial; *in.*

[2] φθάνω, *I arrive, attain.* MH: root is φθα.

[3] TH: the aor. act. indic. 3rd pl. of διώκω, ἐδίωξαν, is implied by the prtc. in the previous verse; *they pursued it.*

[4] προσκόπτω, *I stumble.* MH: root is προσκοπ; π + σ = ψ.

[5] πρόσκομμα, ατος, τό, *hindrance, obstacle,* ***stumbling***.

[6] Σιών, ἡ, *Zion.*

[7] πρόσκομμα, ατος, τό, *hindrance, obstacle,* ***stumbling***.

[8] πέτρα, ας, ἡ, *rock.*

[9] σκάνδαλον, ου, τό, *trap, offense,* ***stumbling***.

[10] καταισχύνω, *I dishonor, put to shame.*

ROMANS 10

New Vocabulary by Frequency [Chapter, Book, SBLGNT Occurrences]

ἄβυσσος, ου, ἡ, *abyss* [1, 1, 9]
ἀγνοέω, *I am unaware, ignorant (of)* [1, 6, 22]
ἀκοή, ῆς, ἡ, *hearing* [3, 3, 24]
ἀνάγω, *I bring up* [1, 1, 23]
ἀντιλέγω, *I oppose, contradict* [1, 1, 9]
ἀπειθέω, *I disobey, am disobedient* [1, 5, 14]
ἀποτολμάω, *I am bold* [1, 1, 1]
ἆρα, *consequently* [1, 11, 52]
ἀσύνετος, ον, *foolish, senseless* [1, 3, 5]
δέησις, εως, ἡ, *prayer* [1, 1, 18]
διαστολή, ῆς, ἡ, *distinction, difference* [1, 2, 3]
ἐγγύς, *near* [1, 2, 31]
ἐκπετάννυμι, *I spread out* [1,1, 1]
Ἕλλην, ηνος, ὁ, *Greek; civilized* [1, 6, 25]
ἐμφανής, *visible, known* [1, 1, 2]
ἐπίγνωσις, εως, ἡ, *knowledge, recognition* [1, 3, 20]
ἐπικαλέω, *I call on* [3, 3, 30]
εὐδοκία, ας, ἡ, *good will, desire* [1, 1, 9]
ζῆλος, ου, ὁ, *zeal* [1, 2, 16]
Ἠσαΐας, ου, ὁ, *Isaiah* [2, 5, 22]
κατάγω, *I bring down* [1, 1, 9]
καταισχύνω, *I dishonor, put to shame* [1, 3, 13]
μενοῦνγε, *rather, on the contrary* [1, 2, 3]
οἰκουμένη, ης, ἡ, *inhabited world* [1, 1, 15]
ὁμολογέω, *I confess, acknowledge* [2, 2, 26]
παραζηλόω, *I make jealous* [1, 3, 4]
παροργίζω, *I provoke to anger* [1, 1, 2]
πέρας, ατος, τό, *end* [1, 1, 4]
πλουτέω, *I am rich* [1, 1, 12]
σωτηρία, ας, ἡ, *salvation* [2, 5, 46]
τέλος, ους, τό, *end* [1, 5, 40]
ὑπακούω, *I obey, listen* [1, 4, 21]
ὑποτάσσω, *I subject, subordinate* [1, 6, 38]
φθόγγος, ου, ὁ, *voice, sound* [1, 1, 2]
χωρίς, *without, apart* [1, 6, 42]
ὡραῖος, α, ον, *timely, beautiful* [1, 1, 4]

10.1 Ἀδελφοί, ἡ μὲν εὐδοκία[1] τῆς ἐμῆς καρδίας καὶ ἡ
⸀δέησις[2] πρὸς τὸν θεὸν ὑπὲρ ⸀αὐτῶν[3] εἰς σωτηρίαν.[4]
2 μαρτυρῶ γὰρ αὐτοῖς ὅτι ζῆλον[5] θεοῦ ἔχουσιν· ἀλλ' οὐ
κατ' ἐπίγνωσιν,[6] **3** ἀγνοοῦντες[7] γὰρ τὴν τοῦ θεοῦ
δικαιοσύνην, καὶ τὴν ⸀ἰδίαν[8] ζητοῦντες[9] στῆσαι,[10]
τῇ δικαιοσύνῃ τοῦ θεοῦ οὐχ ὑπετάγησαν·[11] **4** τέλος[12] γὰρ
νόμου Χριστὸς εἰς δικαιοσύνην παντὶ τῷ πιστεύοντι.

5 Μωϋσῆς γὰρ γράφει ⸀ὅτι[13] τὴν δικαιοσύνην τὴν[14] ἐκ
⸂τοῦ νόμου⸃ ὁ ⸀ποιήσας[15] ἄνθρωπος ζήσεται[16] ἐν ⸀αὐτῇ.[17]
6 ἡ δὲ ἐκ πίστεως δικαιοσύνη οὕτως λέγει· Μὴ εἴπῃς[18] ἐν
τῇ καρδίᾳ σου· Τίς ἀναβήσεται[19] εἰς τὸν οὐρανόν; τοῦτ'

---

1 εὐδοκία, ας, ἡ, *good will, desire.*

2 δέησις, εως, ἡ, *prayer.*

3 TH: "is" should be supplied after αὐτῶν.

4 σωτηρία, ας, ἡ, *salvation.*

5 ζῆλος, ου, ὁ, *zeal.*

6 ἐπίγνωσις, εως, ἡ, *knowledge, recognition.*

7 ἀγνοέω, *I am unaware, ignorant (of).* MH: the root (ἀγνοε) ends in a vowel, so the connecting vowel contracts (ε + ο = ου).

8 TH: δικαιοσύνην is implied from the previous clause; *their own righteousness.* NA has δικαιοσύνην after ἰδίαν, although δικαιοσύνην is in brackets, indicating the questionable nature of its inclusion.

9 MH: the root (ζητε) ends in a vowel, so the connecting vowel contracts (ε + ο = ου).

10 MH: aor. act. inf. of ἵστημι. TH: ζητοῦντες στῆσαι, *seeking to establish.*

11 ὑποτάσσω, *I subject, subordinate.* MH: the root is υποταγ; 2nd aor. pass. does not include θ in tense formative.

12 τέλος, ους, τό, *end.* TH: pred. nom. to Χριστὸς.

13 NA has ὅτι after νόμου, which marks ὁ ποιήσας ἄνθρωπος ζήσεται ἐν αὐτῇ as the content of what Μωϋσῆς writes.

14 TH: τὴν substantivizes the prep. phrase ἐκ τοῦ νόμου; with δικαιοσύνην, *the righteousness that is from the law.*

15 TH: ποιήσας is attrib. to ἄνθρωπος; *the person who does.* NA has αὐτὰ after ποιήσας.

16 MH: from ζάω; in Classical Greek, the root was ζη, which is retained in Koine.

17 TH: αὐτῇ refers to τὴν δικαιοσύνην. NA has αὐτοῖς instead of αὐτῇ.

18 MH: aor. act. subj. 2nd sg. of λέγω.

19 MH: from ἀναβαίνω; root is ἀναβα. The α lengthens to η before the tense formative.

ἔστιν Χριστὸν καταγαγεῖν·[1] **7** ἤ· Τίς καταβήσεται[2] εἰς
τὴν ἄβυσσον; [3] τοῦτ' ἔστιν Χριστὸν ἐκ νεκρῶν
ἀναγαγεῖν.[4] **8** ἀλλὰ τί λέγει; Ἐγγύς[5] σου τὸ ῥῆμά ἐστιν,
ἐν τῷ στόματί σου καὶ ἐν τῇ καρδίᾳ σου, τοῦτ' ἔστιν τὸ
ῥῆμα τῆς πίστεως ὃ[6] κηρύσσομεν. **9** ὅτι ἐὰν ˹ὁμολογήσῃς[7]
ἐν τῷ στόματί ˹σου κύριον Ἰησοῦν, καὶ πιστεύσῃς[8] ἐν τῇ
καρδίᾳ σου ὅτι ὁ θεὸς αὐτὸν ἤγειρεν [9] ἐκ νεκρῶν,
σωθήσῃ· [10] **10** καρδίᾳ γὰρ πιστεύεται εἰς δικαιοσύνην,
στόματι δὲ ὁμολογεῖται[11] εἰς σωτηρίαν·[12] **11** λέγει γὰρ ἡ
γραφή· Πᾶς ὁ πιστεύων ἐπ' αὐτῷ οὐ καταισχυνθήσεται.[13]
12 οὐ γάρ ἐστιν διαστολὴ[14] Ἰουδαίου τε καὶ Ἕλληνος,[15] ὁ
γὰρ αὐτὸς[16] κύριος[17] πάντων, πλουτῶν[18] εἰς[19] πάντας τοὺς

---

[1] κατάγω, *I bring down*. MH: 2nd aor.; redupl. in the aor. tense (καταγ › καταγαγ).

[2] MH: from καταβαίνω; root is καταβα. The α lengthens to η before the tense formative.

[3] ἄβυσσος, ου, ἡ, *abyss*.

[4] ἀνάγω, *I bring up*. MH: 2nd aor.; redupl. in the aor. tense (ἀναγ › ἀναγαγ).

[5] ἐγγύς, *near*. TH: ἐγγύς σου, *near to you*.

[6] TH: acc. rel. pron. refers to τὸ ῥῆμα.

[7] ὁμολογέω, *I confess, acknowledge*. MH: the ε lengthens to η before the tense formative. Subj. mood has a lengthened connecting vowel (ε › η).

[8] MH: subj. mood has a lengthened connecting vowel (ε › η).

[9] MH: since the root ends in ρ, the aor. tense formative is just α, which shifts to ε in the 3rd sg.

[10] MH: fut. tense stem of σῴζω is σω.

[11] ὁμολογέω, *I confess, acknowledge*. MH: the root (ὁμολογε) ends in a vowel, so the connecting vowel contracts (ε + ε = ει).

[12] σωτηρία, ας, ἡ, *salvation*.

[13] καταισχύνω, *I dishonor, put to shame*.

[14] διαστολή, ῆς, ἡ, *distinction, difference*. TH: *distinction between*.

[15] Ἕλλην, ηνος, ὁ, *Greek; civilized*.

[16] TH: αὐτὸς is intensive; with κύριος, *the same Lord*.

[17] TH: ὁ γὰρ αὐτὸς κύριος, *for he is the same Lord*.

[18] πλουτέω, *I am rich*. MH: the root (πλουτε) ends in a vowel, so the connecting vowel contracts (ε + ω = ω).

[19] TH: εἰς indicates advantage; *for the benefit of*.

ἐπικαλουμένους[1] αὐτόν· **13** Πᾶς γὰρ ὃς ἂν[2] ἐπικαλέσηται[3]
τὸ ὄνομα κυρίου σωθήσεται.[4]
14 Πῶς οὖν ⸀ἐπικαλέσωνται[5] εἰς ὃν οὐκ ἐπίστευσαν;
πῶς δὲ ⸀πιστεύσωσιν[6] οὗ οὐκ ἤκουσαν; πῶς δὲ ⸀ἀκούσωσιν[7]
χωρὶς[8] κηρύσσοντος; **15** πῶς δὲ ⸀κηρύξωσιν[9] ἐὰν μὴ
ἀποσταλῶσιν;[10] ⸀καθὼς γέγραπται· Ὡς ὡραῖοι[11] οἱ πόδες
τῶν ⸀εὐαγγελιζομένων ⸀τὰ ἀγαθά. **16** ἀλλ᾽ οὐ πάντες
ὑπήκουσαν[12] τῷ εὐαγγελίῳ· Ἠσαΐας[13] γὰρ λέγει· Κύριε,
τίς ἐπίστευσεν τῇ ἀκοῇ[14] ἡμῶν; **17** ἄρα[15] ἡ πίστις[16]
ἐξ ἀκοῆς,[17] ἡ δὲ ἀκοὴ[18] διὰ ῥήματος ⸀Χριστοῦ.
18 Ἀλλὰ λέγω, μὴ οὐκ ἤκουσαν; μενοῦνγε·[19] Εἰς πᾶσαν
τὴν γῆν ἐξῆλθεν[20] ὁ φθόγγος[21] αὐτῶν, καὶ εἰς τὰ πέρατα[22]

---

[1] ἐπικαλέω, *I call on*. MH: the root (ἐπικαλε) ends in a vowel, so the connecting vowel contracts (ε + ο = ου).

[2] TH: ὃς ἄν, *whoever*, but with πᾶς, *anyone who*.

[3] ἐπικαλέω, *I call on*. MH: subj. mood has a lengthened connecting vowel (ε › η).

[4] MH: fut. tense stem of σῴζω is σω.

[5] ἐπικαλέω, *I call on*. MH: subj. mood has a lengthened connecting vowel (ο › ω).

[6] MH: subj. mood has a lengthened connecting vowel (ο › ω).

[7] MH: subj. mood has a lengthened connecting vowel (ο › ω).

[8] χωρίς, *without, apart*.

[9] MH: from κηρύσσω. The root ends with a velar (κ, γ, χ); velar + σ = ξ. Subj. mood has a lengthened connecting vowel (ο › ω).

[10] MH: 2nd aor. pass. from ἀποστέλλω; stem vowel shifts to α. Subj. mood has a lengthened connecting vowel (ο › ω).

[11] ὡραῖος, α, ον, *timely, beautiful*.

[12] ὑπακούω, *I obey, listen*.

[13] Ἠσαΐας, ου, ὁ, *Isaiah*.

[14] ἀκοή, ῆς, ἡ, *hearing*, ***report***.

[15] ἆρα, *consequently*.

[16] TH: "is" should be supplied after πίστις.

[17] ἀκοή, ῆς, ἡ, *hearing*.

[18] ἀκοή, ῆς, ἡ, *hearing*. TH: "is" should be supplied after ἀκοή.

[19] μενοῦνγε, *rather, on the contrary*.

[20] MH: from ἐξέρχομαι; aor. tense stem is ἐξελθ › ἐξηλθ (aug.).

[21] φθόγγος, ου, ὁ, *voice, sound*.

[22] πέρας, ατος, τό, *end*.

τῆς οἰκουμένης[1] τὰ ῥήματα αὐτῶν. **19** ἀλλὰ λέγω, μὴ
Ἰσραὴλ οὐκ ἔγνω[2]⸆; πρῶτος Μωϋσῆς λέγει· Ἐγὼ
παραζηλώσω[3] ὑμᾶς ἐπ᾽ οὐκ ἔθνει,[4] ἐπ᾽ ἔθνει ἀσυνέτῳ[5]
παροργιῶ[6] ὑμᾶς. **20** Ἠσαΐας[7] δὲ ἀποτολμᾷ[8] καὶ λέγει·
Εὑρέθην[9] ⸀ἐν[10] τοῖς ἐμὲ μὴ ζητοῦσιν, ἐμφανὴς[11]
⸀ἐγενόμην[12] τοῖς ἐμὲ μὴ ἐπερωτῶσιν.[13] **21** πρὸς δὲ τὸν
Ἰσραὴλ λέγει· ⸀Ὅλην τὴν ἡμέραν ἐξεπέτασα[14] τὰς χεῖράς
μου πρὸς λαὸν ἀπειθοῦντα[15] καὶ ἀντιλέγοντα.[16]

---

[1] οἰκουμένη, ης, ἡ, *inhabited world*, ***world***. TH: ἐξῆλθεν is implied from the previous clause.

[2] MH: aor. act. indic. 3rd sg. of γινώσκω.

[3] παραζηλόω, *I make jealous*. MH: the ο lengthens to ω before the tense formative.

[4] TH: οὐκ ἔθνει, *those who are not a nation*.

[5] ἀσύνετος, ον, *foolish, senseless*.

[6] παροργίζω, *I provoke to anger*. MH: παροργιδ (root) + σε (Attic. fut. tense formative) › παροργισσε (δ + σ = σσ) παροργισε (σσ simplifies to σ) › παροργιε (intervocalic σ drops out) + ω (fut. act. indic. 1st sg. ending) › παροργιω (ε + ω = ω).

[7] Ἠσαΐας, ου, ὁ, *Isaiah*.

[8] ἀποτολμάω, *I am bold*. MH: the root (ἀποτολμα) ends in a vowel, so the connecting vowel contracts (α + ε = α; ι subscripts).

[9] MH: from εὑρίσκω; root is εὑρ and inserts ε after tense stem in aor. pass.

[10] TH: ἐν is instrumental; *by*.

[11] ἐμφανής, ές, *visible, known*.

[12] MH: 2nd aor. of γίνομαι; root is γεν.

[13] MH: the root (ἐπερωτα) ends in a vowel, so the connecting vowel contracts (α + ου = ω).

[14] ἐκπετάννυμι, *I spread out*. MH: the root is ἐκπετα.

[15] ἀπειθέω, *I disobey, am disobedient*. MH: the root (ἀπειθε) ends in a vowel, so the connecting vowel contracts (ε + ο = ου).

[16] ἀντιλέγω, *I oppose, contradict*, ***am stubborn***.

10:1 δέησις WH Treg NA28] + ἡ RP
- **αὐτῶν** WH Treg NA28] τοῦ Ἰσραήλ ἐστιν RP

3 ἰδίαν WH Treg] + δικαιοσύνην NA28 RP

5 ὅτι τὴν ... νόμου WH] τὴν ... νόμου ὅτι Treg NA28 RP
- **τοῦ** NA28 RP] – WH Treg

5 ὅτι τὴν ... νόμου WH] τὴν ... νόμου ὅτι Treg NA28 RP
- **ποιήσας** WH] +**αὐτὰ** Treg NA28 RP
- **αὐτῇ** WH Treg] αὐτοῖς NA28 RP

9 ὁμολογήσῃς Treg NA28 RP] + τὸ ῥῆμα WH
- **σου** Treg NA28 RP] + ὅτι WH

14 ἐπικαλέσωνται WH Treg NA28] ἐπικαλέσονται RP
- **πιστεύσωσιν** WH Treg NA28] πιστεύσουσιν RP
- **ἀκούσωσιν** WH Treg NA28] ἀκούσουσιν RP

15 κηρύξωσιν WH Treg NA28] κηρύξουσιν RP
- **καθὼς** Treg NA28 RP] καθάπερ WH
- **εὐαγγελιζομένων** WH Treg NA28] + εἰρήνην τῶν εὐαγγελιζομένων RP
- **τὰ** NA28 RP] – WH Treg

17 Χριστοῦ WH Treg NA28] θεοῦ RP

19 Ἰσραὴλ οὐκ ἔγνω WH Treg NA28] οὐκ ἔγνω Ἰσραὴλ RP

19 Ἰσραὴλ οὐκ ἔγνω WH Treg NA28] οὐκ ἔγνω Ἰσραὴλ RP

20 ἐν Treg NA28] – WH RP
- **ἐγενόμην** WH NA28 RP] + ἐν Treg

ROMANS 11

New Vocabulary by Frequency [Chapter, Book, SBLGNT Occurrences]

ἀγνοέω, *I am unaware, ignorant (of)* [1, 6, 22]
ἀγριέλαιος, ου, ἡ, *wild olive tree* [2, 2, 2]
ἀμεταμέλητος, ον, *without regret* [1, 1, 2]
ἀνεξεραύνητος, ον, *unsearchable, unfathomable* [1, 1, 1]
ἀνταποδίδωμι, *I repay, give back* [1, 2, 7]
ἀνταπόδομα, ατος, τό, *repayment* [1, 1, 2]
ἀπαρχή, ῆς, ἡ, *first fruit* [1, 3, 9]
ἀπείθεια, ας, ἡ, *disobedience* [2, 2, 7]
ἀπειθέω, *I disobey, am disobedient* [2, 5, 14]
ἀπιστία, ας, ἡ, *unbelief, distrust* [2, 4, 11]
ἀποβολή, ῆς, ἡ, *rejection, loss* [1, 1, 2]
ἀποστρέφω, *I turn away* [1, 1, 9]
ἀποτομία, ας, ἡ, *severity* [2, 2, 2]
ἀπωθέω, *I reject* [2, 2, 6]
ἀσέβεια, ας, ἡ, *ungodliness, impiety* [1, 2, 6]
ἀφαιρέω, *I take away* [1, 1, 10]
ἄχρι, *until* [1, 4, 49]
Βάαλ, ὁ, *Baal* [1, 1, 1]
βάθος, ους, τό, *depth* [1, 2, 8]
βαστάζω, *I bear, lift up* [1, 2, 27]
Βενιαμίν, ὁ, *Benjamin* [1, 1, 4]
γνῶσις, εως, ἡ, *knowledge* [1, 3, 29]
γόνυ, ατος, τό, *knee* [1, 2, 12]
διαθήκη, ης, ἡ, *covenant* [1, 2, 33]
διακονία, ας, ἡ, *ministry, service* [1, 4, 34]
δυνατός, ή, όν, *able, capable* [1, 5, 32]
ἐγκεντρίζω, *I graft* [6, 6, 6]
ἐκκλάω, *I break off* [3, 3, 3]
ἐκκόπτω, *I cut off* [2, 2, 10]
ἐκλογή, ῆς, ἡ, *election, choice* [3, 4, 7]
ἐλαία, ας, ἡ, *olive tree* [2, 2, 15]
ἐλεέω, *I have mercy (on)* [3, 6, 28]
ἔλεος, ους, τό, *mercy, compassion* [1, 3, 27]
ἐμαυτοῦ, ῆς, *myself* [1, 1, 37]
ἐντυγχάνω, *I intercede, appeal* [1, 3, 5]
ἐπεί, *because, since* [2, 3, 26]

ἐπιζητέω, *I seek after, search for* [1, 1, 13]
ἐπιμένω, *I remain, continue* [2, 3, 16]
ἐπιτυγχάνω, *I obtain* [2, 2, 5]
ἑπτακισχίλιοι, αι, α, *seven thousand* [1, 1, 1]
ἐχθρός, ά, όν, *hostile, enemy* [1, 3, 32]
ἥκω, *I have come* [1, 1, 27]
Ἠλίας, ου, ὁ, *Elijah* [1, 1, 29]
ἥττημα, ατος, τό, *loss* [1, 1, 2]
θήρα, ας, ἡ, *trap* [1, 1, 1]
θυσιαστήριον, ου, τό, *altar* [1, 1, 23]
Ἰακώβ, ὁ, *Jacob* [1, 2, 27]
Ἰσραηλίτης, ου, ὁ, *Israelite* [1, 2, 9]
κἀκεῖνος, η, ο, *and that one* [1, 1, 22]
καλλιέλαιος, ου, ἡ, *cultivated olive tree* [1, 1, 1]
καλῶς, *well, rightly* [1, 1, 37]
κάμπτω, *I bow, bend* [1, 2, 4]
κατακαυχάομαι, *I boast (over)* [2, 2, 4]
καταλείπω, *I leave behind* [1, 1, 24]
καταλλαγή, ῆς, ἡ, *reconciliation* [1, 2, 4]
κατάνυξις, εως, ἡ, *bewilderment, stupor* [1, 1, 1]
κατασκάπτω, *I tear down* [1, 1, 2]
κλάδος, ου, ὁ, *branch* [5, 5, 11]
κλῆσις, εως, ἡ, *calling* [1, 1, 11]
κρίμα, ατος, τό, *judgment* [1, 6, 27]
λεῖμμα, ατος, τό, *remnant* [1, 1, 1]
μέρος, ους, τό, *part* [1, 3, 42]
μυστήριον, ου, τό, *mystery* [1, 1, 26]
νοῦς, ός, ὁ, *mind, way of thinking* [1, 6, 24]
νῶτος, ου, ὁ, *back* [1, 1, 1]
οὐκέτι, *no longer* [2, 7, 47]
οὖς, ὠτός, τό, *ear* [1, 1, 36]
παγίς, ίδος, ἡ, *snare* [1, 1, 5]
παραζηλόω, *I make jealous* [2, 3, 4]
παράπτωμα, ατος, τό, *wrongdoing, sin* [2, 9, 19]
πιότης, ητος, ἡ, *fattiness* [1, 1, 1]
πλήρωμα, ατος, τό, *fullness* [2, 4, 17]
πλοῦτος, ου, ὁ, *wealth, riches* [3, 5, 22]
πόσος, η, ον, *how many, how much* [2, 2, 27]
ποτέ, *once* [1, 3, 29]
προγινώσκω, *I foreknow* [1, 2, 5]
προδίδωμι, *I give beforehand, give in advance* [1, 1, 1]

πρόσλημψις, εως, ἡ, *acceptance* [1, 1, 1]
πταίω, *I stumble* [1, 1, 5]
πωρόω, *I harden* [1, 1, 5]
πώρωσις, εως, ἡ, *hardness* [1, 1, 3]
ῥίζα, ης, ἡ, *root* [4, 5, 17]
ῥύομαι, *I save, rescue, deliver* [1, 3, 17]
σήμερον, *today* [1, 1, 41]
Σιών, ἡ, *Zion* [1, 2, 7]
σκάνδαλον, ου, τό, *trap, offense* [1, 4, 15]
σκοτίζω, *I become dark, darken* [1, 2, 5]
σπέρμα, ατος, τό, *seed, offspring, descendant* [1, 9, 43]
συγκάμπτω, *I bend, cause to bend* [1, 1, 1]
συγκλείω, *I enclose* [1, 1, 4]
συγκοινωνός, οῦ, ὁ, *partner, participant* [1, 1, 4]
σύμβουλος, ου, ὁ, *conselor, adviser* [1, 1, 1]
σωτηρία, ας, ἡ, *salvation* [1, 5, 46]
τράπεζα, ης, ἡ, *table, meal* [1, 1, 15]
ὑμέτερος, α, ον, *your, yours* [1, 1, 11]
ὑπολείπω, *I leave remaining* [1, 1, 1]
ὑψηλός, ή, όν, *high, lofty* [1, 2, 11]
φείδομαι, *I spare* [2, 3, 10]
φρονέω, *I think, am intent on* [1, 9, 26]
φρόνιμος, ου, ὁ, *wise, prudent* [1, 2, 14]
φυλή, ῆς, ἡ, *tribe, nation* [1, 1, 31]
φύραμα, ατος, τό, *dough* [1, 2, 5]
φύσις, εως, ἡ, *nature* [4, 7, 14]
χάρισμα, ατος, τό, *gift* [1, 6, 17]
χρηματισμός, οῦ, ὁ, *decree* [1, 1, 1]
χρηστότης, ητος, ἡ, *kindness, generosity* [3, 5, 10]
ὦ, *O!, Oh* [1, 4, 17]
ὥσπερ, *just as, even as* [1, 6, 36]

11.1 Λέγω οὖν, μὴ ἀπώσατο[1] ὁ θεὸς τὸν λαὸν αὐτοῦ; μὴ
γένοιτο· καὶ γὰρ ἐγὼ Ἰσραηλίτης[2] εἰμί, ἐκ σπέρματος[3]
Ἀβραάμ, φυλῆς[4] Βενιαμίν.[5] **2** οὐκ ἀπώσατο[6] ὁ θεὸς τὸν
λαὸν αὐτοῦ ὃν[7] προέγνω.[8] ἢ οὐκ οἴδατε ἐν[9] Ἠλίᾳ[10] τί
λέγει ἡ γραφή, ὡς ἐντυγχάνει[11] τῷ θεῷ κατὰ τοῦ ⸀Ἰσραήλ;
3 Κύριε, τοὺς προφήτας σου ἀπέκτειναν,[12] ⸀τὰ
θυσιαστήριά[13] σου κατέσκαψαν,[14] κἀγὼ ὑπελείφθην[15]
μόνος, καὶ ζητοῦσιν[16] τὴν ψυχήν μου. **4** ἀλλὰ τί λέγει αὐτῷ
ὁ χρηματισμός;[17] Κατέλιπον[18] ἐμαυτῷ[19] ἑπτακισχιλίους[20]
ἄνδρας, οἵτινες οὐκ ἔκαμψαν[21] γόνυ[22] τῇ Βάαλ.[23] **5** οὕτως
οὖν καὶ ἐν τῷ νῦν καιρῷ λεῖμμα[24] κατ᾽ ἐκλογὴν[25] χάριτος[26]

---

[1] ἀπωθέω, *I reject*. MH: root is ἀπωθ; θ + σ = σ. Since ω is a long vowel, the aug. is not evident.
[2] Ἰσραηλίτης, ου, ὁ, *Israelite*. TH: pred. nom. to ἐγὼ.
[3] σπέρμα, ατος, τό, *seed, offspring, descendant*.
[4] φυλή, ῆς, ἡ, *tribe, nation*.
[5] Βενιαμίν, ὁ, *Benjamin*.
[6] ἀπωθέω, *I reject*. MH: root is ἀπωθ; θ + σ = σ. Since ω is a long vowel, the aug. is not evident.
[7] TH: rel. pron. refers to τὸν λαὸν.
[8] προγινώσκω, *I foreknow*. MH: aor. act. indic. 3rd sg.; root is προγνο.
[9] TH: ἐν is indicating reference or respect; ἐν Ἠλίᾳ, *about Elijah*.
[10] Ἠλίας, ου, ὁ, *Elijah*.
[11] ἐντυγχάνω, *I intercede, appeal*.
[12] MH: since the root ends in ν, the aor. tense formative is just α.
[13] θυσιαστήριον, ου, τό, *altar*.
[14] κατασκάπτω, *I tear down*. MH: root is κατασκαπ; π + σ = ψ.
[15] ὑπολείπω, *I leave remaining*. MH: π + θ = φθ.
[16] MH: ζητέω is an epsilon contract verb, so a contraction occurs (ε + ου = ου).
[17] χρηματισμός, οῦ, ὁ, *decree, **divine response***.
[18] καταλείπω, *I leave behind*. MH: 2nd aor.; ει › ι.
[19] ἐμαυτοῦ, ῆς, *myself*.
[20] ἑπτακισχίλιοι, αι, α, *seven thousand*.
[21] κάμπτω, *I bow, bend*. MH: root is καμπ; π + σ = ψ.
[22] γόνυ, ατος, τό, *knee*.
[23] Βάαλ, ὁ, *Baal*.
[24] λεῖμμα, ατος, τό, *remnant*.
[25] ἐκλογή, ῆς, ἡ, *election, choice*.
[26] TH: gen. of means; *by grace*.

γέγονεν·[1] **6** εἰ δὲ χάριτι,[2] οὐκέτι[3] ἐξ ἔργων, ἐπεὶ[4] ἡ χάρις
οὐκέτι[5] γίνεται ⸀χάρις.

7 τί οὖν; ὃ[6] ἐπιζητεῖ[7] Ἰσραήλ, τοῦτο οὐκ ἐπέτυχεν,[8]
ἡ δὲ ἐκλογὴ[9] ἐπέτυχεν·[10] οἱ δὲ λοιποὶ ἐπωρώθησαν,[11]
8 ⸀καθὼς γέγραπται· Ἔδωκεν[12] αὐτοῖς ὁ θεὸς πνεῦμα
κατανύξεως,[13] ὀφθαλμοὺς τοῦ μὴ βλέπειν[14] καὶ ὦτα[15] τοῦ
μὴ ἀκούειν,[16] ἕως τῆς σήμερον[17] ἡμέρας. **9** καὶ Δαυὶδ
λέγει· Γενηθήτω[18] ἡ τράπεζα[19] αὐτῶν εἰς παγίδα[20] καὶ εἰς
θήραν[21] καὶ εἰς σκάνδαλον[22] καὶ εἰς ἀνταπόδομα[23] αὐτοῖς,
10 σκοτισθήτωσαν[24] οἱ ὀφθαλμοὶ αὐτῶν τοῦ μὴ βλέπειν,[25]
καὶ τὸν νῶτον[26] αὐτῶν διὰ παντὸς σύγκαμψον.[27]

---

[1] MH: 2nd pf. of γίνομαι. The root (γεν) becomes γον due to ablaut.
[2] TH: dat. of means; *by grace*.
[3] οὐκέτι, *no longer*.
[4] ἐπεί, *because, since,* ***otherwise***.
[5] οὐκέτι, *no longer*.
[6] TH: *that which*.
[7] ἐπιζητέω, *I seek after, search for*.
[8] ἐπιτυγχάνω, *I obtain*. MH: 2nd aor.; tense stem is ἐπι + τυχ.
[9] ἐκλογή, ῆς, ἡ, *election, choice*.
[10] ἐπιτυγχάνω, *I obtain*. MH: 2nd aor.; tense stem is ἐπι + τυχ.
[11] πωρόω, *I harden*. MH: the ο lengthens to ω before the tense formative.
[12] MH: from δίδωμι (a verb among the "kappa" aorists).
[13] κατάνυξις, εως, ἡ, *bewilderment, stupor*.
[14] TH: τοῦ + inf. can indicate result; τοῦ μὴ βλέπειν, *that do not see*.
[15] οὖς, ὠτός, τό, *ear*.
[16] TH: τοῦ + inf. can indicate result; τοῦ μὴ ἀκούειν, *that do not ear*.
[17] σήμερον, *today*. TH: with ἡμέρας, *this very day*.
[18] MH: 2nd aor. of γίνομαι; root is γεν.
[19] τράπεζα, ης, ἡ, *table, meal*.
[20] παγίς, ίδος, ἡ, *snare*.
[21] θήρα, ας, ἡ, *trap*.
[22] σκάνδαλον, ου, τό, *trap, offense,* ***stumbling block***.
[23] ἀνταπόδομα, ατος, τό, *repayment,* ***retribution***.
[24] σκοτίζω, *I become dark, darken*. MH: root ends in δ; δ + θ = σθ.
[25] TH: τοῦ + inf. can indicate result; τοῦ μὴ βλέπειν, *that they do not see*.
[26] νῶτος, ου, ὁ, *back*.
[27] συγκάμπτω, *I bend, cause to bend*. MH: root is συγκαμπ; π + σ = ψ.

11 Λέγω οὖν, μὴ ἔπταισαν[1] ἵνα πέσωσιν;[2] μὴ γένοιτο·
ἀλλὰ τῷ αὐτῶν παραπτώματι[3] ἡ σωτηρία[4] τοῖς ἔθνεσιν,
εἰς τὸ παραζηλῶσαι[5] αὐτούς. **12** εἰ δὲ τὸ παράπτωμα[6]
αὐτῶν πλοῦτος[7] κόσμου καὶ τὸ ἥττημα[8] αὐτῶν πλοῦτος[9]
ἐθνῶν, πόσῳ[10] μᾶλλον τὸ πλήρωμα[11] αὐτῶν.[12]

13 Ὑμῖν ⸀δὲ λέγω τοῖς ἔθνεσιν.[13] ἐφ' ὅσον[14] μὲν ⸀οὖν
εἰμι ἐγὼ ἐθνῶν ἀπόστολος,[15] τὴν διακονίαν[16] μου δοξάζω,
14 εἴ πως παραζηλώσω[17] μου τὴν σάρκα καὶ σώσω[18] τινὰς
ἐξ αὐτῶν. **15** εἰ γὰρ ἡ ἀποβολὴ[19] αὐτῶν καταλλαγὴ[20]
κόσμου, τίς ἡ πρόσλημψις[21] εἰ μὴ ζωὴ ἐκ νεκρῶν;
16 εἰ δὲ ἡ ἀπαρχὴ[22] ἁγία,[23] καὶ τὸ φύραμα·[24] καὶ εἰ ἡ ῥίζα[25]
ἁγία, καὶ οἱ κλάδοι.[26]

---

[1] πταίω, *I stumble.*

[2] MH: aor. act. subj. 3rd pl. of πίπτω. The root is πετ; τ drops out before σ.

[3] παράπτωμα, ατος, τό, *wrongdoing, sin.* TH: dat. of cause; *because of.*

[4] σωτηρία, ας, ἡ, *salvation.* TH: "has come" should be added after σωτηρία.

[5] παραζηλόω, *I make jealous.* TH: εἰς τὸ + inf. = purpose; *to make them jealous.*

[6] παράπτωμα, ατος, τό, *wrongdoing, sin.*

[7] πλοῦτος, ου, ὁ, *wealth, riches.* TH: "brings about" is implied before πλοῦτος.

[8] ἥττημα, ατος, τό, *loss,* ***failure.***

[9] πλοῦτος, ου, ὁ, *wealth, riches.* TH: "brings about" is implied before πλοῦτος.

[10] πόσος, η, ον, *how many, how much.*

[11] πλήρωμα, ατος, τό, *fullness.*

[12] TH: τὸ πλήρωμα αὐτῶν, *will their fullness bring about.*

[13] TH: τοῖς ἔθνεσιν is in app. to Ὑμῖν.

[14] TH: ἐφ' ὅσον, *insofar as.*

[15] TH: pred. nom.

[16] διακονία, ας, ἡ, *ministry, service.*

[17] παραζηλόω, *I make jealous.* MH: ο lengthens to ω before the tense formative.

[18] MH: fut. tense stem of σῴζω is σω.

[19] ἀποβολή, ῆς, ἡ, *rejection, loss.*

[20] καταλλαγή, ῆς, ἡ, *reconciliation.* TH: pred. nom. to ἀποβολή.

[21] πρόσλημψις, εως, ἡ, *acceptance.*

[22] ἀπαρχή, ῆς, ἡ, *first fruit.*

[23] TH: pred. adj. to ἀπαρχὴ.

[24] φύραμα, ατος, τό, *dough.* TH: ἅγιον is implied; (*then*) *also the dough* (*is holy*).

[25] ῥίζα, ης, ἡ, *root.* TH: pred. adj. is ἁγία; *If the root is holy, ….*

[26] κλάδος, ου, ὁ, *branch.* TH: ἅγιοι is implied mirroring the protasis; καὶ οἱ κλάδοι, (*then*) *also the branches are holy.*

17 Εἰ δέ τινες τῶν κλάδων [1] ἐξεκλάσθησαν, [2] σὺ δὲ
ἀγριέλαιος [3] ὢν [4] ἐνεκεντρίσθης [5] ἐν αὐτοῖς καὶ
συγκοινωνὸς [6] τῆς ⸀ῥίζης [7] τῆς πιότητος [8] τῆς ἐλαίας [9]
ἐγένου, [10] **18** μὴ κατακαυχῶ [11] τῶν κλάδων· [12] εἰ δὲ
κατακαυχᾶσαι, [13] οὐ σὺ τὴν ῥίζαν [14] βαστάζεις [15] ἀλλὰ ἡ
ῥίζα [16] σέ. **19** ἐρεῖς [17] οὖν· Ἐξεκλάσθησαν [18] κλάδοι [19] ἵνα
ἐγὼ ἐγκεντρισθῶ. [20] **20** καλῶς· [21] τῇ ἀπιστίᾳ [22] ἐξεκλάσ-

---

[1] κλάδος, ου, ὁ, *branch.*

[2] ἐκκλάω, *I break off.* MH: ἐκ (prep.) + ε (aug.) + κλα (root) › ἐξεκλα (before vowels εκ › εξ) + θη (aor. pass. tense formative) + σαν (3rd pl. ending) › ἐξεκλάσθησαν (inserts σ before tense formative).

[3] ἀγριέλαιος, ου, ἡ, *wild olive tree,* ***wild olive branch***. TH: ἀγριέλαιος is in app. to σύ.

[4] MH: pres. act. prtc. nom. sg. masc. of εἰμί.

[5] ἐγκεντρίζω, *I graft.* MH: compound of ἐν + κεντριδ (ν + κ = γκ); root ends in δ; δ + θ = σθ.

[6] συγκοινωνός, οῦ, ὁ, *partner, participant.* TH: pred. nom. to σύ, the subject of ἐγένου; *you became a partner.*

[7] ῥίζα, ης, ἡ, *root.*

[8] πιότης, ητος, ἡ, *fattiness,* ***richness***. MH: gen. of product; *producing the richness.*

[9] ἐλαία, ας, ἡ, *olive tree.*

[10] MH: 2nd aor. of γίνομαι; root is γεν.

[11] κατακαυχάομαι, *I boast (over).* MH: the root (κατακαυχα) ends in a vowel, so the connecting vowel contracts (α + ου = ω).

[12] κλάδος, ου, ὁ, *branch.*

[13] κατακαυχάομαι, *I boast (over).* MH: pres. mid./pass. indic. 2nd sg. ending is σαι; here, intervocalic σ did not drop out.

[14] ῥίζα, ης, ἡ, *root.*

[15] βαστάζω, *I bear, lift up,* ***support***.

[16] ῥίζα, ης, ἡ, *root.* TH: βαστάζει is implied from the previous clause.

[17] MH: fut. act. indic. 2nd sg. of λέγω.

[18] ἐκκλάω, *I break off.* MH: ἐκ (prep.) + ε (aug.) + κλα (root) › ἐξεκλα (before vowels ἐκ › ἐξ) + θη (aor. pass. tense formative) + σαν (3rd pl. ending) › ἐξεκλάσθησαν (inserts σ before tense formative).

[19] κλάδος, ου, ὁ, *branch.*

[20] ἐγκεντρίζω, *I graft.* MH: root ends in δ; δ + θ = σθ.

[21] καλῶς, *well, rightly,* ***indeed***.

[22] ἀπιστία, ας, ἡ, *unbelief, distrust.*

θησαν,[1] σὺ δὲ τῇ πίστει ἕστηκας.[2] μὴ ⸂ὑψηλὰ[3] φρόνει[4]⸃,
ἀλλὰ φοβοῦ·[5] **21** εἰ γὰρ ὁ θεὸς τῶν κατὰ φύσιν[6] κλάδων[7]
οὐκ ἐφείσατο,[8] ⸀οὐδὲ[9] σοῦ[10] φείσεται.[11] **22** ἴδε[12] οὖν
χρηστότητα[13] καὶ ἀποτομίαν[14] θεοῦ· ἐπὶ μὲν[15] τοὺς
πεσόντας[16] ⸀ἀποτομία,[17] ἐπὶ δὲ σὲ ⸂χρηστότης[18] θεοῦ⸃, ἐὰν
⸀ἐπιμένῃς[19] τῇ χρηστότητι,[20] ἐπεὶ[21] καὶ[22] σὺ ἐκκοπήσῃ.[23]
23 κἀκεῖνοι[24] δέ, ἐὰν μὴ ⸀ἐπιμένωσι[25] τῇ ἀπιστίᾳ,[26]

---

[1] ἐκκλάω, *I break off*. MH: ἐκ (prep.) + ε (aug.) + κλα (root) › ἐξεκλα (before vowels ἐκ › ἐξ) + ϑη (aor. pass. tense formative) + σαν (3rd pl. ending) › ἐξεκλάσϑησαν (inserts σ before tense formative).

[2] MH: pf. act. indic. 2nd sg. of ἵστημι = στα (root) › ἑστη (redupl. of initial σ dissimilates to a rough breathing mark; α lengthens to η) + κα (tense formative) + ς (2nd sg. ending) › ἕστηκας.

[3] ὑψηλός, ή, όν, *high, lofty,* ***proudly***.

[4] φρονέω, *I think, am intent on*.

[5] MH: the root (φοβε) ends in a vowel, so the connecting vowel contracts (ε + ου = ου).

[6] φύσις, εως, ἡ, *nature*.

[7] κλάδος, ου, ὁ, *branch*. TH: gen. dir. obj. of ἐφείσατο.

[8] φείδομαι, *I spare*. MH: δ + σ = σ.

[9] NA has μή πως οὐδὲ, though μή πως is in brackets, indicating the questionable nature of its inclusion.

[10] TH: gen. dir. obj. of φείσεται.

[11] φείδομαι, *I spare*. MH: δ + σ = σ.

[12] MH: aor. act. impv. 2nd sg. of ὁράω.

[13] χρηστότης, ητος, ἡ, *kindness, generosity*.

[14] ἀποτομία, ας, ἡ, *severity*.

[15] TH: μὲν ... δὲ, *on the one hand ... on the other hand*.

[16] MH: aor. act. prtc. acc. pl. masc. of πίπτω. The root is πετ; τ immediately before σ drops out.

[17] ἀποτομία, ας, ἡ, *severity*.

[18] χρηστότης, ητος, ἡ, *kindness, generosity*.

[19] ἐπιμένω, *I remain, continue*. MH: subj. mood has a lengthened connecting vowel (ε › η).

[20] χρηστότης, ητος, ἡ, *kindness, generosity*.

[21] ἐπεί, *because, since,* ***otherwise***.

[22] TH: καί is additive; *also*.

[23] ἐκκόπτω, *I cut off*. MH: 2nd fut. pass does not include ϑ in the tense formative.

[24] κἀκεῖνος, η, ο, *and that one*. MH: crasis of καὶ + ἐκεῖνος. TH: *even those*.

[25] ἐπιμένω, *I remain, continue*.

[26] ἀπιστία, ας, ἡ, *unbelief, distrust*.

ἐγκεντρισθήσονται·[1] δυνατὸς[2] γάρ ⸂ἐστιν ὁ θεὸς⸃ πάλιν
ἐγκεντρίσαι[3] αὐτούς. **24** εἰ γὰρ σὺ ἐκ τῆς κατὰ φύσιν[4]
ἐξεκόπης[5] ἀγριελαίου[6] καὶ παρὰ φύσιν[7] ἐνεκεντρίσθης[8]
εἰς καλλιέλαιον,[9] πόσῳ[10] μᾶλλον οὗτοι οἱ κατὰ φύσιν[11]
ἐγκεντρισθήσονται[12] τῇ ἰδίᾳ ἐλαίᾳ.[13]

25 Οὐ γὰρ θέλω ὑμᾶς ἀγνοεῖν,[14] ἀδελφοί, τὸ
μυστήριον[15] τοῦτο, ἵνα μὴ ⸀ἦτε[16] ἑαυτοῖς φρόνιμοι,[17] ὅτι
πώρωσις[18] ἀπὸ μέρους[19] τῷ Ἰσραὴλ γέγονεν[20] ἄχρι[21] οὗ τὸ
πλήρωμα[22] τῶν ἐθνῶν εἰσέλθῃ,[23] **26** καὶ οὕτως πᾶς Ἰσραὴλ
σωθήσεται·[24] καθὼς γέγραπται· Ἥξει[25] ἐκ Σιὼν[26]

---

[1] ἐγκεντρίζω, *I graft*. MH: root ends in δ; δ + ϑ = σϑ.

[2] δυνατός, ή, όν, *able, capable*. MH: pred. adj.

[3] ἐγκεντρίζω, *I graft*. MH: root ends in δ; δ + σ = σ.

[4] φύσις, εως, ἡ, *nature*.

[5] ἐκκόπτω, *I cut off*. MH: root is ἐκκοπ; 2nd aor. pass. does not include ϑ in the tense formative (before vowels εκ › εξ).

[6] ἀγριέλαιος, ου, ἡ, *wild olive tree*. TH: ἐκ τῆς κατὰ φύσιν … ἀγριελαίου, *from wild olive tree by nature*.

[7] φύσις, εως, ἡ, *nature*.

[8] ἐγκεντρίζω, *I graft*. MH: compound of ἐν + κεντριδ (ν + κ = γκ); root ends in δ; δ + ϑ = σϑ.

[9] καλλιέλαιος, ου, ἡ, *cultivated olive tree*.

[10] πόσος, η, ον, *how many, how much*.

[11] φύσις, εως, ἡ, *nature*. TH: κλάδοι is implied after φύσιν; οἱ κατὰ φύσιν is in app. to οὗτοι; *these, the natural (branches)*.

[12] ἐγκεντρίζω, *I graft*. MH: root ends in δ; δ + ϑ = σϑ.

[13] ἐλαία, ας, ἡ, *olive tree*.

[14] ἀγνοέω, *I am unaware, ignorant (of)*. TH: complementary inf. with θέλω.

[15] μυστήριον, ου, τό, *mystery*.

[16] MH: pres. act. subj. 2nd pl. of εἰμί. NA has παρ' in brackets after ἦτε.

[17] φρόνιμος, ου, ὁ, *wise, prudent*. TH: ἑαυτοῖς φρόνιμοι, *arrogant*.

[18] πώρωσις, εως, ἡ, *hardness*.

[19] μέρος, ους, τό, *part*. TH: πώρωσις ἀπὸ μέρους, *partial hardness*.

[20] MH: 2nd pf. of γίνομαι. The root (γεν) becomes γον due to ablaut.

[21] ἄχρι, *until*. TH: ἄχρι οὗ, *until which time*.

[22] πλήρωμα, ατος, τό, *fullness*.

[23] MH: 2nd aor. of εἰσέρχομαι; root is εἰσελθ.

[24] MH: fut. tense stem of σῴζω is σω.

[25] ἥκω, *I have come*. MH: κ + σ = ξ.

[26] Σιών, ἡ, *Zion*.

ὁ ⸀ῥυόμενος,[1] ἀποστρέψει[2] ἀσεβείας[3] ἀπὸ Ἰακώβ.[4] **27** καὶ
αὕτη αὐτοῖς ἡ παρ' ἐμοῦ διαθήκη,[5] ὅταν ἀφέλωμαι[6] τὰς
ἁμαρτίας αὐτῶν. **28** κατὰ μὲν[7] τὸ εὐαγγέλιον ἐχθροὶ[8] δι'
ὑμᾶς, κατὰ δὲ τὴν ἐκλογὴν[9] ἀγαπητοὶ[10] διὰ τοὺς
πατέρας· **29** ἀμεταμέλητα[11] γὰρ τὰ χαρίσματα[12] καὶ ἡ
κλῆσις[13] τοῦ θεοῦ. **30** ὥσπερ[14] ⸀γὰρ ὑμεῖς ποτε[15]
ἠπειθήσατε[16] τῷ θεῷ, νῦν δὲ ἠλεήθητε[17] τῇ τούτων
ἀπειθείᾳ,[18] **31** οὕτως καὶ οὗτοι νῦν ἠπείθησαν[19] τῷ
ὑμετέρῳ[20] ἐλέει[21] ἵνα καὶ[22] αὐτοὶ ⸀νῦν ἐλεηθῶσιν·[23]

---

[1] ῥύομαι, *I save, rescue, deliver.*

[2] ἀποστρέφω, *I turn away,* ***remove***. MH: φ + σ = ψ.

[3] ἀσέβεια, ας, ἡ, *ungodliness, impiety.*

[4] Ἰακώβ, ὁ, *Jacob.*

[5] διαθήκη, ης, ἡ, *covenant.* MH: pred. nom. to αὕτη.

[6] ἀφαιρέω, *I take away.* MH: aor. mid. subj. 1st sg.

[7] TH: μὲν … δὲ, *on the one hand … on the other hand.*

[8] ἐχθρός, ά, όν, *hostile, enemy.* TH: pred. adj. to an implied subject πᾶς Ἰσραὴλ from v. 26.

[9] ἐκλογή, ῆς, ἡ, *election, choice.*

[10] TH: pred. nom. to an implied subject πᾶς Ἰσραὴλ from v. 26.

[11] ἀμεταμέλητος, ον, *without regret,* ***irrevocable***. TH: pred. adj. to the compound subjects τὰ χαρίσματα καὶ ἡ κλῆσις.

[12] χάρισμα, ατος, τό, *gift.*

[13] κλῆσις, εως, ἡ, *calling.*

[14] ὥσπερ, *just as, even as.*

[15] ποτέ, *once.*

[16] ἀπειθέω, *I disobey, am disobedient.* MH: the ε lengthens to η before the tense formative.

[17] ἐλεέω, *I have mercy (on).* MH: the ε lengthens to η before the tense formative.

[18] ἀπείθεια, ας, ἡ, *disobedience.*

[19] ἀπειθέω, *I disobey, am disobedient.* MH: the ε lengthens to η before the tense formative.

[20] ὑμέτερος, α, ον, *your, yours.*

[21] ἔλεος, ους, τό, *mercy, compassion.* TH: dat. of cause; τῷ ὑμετέρῳ ἐλέει, *because of your mercy.*

[22] TH: καί is additive *also.*

[23] ἐλεέω, *I have mercy (on).* MH: the ε lengthens to η before the tense formative; subj. mood has a lengthened connecting vowel (ο › ω).

32 συνέκλεισεν[1] γὰρ ὁ θεὸς τοὺς πάντας εἰς ἀπείθειαν[2]
ἵνα τοὺς πάντας ἐλεήσῃ.[3]

33 Ὦ[4] βάθος[5] πλούτου[6] καὶ σοφίας καὶ γνώσεως[7] θεοῦ·
ὡς ἀνεξεραύνητα[8] τὰ κρίματα[9] αὐτοῦ καὶ ἀνεξιχνίαστοι[10]
αἱ ὁδοὶ αὐτοῦ. **34** Τίς γὰρ ἔγνω[11] νοῦν[12] κυρίου; ἢ τίς
σύμβουλος[13] αὐτοῦ ἐγένετο;[14] **35** ἢ τίς προέδωκεν[15] αὐτῷ,
καὶ[16] ἀνταποδοθήσεται[17] αὐτῷ; **36** ὅτι ἐξ αὐτοῦ καὶ δι'
αὐτοῦ καὶ εἰς αὐτὸν τὰ πάντα· αὐτῷ[18] ἡ δόξα εἰς τοὺς
αἰῶνας, ἀμήν.

---

[1] συγκλείω, *I enclose*, ***consign***.

[2] ἀπείθεια, ας, ἡ, *disobedience*.

[3] ἐλεέω, *I have mercy (on)*. MH: the ε lengthens to η before the tense formative; subj. mood has a lengthened connecting vowel (ε › η).

[4] ὦ, *O!, Oh*.

[5] βάθος, ους, τό, *depth*.

[6] πλοῦτος, ου, ὁ, *wealth, riches*.

[7] γνῶσις, εως, ἡ, *knowledge*.

[8] ἀνεξεραύνητος, ον, *unsearchable, unfathomable*. MH: pred. adj. to τὰ κρίματα.

[9] κρίμα, ατος, τό, *judgment*.

[10] ἀνεξιχνίαστος, ον, *inscrutable, incomprehensible*. MH: pred. adj. to αἱ ὁδοὶ.

[11] MH: aor. act. indic. 3rd sg. of γινώσκω.

[12] νοῦς, ός, ὁ, *mind, way of thinking*.

[13] σύμβουλος, ου, ὁ, *conselor, adviser*.

[14] MH: 2nd aor. of γίνομαι; root is γεν.

[15] προδίδωμι, *I give beforehand, give in advance*. MH: root is προδο. The ο lengthens to ω before the tense formative. δίδωμι (and its compound forms) belongs to a small category of words that are called "kappa aorists" because they use kappa in the tense formative instead of sigma.

[16] TH: *that*.

[17] ἀνταποδίδωμι, *I repay, give back*. MH: root is ἀντιαποδο.

[18] TH: "is" should be supplied after αὐτῷ.

11:2 Ἰσραήλ WH Treg NA28] + λέγων RP
3 τὰ WH Treg NA28] καὶ τὰ RP
6 χάρις WH Treg NA28] + Εἰ δὲ ἐξ ἔργων οὐκέτι ἐστὶν χάρις ἐπεὶ τὸ ἔργον οὐκέτι ἐστὶν ἔργον RP
8 καθὼς NA28 RP] καθάπερ WH Treg
13 δὲ WH Treg NA28] γὰρ RP
- **οὖν** WH Treg NA28] – RP

17 ῥίζης WH NA28] + καὶ Treg RP
20 ὑψηλὰ φρόνει WH Treg NA28] ὑψηλοφρόνει RP
20 ὑψηλὰ φρόνει WH Treg NA28] ὑψηλοφρόνει RP
21 οὐδὲ WH Treg NIV] μήπως οὐδέ RP NA28
22 ἀποτομία WH Treg NA28] ἀποτομίαν RP
- **χρηστότης θεοῦ** WH Treg NA28] χρηστότητα RP
- **χρηστότης θεοῦ** WH Treg NA28] χρηστότητα RP
- **ἐπιμένης** WH Treg NA28] ἐπιμείνῃς RP

23 ἐπιμένωσι WH Treg NA28] ἐπιμείνωσιν RP
- **ἐστιν ὁ θεὸς** WH Treg NA28] ὁ θεὸς ἐστιν RP
- **ἐστιν ὁ θεὸς** WH Treg NA28] ὁ θεὸς ἐστιν RP

25 ἦτε Holmes] + ἐν WH Treg; + παρ’ NA28 RP
26 ῥυόμενος WH Treg NA28] + καὶ RP
30 γὰρ WH Treg NA28] + καὶ RP
31 νῦν WH NA28] – Treg RP

ROMANS 12

New Vocabulary by Frequency [Chapter, Book, SBLGNT Occurrences]

ἀνακαίνωσις, εως, ἡ, *renewal* [1, 1, 2]
ἀναλογία, ας, ἡ, *proportion* [1, 1, 1]
ἄνθραξ, ακος, ὁ, *coal* [1, 1, 1]
ἀνταποδίδωμι, *I repay, give back* [1, 2, 7]
ἀντί, *for, in place of* [1, 1, 22]
ἀνυπόκριτος, ον, *genuine, without hypocrisy* [1, 1, 6]
ἁπλότης, ητος, ἡ, *sincerity, generosity* [1, 1, 7]
ἀποδίδωμι, *I repay, render* [1, 3, 48]
ἀποστυγέω, *I abhor, detest* [1, 1, 1]
διακονία, ας, ἡ, *ministry, service* [2, 4, 34]
διάφορος, ον, *different* [1, 1, 4]
διδασκαλία, ας, ἡ, *teaching, instruction* [1, 2, 21]
διψάω, *I am thirsty* [1, 1, 16]
διώκω, *I pursue, chase* [2, 5, 45]
δοκιμάζω, *I test, approve* [1, 4, 22]
δουλεύω, *I serve* [1, 7, 25]
δυνατός, ή, όν, *able, capable* [1, 5, 32]
εἰρηνεύω, *I keep peace, live peaceably* [1, 1, 4]
ἐκδικέω, *I avenge* [1, 1, 6]
ἐκδίκησις, εως, ἡ, *vengeance* [1, 1, 9]
ἐλεέω, *I have mercy (on)* [1, 8, 32]
εὐάρεστος, ον, *pleasing, acceptable* [2, 3, 9]
εὐλογέω, *I bless, praise* [2, 2, 41]
ἐχθρός, ά, όν, *hostile, enemy* [1, 3, 32]
ζέω, *I boil, am stirred up* [1, 1, 2]
θλῖψις, εως, ἡ, *affliction, tribulation* [1, 5, 45]
θυσία, ας, ἡ, *sacrifice* [1, 1, 28]
ἱλαρότης, ητος, ἡ, *cheerfulness* [1, 1, 1]
καθάπερ, *just as* [1, 2, 13]
καταράομαι, *I curse* [1, 1, 5]
κλαίω, *I weep, cry* [2, 2, 40]
κοινωνέω, *I share, participate* [1, 2, 8]
κολλάω, *I attach firmly, unite* [1, 1, 12]
λατρεία, ας, ἡ, *service, worship* [1, 2, 5]
λογικός, ή, όν, *rational, reasonable* [1, 1, 2]
μέλος, ους, τό, *member, part* [3, 10, 34]

μερίζω, *I distribute, divide* [1, 1, 14]
μεταδίδωμι, *I give, share* [1, 2, 5]
μεταμορφόω, *I transform* [1, 1, 4]
μέτρον, ου, τό, *measure* [1, 1, 14]
νικάω, *I conquer, overcome* [2, 3, 28]
νοῦς, ός, ὁ, *mind, way of thinking* [1, 6, 24]
οἰκτιρμός, οῦ, ὁ, *pity, compassion* [1, 1, 5]
ὀκνηρός, ά, όν, *timid, idle* [1, 1, 3]
ὀργή, ῆς, ἡ, *wrath* [1, 12, 36]
παράκλησις, εως, ἡ, *exhortation, encouragement* [1, 3, 29]
παρίστημι, *I present, demonstrate* [1, 8, 41]
πεινάω, *I am hungry* [1, 1, 23]
ποτίζω, *I give to drink* [1, 1, 15]
πρᾶξις, εως, ἡ, *act, deed* [1, 2, 6]
προηγέομαι, *I go first, precede* [1, 1, 1]
προΐστημι, *I lead, direct* [1, 1, 8]
προνοέω, *I think first, preconceive* [1, 1, 3]
προσευχή, ῆς, ἡ, *prayer* [1, 3, 36]
προσκαρτερέω, *I am devoted* [1, 2, 10]
προφητεία, ας, ἡ, *prophecy* [1, 1, 19]
σπουδή, ῆς, ἡ, *diligence, eagerness* [2, 2, 12]
συναπάγω, *I lead away with, accommodate* [1, 1, 3]
συσχηματίζω, *I correct* [1, 1, 2]
σωρεύω, *I heap up* [1, 1, 2]
σωφρονέω, *I am reasonable, of sound mind* [1, 1, 6]
ταπεινός, ή, όν, *humble, lowly* [1, 1, 8]
τέλειος, α, ον, *perfect, complete* [1, 1, 19]
τιμή, ῆς, ἡ, *honor* [1, 6, 41]
ὑπερφρονέω, *I am proud* [1, 1, 1]
ὑπομένω, *I stay, remain* [1, 1, 17]
ὑψηλός, ή, όν, *high, lofty* [1, 2, 11]
φιλαδελφία, ας, ἡ, *brotherly love* [1, 1, 6]
φιλοξενία, ας, ἡ, *hospitality* [1, 1, 2]
φιλόστοργος, ον, *loving dearly, affectionate* [1, 1, 1]
φρονέω, *I think, am intent on* [4, 9, 26]
φρόνιμος, ου, ὁ, *wise, prudent* [1, 2, 14]
χάρισμα, ατος, τό, *gift* [1, 6, 17]
χρεία, ας, ἡ, *need* [1, 1, 49]
ψωμίζω, *I feed* [1, 1, 2]

12.1 Παρακαλῶ οὖν ὑμᾶς, ἀδελφοί, διὰ τῶν οἰκτιρμῶν[1]
τοῦ θεοῦ παραστῆσαι[2] τὰ σώματα ὑμῶν θυσίαν[3] ζῶσαν[4]
ἁγίαν ⸂εὐάρεστον[5] τῷ θεῷ⸃, τὴν λογικὴν[6] λατρείαν[7] ὑμῶν·
2 καὶ μὴ ⸀συσχηματίζεσθε[8] τῷ αἰῶνι τούτῳ, ἀλλὰ
⸀μεταμορφοῦσθε[9] τῇ ἀνακαινώσει[10] τοῦ ⸀νοός,[11] εἰς τὸ
δοκιμάζειν[12] ὑμᾶς[13] τί τὸ θέλημα τοῦ θεοῦ, τὸ ἀγαθὸν
καὶ εὐάρεστον[14] καὶ τέλειον.[15]

3 Λέγω γὰρ διὰ τῆς χάριτος τῆς δοθείσης[16] μοι παντὶ
τῷ ὄντι[17] ἐν ὑμῖν[18] μὴ ὑπερφρονεῖν[19] παρ᾽[20] ὃ δεῖ
φρονεῖν,[21] ἀλλὰ φρονεῖν[22] εἰς τὸ σωφρονεῖν,[23] ἑκάστῳ ὡς

---

[1] οἰκτιρμός, οῦ, ὁ, *pity, compassion.*

[2] παρίστημι, *I present, demonstrate.* MH: root is περιστα.

[3] θυσία, ας, ἡ, *sacrifice.*

[4] MH: the root (ζα) ends in a vowel, so the connecting vowel contracts (α + ου = ω). TH: pred. prtc.; θυσίαν ζῶσαν ἁγίαν εὐάρεστον, *a sacrifice—living, holy, acceptable.*

[5] εὐάρεστος, ον, *pleasing, acceptable.*

[6] λογικός, ή, όν, *rational, reasonable.*

[7] λατρεία, ας, ἡ, *service, worship.* TH: τὴν λογικὴν λατρείαν ὑμῶν is in app. to the preceding clause.

[8] συσχηματίζω, *I correct,* ***conform.***

[9] μεταμορφόω, *I transform.* MH: the root (μεταμορφο) ends in a vowel, so the connecting vowel contracts (ο + ε = ου).

[10] ἀνακαίνωσις, εως, ἡ, *renewal.* TH: instrumental dat.; *by the renewal.*

[11] νοῦς, ός, ὁ, *mind, way of thinking.*

[12] δοκιμάζω, *I test, approve.* TH: εἰς τὸ + inf. indicates purpose; *in order that you test.*

[13] TH: acc. is the subject of the inf. δοκιμάζειν.

[14] εὐάρεστος, ον, *pleasing, acceptable.*

[15] τέλειος, α, ον, *perfect, complete.* TH: τὸ ἀγαθὸν … εὐάρεστον … τέλειον are in app. to τὸ θέλημα; *that which is good, … pleasing, … perfect.*

[16] MH: aor. pass. prtc. gen. sg. fem. of δίδωμι; root is δο.

[17] MH: pres. act. prtc. dat. sg. masc. of εἰμί.

[18] TH: παντὶ τῷ ὄντι ἐν ὑμῖν, *to everyone among you.*

[19] ὑπερφρονέω, *I am proud,* ***think higher of myself.***

[20] TH: παρ᾽ is indicating comparison; *than.*

[21] φρονέω, *I think, am intent on.* TH: complementary inf. with δεῖ.

[22] φρονέω, *I think, am intent on.*

[23] σωφρονέω, *I am reasonable, of sound mind.* TH: εἰς τὸ + inf. indicates purpose; *in order to be reasonable.*

ὁ θεὸς ἐμέρισεν[1] μέτρον[2] πίστεως. **4** καθάπερ[3] γὰρ ἐν ἑνὶ
σώματι ʽπολλὰ μέλη[4]ʼ ἔχομεν, τὰ δὲ μέλη[5] πάντα οὐ τὴν
αὐτὴν[6] ἔχει πρᾶξιν,[7] **5** οὕτως οἱ πολλοὶ[8] ἓν σῶμά[9] ἐσμεν ἐν
Χριστῷ, ʽτὸ[10] δὲ καθ' εἷς ἀλλήλων μέλη.[11] **6** ἔχοντες δὲ
χαρίσματα [12] κατὰ τὴν χάριν τὴν δοθεῖσαν [13] ἡμῖν
διάφορα, [14] εἴτε [15] προφητείαν [16] κατὰ [17] τὴν ἀναλογίαν [18]
τῆς πίστεως, **7** εἴτε διακονίαν [19] ἐν τῇ διακονίᾳ, [20] εἴτε
ὁ διδάσκων ἐν τῇ διδασκαλίᾳ, [21] **8** εἴτε ὁ παρακαλῶν
ἐν τῇ παρακλήσει, [22] ὁ μεταδιδοὺς [23] ἐν ἁπλότητι, [24]
ὁ προϊστάμενος[25] ἐν σπουδῇ,[26] ὁ ἐλεῶν[27] ἐν ἱλαρότητι.[28]

---

[1] μερίζω, *I distribute, divide*. MH: the root ends in δ; δ + σ = σ.
[2] μέτρον, ου, τό, *measure*.
[3] καθάπερ, *just as*.
[4] μέλος, ους, τό, *member, part*.
[5] μέλος, ους, τό, *member, part*.
[6] TH: αὐτὴν is intensive; with πρᾶξιν, *the same function*.
[7] πρᾶξις, εως, ἡ, *act, deed,* ***function.***
[8] TH: οἱ πολλοὶ is in app. to the subject of ἐσμεν; *we, the many*.
[9] TH: pred. nom. to the subject of ἐσμεν.
[10] TH: τὸ substantivizes the prep. phrase καθ' εἷς; *each one*.
[11] μέλος, ους, τό, *member, part*. TH: ἐσμεν is implied; τὸ δὲ καθ' εἷς ἀλλήλων μέλη, *and we are, each one, members of one another*.
[12] χάρισμα, ατος, τό, *gift*.
[13] MH: aor. pass. prtc. acc. sg. fem. of δίδωμι; root is δο.
[14] διάφορος, ον, *different*. TH: modifies χαρίσματα; *different gifts*.
[15] TH: the nom. χάρισμα is implied after εἴτε. With the subsequent uses of εἴτε; *whether the gift is … or … or … or*.
[16] προφητεία, ας, ἡ, *prophecy*.
[17] TH: κατὰ is indicating standard; *in accordance with*.
[18] ἀναλογία, ας, ἡ, *proportion*.
[19] διακονία, ας, ἡ, *ministry, service*.
[20] διακονία, ας, ἡ, *ministry, service*.
[21] διδασκαλία, ας, ἡ, *teaching, instruction*.
[22] παράκλησις, εως, ἡ, *exhortation, encouragement*.
[23] μεταδίδωμι, *I impart, give, share*. MH: pres. act. prtc. nom. sg. masc.
[24] ἁπλότης, ητος, ἡ, *sincerity, generosity*.
[25] προΐστημι, *I lead, direct*.
[26] σπουδή, ῆς, ἡ, *diligence, eagerness*.
[27] ἐλεέω, *I have mercy (on)*.
[28] ἱλαρότης, ητος, ἡ, *cheerfulness*.

9 Ἡ ἀγάπη ἀνυπόκριτος.[1] ἀποστυγοῦντες[2] τὸ
πονηρόν, κολλώμενοι[3] τῷ ἀγαθῷ· **10** τῇ φιλαδελφίᾳ[4] εἰς
ἀλλήλους φιλόστοργοι,[5] τῇ τιμῇ[6] ἀλλήλους προηγ-
ούμενοι,[7] **11** τῇ σπουδῇ[8] μὴ ὀκνηροί,[9] τῷ πνεύματι
ζέοντες,[10] τῷ κυρίῳ δουλεύοντες,[11] **12** τῇ ἐλπίδι χαίροντες,
τῇ θλίψει[12] ὑπομένοντες,[13] τῇ προσευχῇ[14] προσκαρτερ-
οῦντες,[15] **13** ταῖς χρείαις[16] τῶν ἁγίων κοινωνοῦντες,[17] τὴν
φιλοξενίαν[18] διώκοντες.[19] **14** εὐλογεῖτε[20] τοὺς ⸀διώκοντας,[21]

---

[1] ἀνυπόκριτος, ον, *genuine, without hypocrisy*. TH: pred. adj. to ἀγάπη.

[2] ἀποστυγέω, *I abhor, detest*. MH: the root (ἀποστυγε) ends in a vowel, so the connecting vowel contracts (ε + ο = ου).

[3] κολλάω, *I attach firmly, unite,* ***cling***. MH: the root (κολλα) ends in a vowel, so the connecting vowel contracts (α + ο = ω).

[4] φιλαδελφία, ας, ἡ, *brotherly love*. TH: dat. of reference; *with reference to brotherly love*.

[5] φιλόστοργος, ον, *loving dearly, affectionate*.

[6] τιμή, ῆς, ἡ, *honor*. TH: dat. of reference; *with reference to honor*.

[7] προηγέομαι, *I go first, precede*. MH: the root (προηγε) ends in a vowel, so the connecting vowel contracts (ε + ο = ου).

[8] σπουδή, ῆς, ἡ, *diligence, eagerness*. TH: dat. of reference; *with reference to diligence*.

[9] ὀκνηρός, ά, όν, *timid, idle*. TH: μὴ ὀκνηροί, *not being timid*.

[10] ζέω, *I boil, am stirred up,* ***am excited***.

[11] δουλεύω, *I serve*.

[12] θλῖψις, εως, ἡ, *affliction, tribulation*.

[13] ὑπομένω, *I stay, remain,* ***endure***.

[14] προσευχή, ῆς, ἡ, *prayer*.

[15] προσκαρτερέω, *I am devoted*. MH: the root (προσκαρτερε) ends in a vowel, so the connecting vowel contracts (ε + ο = ου).

[16] χρεία, ας, ἡ, *need*.

[17] κοινωνέω, *I share, participate*. MH: the verb stem (κοινωνε) ends in a vowel, so the connecting vowel contracts (ε + ο = ου).

[18] φιλοξενία, ας, ἡ, *hospitality*.

[19] διώκω, *I pursue, chase*.

[20] εὐλογέω, *I bless, praise*. MH: the root (εὐλογε) ends in a vowel, so the connecting vowel contracts (ε + ε = ει).

[21] διώκω, *I pursue, chase,* ***persecute***. NA has διώκοντας ὑμᾶς, though ὑμᾶς is in brackets, indicating the questionable nature of its inclusion.

εὐλογεῖτε[1] καὶ μὴ καταρᾶσθε.[2] **15** χαίρειν[3] μετὰ
⸀χαιρόντων,[4] κλαίειν[5] μετὰ κλαιόντων.[6] **16** τὸ αὐτὸ[7] εἰς
ἀλλήλους φρονοῦντες,[8] μὴ τὰ ὑψηλὰ[9] φρονοῦντες[10] ἀλλὰ
τοῖς ταπεινοῖς[11] συναπαγόμενοι.[12] μὴ γίνεσθε φρόνιμοι[13]
παρ' ἑαυτοῖς. **17** μηδενὶ κακὸν ἀντὶ[14] κακοῦ ἀποδιδ-
όντες·[15] προνοούμενοι[16] καλὰ ἐνώπιον πάντων ἀνθρώπων·
18 εἰ δυνατόν,[17] τὸ ἐξ ὑμῶν[18] μετὰ πάντων ἀνθρώπων
εἰρηνεύοντες·[19] **19** μὴ ἑαυτοὺς ἐκδικοῦντες,[20] ἀγαπητοί,
ἀλλὰ δότε[21] τόπον τῇ ὀργῇ,[22] γέγραπται γάρ· Ἐμοὶ[23]
ἐκδίκησις,[24] ἐγὼ ἀνταποδώσω,[25] λέγει κύριος.

---

[1] εὐλογέω, *I bless, praise*. MH: the root (εὐλογε) ends in a vowel, so the connecting vowel contracts (ε + ε = ει).

[2] καταράομαι, *I curse*. MH: the root (καταρα) ends in a vowel, so the connecting vowel contracts (α + ε = α).

[3] TH: inf. is functioning like an impv.

[4] TH: subst. prtc.

[5] κλαίω, *I weep, cry*. TH: inf. is functioning like an impv.

[6] κλαίω, *I weep, cry*. TH: subst. prtc.

[7] TH: τὸ αὐτὸ is intensive; with φρονοῦντες, *thinking the same*.

[8] φρονέω, *I think, am intent on*.

[9] ὑψηλός, ή, όν, *high, lofty,* ***proud***. TH: with φρονοῦντες, *thinking proudly*.

[10] φρονέω, *I think, am intent on*.

[11] ταπεινός, ή, όν, *humble, lowly*. TH: dat. of association; *with*.

[12] συναπάγω, *I lead away with, accomodate,* ***associate***.

[13] φρόνιμος, ου, ὁ, *wise, prudent*. TH: φρόνιμοι παρ' ἑαυτοῖς, *arrogant*.

[14] ἀντί, *for, in place of*.

[15] ἀποδίδωμι, *I repay, render*.

[16] προνοέω, *I think first, preconceive,* ***consider***. MH: the verb stem (προνοε) ends in a vowel, so the connecting vowel contracts (ε + ο = ου).

[17] δυνατός, ή, όν, *able, capable,* ***possible***.

[18] TH: τὸ ἐξ ὑμῶν, *as it depends on you*.

[19] εἰρηνεύω, *I keep peace, live peaceably*.

[20] ἐκδικέω, *I avenge*. MH: the root (ἐκδικε) ends in a vowel, so the connecting vowel contracts (ε + ο = ου).

[21] MH: aor. act. impv. 2nd pl. of δίδωμι; root is δο.

[22] ὀργή, ῆς, ἡ, *wrath*.

[23] TH: dat. of possession; *mine*.

[24] ἐκδίκησις, εως, ἡ, *vengeance*.

[25] ἀνταποδίδωμι, *I repay, give back*. MH: root is ἀντιαποδο; the ο lengthens to ω before the tense formative.

20 ʼἀλλὰ ἐὰνʼ πεινᾷ[1] ὁ ἐχθρός[2] σου, ψώμιζε[3] αὐτόν· ἐὰν
διψᾷ,[4] πότιζε[5] αὐτόν· τοῦτο γὰρ ποιῶν ἄνθρακας[6] πυρὸς
σωρεύσεις[7] ἐπὶ τὴν κεφαλὴν αὐτοῦ. 21 μὴ νικῶ[8] ὑπὸ τοῦ
κακοῦ, ἀλλὰ νίκα[9] ἐν[10] τῷ ἀγαθῷ τὸ κακόν.

12:1 εὐάρεστον τῷ θεῷ Treg NA28 RP] τῷ θεῷ εὐάρεστον WH
12:1 εὐάρεστον τῷ θεῷ Treg NA28 RP] τῷ θεῷ εὐάρεστον WH
2 συσχηματίζεσθε WH Treg NA28] συσχηματίζεσθαι RP
- **μεταμορφοῦσθε** WH Treg NA28] μεταμορφοῦσθαι RP
- **νοός** WH Treg NA28] + ὑμῶν RP

4 πολλὰ μέλη WH Treg NA28] μέλη πολλὰ RP
4 πολλὰ μέλη WH Treg NA28] μέλη πολλὰ RP
5 τὸ WH Treg NA28] ὁ RP
14 διώκοντας WH] + ὑμᾶς Treg NA28 RP
15 χαιρόντων WH Treg NA28] + καὶ RP
20 ἀλλὰ ἐὰν WH Treg NA28] Ἐὰν οὖν RP
20 ἀλλὰ ἐὰν WH Treg NA28] Ἐὰν οὖν RP

---

[1] πεινάω, *I am hungry*. MH: πεινα (root) + ῃ (pres. act. subj. 3rd sg. ending) › πεινᾷ (α + ῃ = ᾳ).
[2] ἐχθρός, ά, όν, *hostile, enemy*.
[3] ψωμίζω, *I feed*.
[4] διψάω, *I am thirsty*. MH: διψα (root) + ῃ (pres. act. subj. 3rd sg. ending) › διψᾷ (α + ῃ = ᾳ).
[5] ποτίζω, *I give to drink*.
[6] ἄνθραξ, ακος, ὁ, *coal*.
[7] σωρεύω, *I heap up*.
[8] νικάω, *I conquer, overcome*. MH: pres. pass. impv. 2nd sg. (α + ου = ω).
[9] νικάω, *I conquer, overcome*. MH: pres. act. impv. 2nd sg. (α + ε = α).
[10] TH: ἐν is instrumental; *with*.

ROMANS 13

New Vocabulary by Frequency [Chapter, Book, SBLGNT Occurrences]

ἀνάγκη, ης, ἡ, *necessity* [1, 1, 17]
ἀνακεφαλαιόω, *I sum up* [1, 1, 2]
ἀνθίστημι, *I oppose, resist* [2, 3, 14]
ἀντιτάσσω, *I resist* [1, 1, 5]
ἀποβάλλω, *I throw off* [1, 1, 3]
ἀποδίδωμι, *I repay, render* [1, 3, 48]
ἄρχων, οντος, ὁ, *ruler, leader* [1, 1, 37]
ἀσέλγεια, ας, ἡ, *licentiousness* [1, 1, 10]
διάκονος, ου, ὁ, *servant, minister* [2, 4, 29]
διαταγή, ῆς, ἡ, *ordinance* [1, 1, 2]
ἐγγίζω, *I bring near* [1, 1, 42]
ἐγγύς, *near* [1, 2, 31]
εἰκῇ, *without cause, for no reason, in vain* [1, 1, 6]
ἔκδικος, ου, ὁ, *avenger* [1, 1, 2]
ἐνδύω, *I put on, clothe* [2, 2, 28]
ἔπαινος, ου, ὁ, *praise, approval* [1, 2, 11]
ἐπιθυμέω, *I covet, desire* [1, 2, 16]
ἐπιθυμία, ας, ἡ, *desire, lust* [1, 5, 38]
ἐργάζομαι, *I work, labor, do* [1, 4, 41]
ἔρις, ιδος, ἡ, *strife* [1, 2, 9]
εὐσχημόνως, *decently* [1, 1, 3]
ζῆλος, ου, ὁ, *zeal* [1, 2, 16]
κλέπτω, *I steal* [1, 3, 13]
κοίτη, ης, ἡ, *bed* [1, 2, 4]
κρίμα, ατος, τό, *judgment* [1, 6, 27]
κῶμος, ου, ὁ, *celebration, feasting* [1, 1, 3]
λειτουργός, οῦ, ὁ, *servant, minister* [1, 2, 5]
μάχαιρα, ης, ἡ, *sword* [1, 2, 29]
μέθη, ης, ἡ, *drunkenness* [1, 1, 3]
μοιχεύω, *I commit adultery* [1, 3, 15]
ὅπλον, ου, τό, *tool, weapon* [1, 3, 6]
ὀργή, ῆς, ἡ, *wrath* [2, 12, 36]
ὀφειλή, ῆς, ἡ, *obligation, duty* [1, 1, 3]
ὀφείλω, *I owe* [1, 3, 35]
πλήρωμα, ατος, τό, *fullness* [1, 4, 17]
πλησίον, *near* [2, 3, 17]

πράσσω, *I do, engage in* [1, 10, 38]
προκόπτω, *I advance, progress* [1, 1, 6]
πρόνοια, ας, ἡ, *provision* [1, 1, 2]
προσκαρτερέω, *I am devoted* [1, 2, 10]
σεαυτοῦ, ῆς, *yourself* [1, 6, 43]
σκότος, ους, τό, *darkness* [1, 2, 30]
συνείδησις, εως, ἡ, *conscience* [1, 3, 31]
σωτηρία, ας, ἡ, *salvation* [1, 5, 46]
τάσσω, *I arrange, appoint* [1, 1, 8]
τελέω, *I fulfill, complete* [1, 2, 28]
τέλος, ους, τό, *end* [2, 5, 40]
τιμή, ῆς, ἡ, *honor* [2, 6, 41]
ὑπερέχω, *I surpass, have power over* [1, 1, 5]
ὕπνος, ου, ὁ, *sleep* [1, 1, 6]
ὑποτάσσω, *I subject, subordinate* [2, 6, 38]
φόβος, ου, ὁ, *fear, reverence* [3, 5, 47]
φονεύω, *I murder, kill* [1, 1, 12]
φορέω, *I bear, carry* [1, 1, 6]
φόρος, ου, ὁ, *tribute, tax* [3, 3, 5]

13.1 Πᾶσα ψυχὴ ἐξουσίαις ὑπερεχούσαις[1] ὑποτασσ-
έσθω,[2] οὐ γὰρ ἔστιν ἐξουσία[3] εἰ μὴ ὑπὸ θεοῦ, αἱ δὲ ⸀οὖσαι[4]
⸀ὑπὸ θεοῦ τεταγμέναι[5] εἰσίν. **2** ὥστε ὁ ἀντιτασσόμενος[6] τῇ
ἐξουσίᾳ τῇ τοῦ θεοῦ διαταγῇ[7] ἀνθέστηκεν,[8] οἱ δὲ
ἀνθεστηκότες[9] ἑαυτοῖς κρίμα[10] λήμψονται.[11] **3** οἱ γὰρ
ἄρχοντες[12] οὐκ εἰσὶν φόβος[13] ⸂τῷ ἀγαθῷ ἔργῳ⸃ ἀλλὰ ⸂τῷ
κακῷ⸃. θέλεις δὲ μὴ φοβεῖσθαι[14] τὴν ἐξουσίαν; τὸ ἀγαθὸν
ποίει, καὶ ἕξεις[15] ἔπαινον[16] ἐξ αὐτῆς· **4** θεοῦ γὰρ
διάκονός[17] ἐστιν σοὶ εἰς τὸ ἀγαθόν. ἐὰν δὲ τὸ κακὸν
ποιῇς, φοβοῦ· οὐ γὰρ εἰκῇ[18] τὴν μάχαιραν[19] φορεῖ·[20]

---

[1] ὑπερέχω, *I surpass, have power over,* ***govern***. TH: attrib. adj. prtc.; ἐξουσίαις ὑπερεχούσαις, *governing authorities*.

[2] ὑποτάσσω, *I subject, subordinate*.

[3] TH: pred. nom. to the implied subject of the verb ἔστιν.

[4] MH: pres. act. prtc. nom. pl. fem. TH: αἱ ... οὖσαι, *the ones (authorities) that exist*.

[5] τάσσω, *I arrange, appoint,* ***institute.*** MH: pf. tense stem is ταχ; χ + μ = γμ. TH: periphr. prtc. The pres. tense εἰσίν followed by the pf. prtc. indicates pf. tense; *have been instituted*.

[6] ἀντιτάσσω, *I resist*.

[7] διαταγή, ῆς, ἡ, *ordinance*. TH: dir. obj. of ἀνθέστηκεν.

[8] ἀνθίστημι, *I oppose, resist*. MH: pf. act. indic. 3rd sg.

[9] ἀνθίστημι, *I oppose, resist*. MH: pf. act. prtc. nom. pl. masc.

[10] κρίμα, ατος, τό, *judgment*.

[11] MH: fut. mid. indic. 3rd pl. of λαμβανω = λαβ (root) › λανβ (ν is inserted to assist with pronounciation; called epenthesis) › λαμβ (ν + β = μβ) › λημβ (vowel shifts; α › η) › λημψονται (β + σ = ψ).

[12] ἄρχων, οντος, ὁ, *ruler, leader*.

[13] φόβος, ου, ὁ, *fear, reverence,* ***terrible***. TH: pred. nom. to ἄρχοντες.

[14] TH: complementary inf. with θέλεις.

[15] MH: fut. act. indic. 2nd sg. of ἔχω = σεχ (root) › ἑχ (σ drops and is replaced by a rough breathing mark) › ἐχ (rough breathing mark deaspirates due to χ) + σ (tense formative) › ἑξ (χ + σ = ξ; since χ is lost, the rough breathing mark returns) › ἕξεις.

[16] ἔπαινος, ου, ὁ, *praise, approval*.

[17] διάκονος, ου, ὁ, *servant, minister*. TH: pred. nom. of the verb ἐστιν.

[18] εἰκῇ, *without cause, for no reason, in vain*.

[19] μάχαιρα, ης, ἡ, *sword*.

[20] φορέω, *I bear, carry*. MH: the root (φορε) ends in a vowel, so the connecting vowel contracts (ε + ει = ει).

θεοῦ γὰρ διάκονός[1] ἐστιν, ἔκδικος[2] εἰς ὀργὴν[3] τῷ τὸ
κακὸν πράσσοντι.[4] **5** διὸ ἀνάγκη[5] ὑποτάσσεσθαι,[6] οὐ
μόνον διὰ τὴν ὀργὴν[7] ἀλλὰ καὶ διὰ τὴν συνείδησιν,[8] **6** διὰ
τοῦτο γὰρ καὶ φόρους[9] τελεῖτε,[10] λειτουργοὶ[11] γὰρ θεοῦ
εἰσιν εἰς αὐτὸ τοῦτο[12] προσκαρτεροῦντες.[13] **7** ⸀ἀπόδοτε[14]
πᾶσι τὰς ὀφειλάς,[15] τῷ τὸν φόρον[16] τὸν φόρον,[17] τῷ τὸ
τέλος[18] τὸ τέλος,[19] τῷ τὸν φόβον[20] τὸν φόβον,[21] τῷ τὴν
τιμὴν[22] τὴν τιμήν.[23]
8 Μηδενὶ μηδὲν[24] ὀφείλετε,[25] εἰ μὴ τὸ[26] ⸂ἀλλήλους
ἀγαπᾶν⸃· ὁ γὰρ ἀγαπῶν τὸν ἕτερον νόμον πεπλήρωκεν.[27]

---

[1] διάκονος, ου, ὁ, *servant, minister*. TH: pred. nom. to the subject of ἐστιν.
[2] ἔκδικος, ου, ὁ, *avenger*. TH: app. to διάκονός.
[3] ὀργή, ῆς, ἡ, *wrath*.
[4] πράσσω, *I do, engage in*.
[5] ἀνάγκη, ης, ἡ, *necessity*. TH: *it is necessary*.
[6] ὑποτάσσω, *I subject, subordinate*.
[7] ὀργή, ῆς, ἡ, *wrath*.
[8] συνείδησις, εως, ἡ, *conscience*.
[9] φόρος, ου, ὁ, *tribute, tax*.
[10] τελέω, *I fulfill, complete,* ***pay***. MH: the root (τελε) ends in a vowel, so the connecting vowel contracts (ε + ε = ει).
[11] λειτουργός, οῦ, ὁ, *servant, minister*. TH: pred. nom. to implied subject of εἰσιν.
[12] TH: εἰς αὐτὸ τοῦτο, *in this same thing*.
[13] προσκαρτερέω, *I am devoted*. MH: the root (προσκαρτερε) ends in a vowel, so the connecting vowel contracts (ε + ο = ου).
[14] ἀποδίδωμι, *I repay, render*. MH: 2nd aor.; root is ἀποδο.
[15] ὀφειλή, ῆς, ἡ, *obligation, duty*.
[16] φόρος, ου, ὁ, *tribute, tax*. TH: τῷ τὸν φόρον, *to the (one owed) tribute*.
[17] φόρος, ου, ὁ, *tribute, tax*. TH: τὸν φόρον, *(pay) tribute*.
[18] τέλος, ους, τό, *end,* ***tax***. TH: τῷ τὸ τέλος, *to the (one owed) tax*.
[19] τέλος, ους, τό, *end,* ***tax***. TH: τὸ τέλος, *(pay) tax*.
[20] φόβος, ου, ὁ, *fear, reverence*. TH: τῷ τὸν φόβον, *to the (one owed) reverence*.
[21] φόβος, ου, ὁ, *fear, reverence*. TH: τὸν φόβον, *(give) reverence*.
[22] τιμή, ῆς, ἡ, *honor*. TH: τῷ τὴν τιμὴν, *to the (one owed) honor*.
[23] τιμή, ῆς, ἡ, *honor*. TH: τὴν τιμήν, *(give) honor*.
[24] TH: double negative; *nothing to anyone*.
[25] ὀφείλω, *I owe*.
[26] TH: τὸ nominalizes the inf. ἀγαπᾶν.
[27] MH: the ο lengthens to a ω before the tense formative.

9 τὸ[1] γάρ· Οὐ μοιχεύσεις,[2] Οὐ φονεύσεις,[3] Οὐ κλέψεις,[4]
Οὐκ ἐπιθυμήσεις,[5] καὶ εἴ τις ἑτέρα ἐντολή, ἐν ⸂τῷ λόγῳ
τούτῳ⸃ ἀνακεφαλαιοῦται,[6] ⸂ἐν τῷ[7]⸃· Ἀγαπήσεις τὸν
πλησίον[8] σου ὡς σεαυτόν.[9] **10** ἡ ἀγάπη τῷ πλησίον[10] κακὸν
οὐκ ἐργάζεται·[11] πλήρωμα[12] οὖν νόμου ἡ ἀγάπη.

11 Καὶ τοῦτο εἰδότες[13] τὸν καιρόν, ὅτι ὥρα ⸂ἤδη ὑμᾶς[14]⸃
ἐξ ὕπνου[15] ἐγερθῆναι, νῦν γὰρ ἐγγύτερον[16] ἡμῶν ἡ
σωτηρία[17] ἢ ὅτε ἐπιστεύσαμεν. **12** ἡ νὺξ προέκοψεν,[18] ἡ δὲ
ἡμέρα ἤγγικεν.[19] ⸀ἀποβαλώμεθα[20] οὖν τὰ ἔργα τοῦ
σκότους,[21] ⸂ἐνδυσώμεθα[22] δὲ⸃ τὰ ὅπλα[23] τοῦ φωτός.

---

[1] TH: τὸ introduces the quotation that follows and does not need to be translated.
[2] μοιχεύω, *I commit adultery*.
[3] φονεύω, *I murder, kill*.
[4] κλέπτω, *I steal*.
[5] ἐπιθυμέω, *I covet, desire*. MH: the ε lengthens to η before the tense formative.
[6] ἀνακεφαλαιόω, *I sum up*. MH: the root (ἀνακεφαλαιο) ends in a vowel, so the connecting vowel contracts (ο + ε = ου).
[7] TH: ἐν τῷ is repetitive, referring back to ἐν τῷ λόγῳ τούτῳ, and introduces the quote that follows.
[8] πλησίον, *near*, ***neighbor***.
[9] σεαυτοῦ, ῆς, *yourself*.
[10] πλησίον, *near*, ***neighbor***.
[11] ἐργάζομαι, *I work, labor, do*.
[12] πλήρωμα, ατος, τό, *fullness*, ***fulfilment***. TH: pred. nom. to ἀγάπη.
[13] MH: pf. act. prtc. nom. pl. masc. of οἶδα.
[14] TH: the acc. is the subject of the inf.; ὅτι ὥρα ἤδη ὑμᾶς … ἐγερθῆναι, *that (it is) the hour already for you to wake up*.
[15] ὕπνος, ου, ὁ, *sleep*.
[16] ἐγγύς, *near*. TH: ἐγγύτερον is the comparative form; with ἤ, *nearer … than*.
[17] σωτηρία, ας, ἡ, *salvation*.
[18] προκόπτω, *I advance, progress*. MH: the root is προκοπ; π + σ = ψ.
[19] ἐγγίζω, *I bring near*, ***am near***. MH: pf. act. indic. 3rd sg.
[20] ἀποβάλλω, *I throw off*. MH: 2nd aor.; root is ἀποβαλ. NA has ἀποθώμεθα.
[21] σκότος, ους, τό, *darkness*.
[22] ἐνδύω, *I put on, clothe*.
[23] ὅπλον, ου, τό, *tool, weapon*.

13 ὡς ἐν ἡμέρᾳ εὐσχημόνως[1] περιπατήσωμεν,[2] μὴ κώμοις[3]
καὶ μέθαις,[4] μὴ κοίταις[5] καὶ ἀσελγείαις,[6] μὴ ἔριδι[7] καὶ
ζήλῳ,[8] **14** ἀλλὰ ἐνδύσασθε[9] τὸν κύριον Ἰησοῦν Χριστόν,
καὶ τῆς σαρκὸς πρόνοιαν[10] μὴ ποιεῖσθε[11] εἰς ἐπιθυμίας.[12]

13:1 οὖσαι WH Treg NA28] + ἐξουσίαι RP
- **ὑπὸ** WH Treg NA28] + τοῦ RP

3 τῷ ἀγαθῷ ἔργῳ WH Treg NA28] τῶν ἀγαθῶν ἔργων RP
3 τῷ ἀγαθῷ ἔργῳ WH Treg NA28] τῶν ἀγαθῶν ἔργων RP
- **τῷ κακῷ** WH Treg NA28] τῶν κακῶν RP
- **τῷ κακῷ** WH Treg NA28] τῶν κακῶν RP

7 ἀπόδοτε WH Treg NA28] + οὖν RP
8 ἀλλήλους ἀγαπᾶν WH Treg NA28] ἀγαπᾶν ἀλλήλους RP
8 ἀλλήλους ἀγαπᾶν WH Treg NA28] ἀγαπᾶν ἀλλήλους RP
9 τῷ λόγῳ τούτῳ WH Treg NA28] τούτῳ τῷ λόγῳ RP
9 τῷ λόγῳ τούτῳ WH Treg NA28] τούτῳ τῷ λόγῳ RP
- **ἐν τῷ** WH Treg RP NA28] – NIV
- **ἐν τῷ** WH Treg RP NA28] – NIV

11 ἤδη ὑμᾶς WH NA28] ἤδη ἡμᾶς Treg; ἡμᾶς ἤδη RP
11 ἤδη ὑμᾶς WH NA28] ἤδη ἡμᾶς Treg; ἡμᾶς ἤδη RP
12 ἀποβαλώμεθα Holmes] ἀποθώμεθα WH Treg NA28 RP
- **ἐνδυσώμεθα δὲ** WH Treg NA28] καὶ ἐνδυσώμεθα RP
- **ἐνδυσώμεθα δὲ** WH Treg NA28] καὶ ἐνδυσώμεθα RP

---

[1] εὐσχημόνως, *decently*.
[2] MH: the ε lengthens to η before the tense formative.
[3] κῶμος, ου, ὁ, *celebration, feasting,* ***revelry***.
[4] μέθη, ης, ἡ, *drunkenness*.
[5] κοίτη, ης, ἡ, *bed,* ***sexual immorality***.
[6] ἀσέλγεια, ας, ἡ, *licentiousness*.
[7] ἔρις, ιδος, ἡ, *strife*.
[8] ζῆλος, ου, ὁ, *zeal,* ***jealousy***.
[9] ἐνδύω, *I put on, clothe*.
[10] πρόνοια, ας, ἡ, *provision*.
[11] MH: the root (ποιε) ends in a vowel, so there is a contraction (ε + ε = ει).
[12] ἐπιθυμία, ας, ἡ, *desire, lust*. TH: εἰς indicates purpose; *for desire*.

ROMANS 14

New Vocabulary by Frequency [Chapter, Book, SBLGNT Occurrences]

ἀλλότριος, α, ον, *someone else's, belong to another* [1, 2, 14]
ἆρα, *consequently* [2, 11, 52]
ἀσθενέω, *I am weak, sick* [3, 5, 34]
βῆμα, ατος, τό, *step* [1, 1, 12]
βλασφημέω, *I slander, blaspheme* [1, 3, 34]
βρῶμα, ατος, τό, *food* [3, 3, 17]
βρῶσις, εως, ἡ, *food, meat* [1, 1, 11]
γόνυ, ατος, τό, *knee* [1, 2, 12]
διακρίνω, *I separate, evaluate* [1, 2, 19]
διάκρισις, εως, ἡ, *separation, division* [1, 1, 3]
διαλογισμός, ου, ὁ, *reasoning* [1, 2, 14]
διώκω, *I pursue, chase* [1, 5, 45]
δοκιμάζω, *I test, approve* [1, 4, 22]
δόκιμος, ον, *approved* [1, 2, 7]
δουλεύω, *I serve* [1, 7, 25]
δυνατέω, *I am able* [1, 1, 3]
ἕνεκα, *on account of, for the sake of* [1, 2, 26]
ἐξομολογέω, *I confess, acknowledge, give thanks* [1, 2, 10]
ἐξουθενέω, *I despise* [2, 2, 11]
εὐάρεστος, ον, *pleasing, acceptable* [1, 3, 19]
εὐχαριστέω, *I give thanks* [2, 5, 38]
καθαρός, ά, όν, *clean, pure* [1, 1, 26]
κάμπτω, *I bow, bend* [1, 2, 4]
κατακρίνω, *I pronounce a sentence on* [1, 4, 17]
καταλύω, *I destroy, demolish* [1, 1 17]
κοινός, ή, όν, *unclean, common* [3, 3, 14]
κρέας, ως, τό, *meat* [1, 1, 2]
κυριεύω, *I rule, am master of* [1, 4, 7]
λάχανον, ου, τό, *vegetable* [1, 1, 4]
λογίζομαι, *I regard, consider* [1, 19, 40]
λυπέω, *I grieve, am distressed* [1, 1, 26]
μηκέτι, *no longer* [1, 3, 22]
νοῦς, ός, ὁ, *mind, way of thinking* [1, 6, 24]
οἰκέτης, ου, ὁ, *household slave* [1, 1, 4]
οἰκοδομή, ῆς, ἡ, *building* [1, 2, 18]
οἶνος, ου, ὁ, *wine* [1, 1, 34]

οὐκέτι, *no longer* [1, 7, 47]
παρίστημι, *I present, demonstrate* [1, 8, 41]
πληροφορέω, *I fulfill, fully convince* [1, 2, 6]
πόσις, εως, ἡ, *drink, beverage* [1, 1, 3]
πρόσκομμα, ατος, τό, *hindrance, obstacle* [2, 4, 6]
προσκόπτω, *I stumble* [1, 2, 8]
προσλαμβάνω, *I receive, take in* [2, 4, 12]
σεαυτοῦ, ῆς, *yourself* [1, 6, 43]
σκανδαλίζω, *I cause to stumble* [1, 1, 30]
σκάνδαλον, ου, τό, *trap, offense* [1, 4, 15]
στήκω, *I stand* [1, 1, 9]
φρονέω, *I think, am intent on* [2, 9, 26]

14.1 Τὸν δὲ ἀσθενοῦντα[1] τῇ πίστει προσλαμβάνεσθε,[2]
μὴ εἰς διακρίσεις[3] διαλογισμῶν.[4] 2 ὃς[5] μὲν[6] πιστεύει
φαγεῖν[7] πάντα, ὁ δὲ ἀσθενῶν[8] λάχανα[9] ἐσθίει. 3 ὁ ἐσθίων
τὸν μὴ ἐσθίοντα μὴ ἐξουθενείτω,[10] ⸂ὁ δὲ⸃ μὴ ἐσθίων τὸν
ἐσθίοντα μὴ κρινέτω, ὁ θεὸς γὰρ αὐτὸν προσελάβετο.[11]
4 σὺ[12] τίς εἶ ὁ κρίνων ἀλλότριον[13] οἰκέτην;[14] τῷ ἰδίῳ κυρίῳ
στήκει[15] ἢ πίπτει· σταθήσεται[16] δέ, ⸂δυνατεῖ[17] γὰρ⸃ ὁ
⸀κύριος στῆσαι[18] αὐτόν.

5 ⸆Ὃς[19] ⸀μὲν[20] κρίνει ἡμέραν παρ’[21] ἡμέραν, ὃς δὲ κρίνει
πᾶσαν ἡμέραν· ἕκαστος ἐν τῷ ἰδίῳ νοῒ[22] πληρο-
φορείσθω·[23] 6 ὁ φρονῶν[24] τὴν ἡμέραν κυρίῳ ⸀φρονεῖ.[25] καὶ

---

[1] ἀσθενέω, *I am weak, sick*. MH: the root (ἀσθενε) ends in a vowel, so the connecting vowel contracts (ε + ο = ου).

[2] προσλαμβάνω, *I receive, take in*.

[3] διάκρισις, εως, ἡ, *separation, division, **argument***.

[4] διαλογισμός, ου, ὁ, *reasoning, **opinion***.

[5] TH: ὃς contains an embedded dem.; *the one who*.

[6] TH: μὲν … δὲ, *on the one hand … on the other*.

[7] MH: aor. act. inf. of ἐσθίω. TH: *he may eat*.

[8] ἀσθενέω, *I am weak, sick*.

[9] λάχανον, ου, τό, *vegetable*.

[10] ἐξουθενέω, *I despise*. MH: the connecting vowel contracts (ε + ε = ει).

[11] προσλαμβάνω, *I receive, take in*. MH: 2nd aor.; root is προσλαβ.

[12] TH: pred. nom. to the subject τίς.

[13] ἀλλότριος, α, ον, *someone else's, belong to another*.

[14] οἰκέτης, ου, ὁ, *household slave*.

[15] στήκω, *I stand*.

[16] MH: fut. pass. indic. 3rd sg. of ἵστημι.

[17] δυνατέω, *I am able*.

[18] TH: στῆσαι αὐτόν, *to make him stand*.

[19] TH: Ὃς μὲν … ὃς δὲ, *one person … another person*.

[20] NA has γὰρ after μὲν, though γὰρ is in brackets, indicating the questionable nature of its inclusion.

[21] TH: παρά is indicating comparison; *more than*.

[22] νοῦς, ός, ὁ, *mind, way of thinking*.

[23] πληροφορέω, *I fulfill, fully convince*. MH: the root (πληροφορε) ends in a vowel, so the connecting vowel contracts (ε + ε = ει).

[24] φρονέω, *I think, am intent on, **observe***.

[25] φρονέω, *I think, am intent on, **observe***.

ὁ ἐσθίων κυρίῳ ἐσθίει, εὐχαριστεῖ[1] γὰρ τῷ θεῷ· καὶ ὁ μὴ
ἐσθίων κυρίῳ οὐκ ἐσθίει, καὶ εὐχαριστεῖ[2] τῷ θεῷ.
7 Οὐδεὶς γὰρ ἡμῶν[3] ἑαυτῷ ζῇ,[4] καὶ οὐδεὶς ἑαυτῷ
ἀποθνήσκει· **8** ἐάν τε γὰρ ζῶμεν,[5] τῷ κυρίῳ ζῶμεν,[6] ἐάν τε
ἀποθνήσκωμεν, τῷ κυρίῳ ἀποθνήσκομεν. ἐάν τε οὖν
ζῶμεν[7] ἐάν τε ἀποθνήσκωμεν, τοῦ κυρίου ἐσμέν.
9 εἰς τοῦτο γὰρ ⸀Χριστὸς ⸀ἀπέθανεν[8] καὶ ἔζησεν ἵνα καὶ[9]
νεκρῶν καὶ ζώντων κυριεύσῃ.[10]
10 Σὺ δὲ τί κρίνεις τὸν ἀδελφόν σου; ἢ καὶ σὺ τί
ἐξουθενεῖς[11] τὸν ἀδελφόν σου; πάντες γὰρ
παραστησόμεθα[12] τῷ βήματι[13] τοῦ ⸀θεοῦ, **11** γέγραπται
γάρ· Ζῶ[14] ἐγώ, λέγει κύριος, ὅτι ἐμοὶ κάμψει[15] πᾶν γόνυ,[16]

---

[1] εὐχαριστέω, *I give thanks*. MH: the root (εὐχαριστε) ends in a vowel, so the connecting vowel contracts (ε + ε = ει).

[2] εὐχαριστέω, *I give thanks*. MH: the root (εὐχαριστε) ends in a vowel, so the connecting vowel contracts (ε + ε = ει).

[3] TH: Οὐδεὶς … ἡμῶν, *none of us*.

[4] MH: from ζάω; in Classical Greek, the root was ζη, which is retained in some forms in Koine (η + ει = ῃ).

[5] MH: from ζάω; in Classical Greek, the root was ζη, which is retained in some forms in Koine (η + ο = ω).

[6] MH: from ζάω; in Classical Greek, the root was ζη, which is retained in some forms in Koine (η + ο = ω).

[7] MH: from ζάω; in Classical Greek, the root was ζη, which is retained in some forms in Koine (η + ο = ω).

[8] MH: 2nd aor. of ἀποθνήσκω; the root is ἀποθαν.

[9] TH: καὶ ... καὶ, *both … and*.

[10] κυριεύω, *I rule, am master of*.

[11] ἐξουθενέω, *I despise*. MH: the root (ἐξουθενε) ends in a vowel, so the connecting vowel contracts (ε + ε = ει).

[12] παρίστημι, *I present, demonstrate, **stand***. MH: fut. mid. indic. 1st pl.

[13] βῆμα, ατος, τό, *step, **judgment seat***.

[14] MH: from ζάω; in Classical Greek, the root was ζη, which is retained in some forms in Koine (η + ο = ω).

[15] κάμπτω, *I bow, bend*. MH: root is καμπ; π + σ = ψ.

[16] γόνυ, ατος, τό, *knee*.

καὶ ⸂πᾶσα γλῶσσα ἐξομολογήσεται[1]⸃ τῷ θεῷ. **12** ⸀ἄρα[2]
ἕκαστος ἡμῶν περὶ ἑαυτοῦ λόγον[3] ⸀δώσει.[4]

13 Μηκέτι[5] οὖν ἀλλήλους κρίνωμεν· ἀλλὰ τοῦτο
κρίνατε[6] μᾶλλον, τὸ μὴ τιθέναι πρόσκομμα[7] τῷ ἀδελφῷ ἢ
σκάνδαλον.[8] **14** οἶδα καὶ πέπεισμαι[9] ἐν κυρίῳ Ἰησοῦ ὅτι
οὐδὲν κοινὸν[10] δι' ⸀ἑαυτοῦ· εἰ μὴ τῷ λογιζομένῳ[11] τι[12]
κοινὸν[13] εἶναι, ἐκείνῳ κοινόν.[14] **15** εἰ ⸀γὰρ διὰ βρῶμα[15] ὁ
ἀδελφός σου λυπεῖται,[16] οὐκέτι[17] κατὰ ἀγάπην
περιπατεῖς.[18] μὴ τῷ βρώματί[19] σου ἐκεῖνον ἀπόλλυε ὑπὲρ
οὗ Χριστὸς ἀπέθανεν. **16** μὴ βλασφημείσθω[20] οὖν ὑμῶν τὸ

---

[1] ἐξομολογέω, *I confess, acknowledge, give thanks.* MH: the ε lengthens to η before the tense formative.

[2] ἄρα, *consequently.* NA has οὖν after ἄρα, though οὖν is in brackets, indicating the questionable nature of its inclusion.

[3] TH: *account.*

[4] MH: root is δο; the ο of the root lengthens to ω before the tense formative. NA has τῷ θεῷ after δώσει, though τῷ θεῷ is in brackets, indicating the questionable nature of its inclusion.

[5] μηκέτι, *no longer.*

[6] MH: since the root (κριν) ends in ν, the aor. tense formative is α.

[7] πρόσκομμα, ατος, τό, *hindrance, obstacle,* ***stumbling***.

[8] σκάνδαλον, ου, τό, *trap, offense,* ***stumbling block***.

[9] MH: from πείθω; πειθ (root) › πεπειθ (redupl.) + μαι (pf. pass. indic. 1st sg. ending) › πέπεισμαι (θ + μ = σμ).

[10] κοινός, ή, όν, *unclean, common.* TH: pred. adj. to οὐδὲν.

[11] λογίζομαι, *I regard, consider.*

[12] TH: acc. is the subject of the inf. εἶναι.

[13] κοινός, ή, όν, *unclean, common.*

[14] κοινός, ή, όν, *unclean, common.* TH: ἐκείνῳ κοινόν, *it is unclean to that one.*

[15] βρῶμα, ατος, τό, *food.*

[16] λυπέω, *I grieve, am distressed.* MH: the root (λυπε) ends in a vowel, so the connecting vowel contracts (ε + ε = ει).

[17] οὐκέτι, *no longer.*

[18] MH: the root (περιπατε) ends in a vowel, so the connecting vowel contracts (ε + ε = ει).

[19] βρῶμα, ατος, τό, *food.*

[20] βλασφημέω, *I slander, blaspheme.* MH: the root (βλασφημε) ends in a vowel, so the connecting vowel contracts (ε + ε = ει).

ἀγαθόν. **17** οὐ γάρ ἐστιν ἡ βασιλεία τοῦ θεοῦ βρῶσις[1] καὶ
πόσις,[2] ἀλλὰ δικαιοσύνη καὶ εἰρήνη καὶ χαρὰ ἐν
πνεύματι ἁγίῳ· **18** ὁ γὰρ ἐν ⸀τούτῳ[3] δουλεύων[4] τῷ Χριστῷ
εὐάρεστος[5] τῷ θεῷ καὶ δόκιμος[6] τοῖς ἀνθρώποις. **19** ἄρα[7]
οὖν τὰ[8] τῆς εἰρήνης διώκωμεν[9] καὶ τὰ τῆς οἰκοδομῆς[10]
τῆς[11] εἰς ἀλλήλους. **20** μὴ ἕνεκεν[12] βρώματος[13] κατάλυε[14] τὸ
ἔργον τοῦ θεοῦ. πάντα μὲν καθαρά,[15] ἀλλὰ κακὸν τῷ
ἀνθρώπῳ τῷ διὰ προσκόμματος[16] ἐσθίοντι. **21** καλὸν[17] τὸ
μὴ φαγεῖν[18] κρέα[19] μηδὲ πιεῖν[20] οἶνον[21] μηδὲ ἐν ᾧ[22] ὁ
ἀδελφός σου προσκόπτει[23] ⸂ἢ σκανδαλίζεται[24] ἢ
ἀσθενεῖ⸃.[25] **22** σὺ πίστιν ⸀ἣν ἔχεις κατὰ σεαυτὸν[26] ἔχε[27]

---

[1] βρῶσις, εως, ἡ, *food, meat*.
[2] πόσις, εως, ἡ, *drink, beverage*.
[3] TH: ἐν τούτῳ, *in this way*.
[4] δουλεύω, *I serve*.
[5] εὐάρεστος, ον, *pleasing, acceptable*. TH: pred. adj. to ὁ … δουλεύων.
[6] δόκιμος, ον, *approved*. TH: pred. adj. to ὁ … δουλεύων.
[7] ἄρα, *consequently*.
[8] TH: τὰ τῆς εἰρήνης … τῆς οἰκοδομῆς *the things of peace … of edification*
[9] διώκω, *I pursue, chase*.
[10] οἰκοδομή, ῆς, ἡ, *building*, ***edification***.
[11] TH: τῆς substantivizes the prep. phrase εἰς ἀλλήλους.
[12] ἕνεκα, *on account of, for the sake of*.
[13] βρῶμα, ατος, τό, *food*.
[14] καταλύω, *I destroy, demolish*.
[15] καθαρός, ά, όν, *clean, pure*. TH: pred. adj. to πάντα.
[16] πρόσκομμα, ατος, τό, *hindrance, obstacle*, ***stumbling***.
[17] TH: *It is good*.
[18] MH: aor. act. inf. of ἐσθίω.
[19] κρέας, ως, τό, *meat*.
[20] MH: aor. act. inf. of πίνω.
[21] οἶνος, ου, ὁ, *wine*.
[22] TH: μηδὲ ἐν ᾧ, *nor do anything by which*.
[23] προσκόπτω, *I stumble*.
[24] σκανδαλίζω, *I cause to stumble*.
[25] ἀσθενέω, *I am weak, sick*. MH: the root (ἀσθενε) ends in a vowel, so the connecting vowel contracts (ε + ε = ει). NA omits ἢ σκανδαλίζεται ἢ ἀσθενεῖ.
[26] σεαυτοῦ, ῆς, *yourself*.
[27] TH: imperative from ἔχω; *keep*.

ἐνώπιον τοῦ θεοῦ. μακάριος ὁ μὴ κρίνων ἑαυτὸν ἐν ᾧ[1]
δοκιμάζει·[2] **23** ὁ δὲ διακρινόμενος[3] ἐὰν φάγῃ κατα-
κέκριται,[4] ὅτι οὐκ ἐκ πίστεως· πᾶν δὲ ὃ οὐκ ἐκ πίστεως
ἁμαρτία[5] ἐστίν.

14:3 ὁ δὲ WH Treg NA28] καὶ ὁ RP
14:3 ὁ δὲ WH Treg NA28] καὶ ὁ RP
4 δυνατεῖ γὰρ WH Treg NA28] δυνατὸς γάρ ἐστιν RP
4 δυνατεῖ γὰρ WH Treg NA28] δυνατὸς γάρ ἐστιν RP
• **κύριος** WH Treg NA28] θεὸς RP
5 μὲν Treg NIV RP] + γάρ WH NA28
6 φρονεῖ WH Treg NA28] + καὶ ὁ μὴ φρονῶν τὴν ἡμέραν κυρίῳ οὐ φρονεῖ RP
9 Χριστὸς WH Treg NA28] + καὶ RP
• **ἀπέθανεν** WH Treg NA28] + καὶ ἀνέστη RP
10 θεοῦ WH Treg NA28] χριστοῦ RP
11 πᾶσα γλῶσσα ἐξομολογήσεται WH NA28 RP] ἐξομολογήσεται πᾶσα γλῶσσα Treg
11 πᾶσα γλῶσσα ἐξομολογήσεται WH NA28 RP] ἐξομολογήσεται πᾶσα γλῶσσα Treg
12 ἄρα Treg] + οὖν WH NA28 RP
• **δώσει** Holmes WH[marg]] + τῷ θεῷ WH NA28 RP; ἀποδώσει τῷ θεῷ Treg
14 ἑαυτοῦ WH NA28] αὐτοῦ Treg RP
15 γὰρ WH Treg NA28] δὲ RP
18 τούτῳ WH Treg NA28] τούτοις RP
21 ἢ σκανδαλίζεται ἢ ἀσθενεῖ Treg RP] – WH NA28
21 ἢ σκανδαλίζεται ἢ ἀσθενεῖ Treg RP] – WH NA28
22 ἣν WH Treg NA28] – RP
23 ἐστίν WH Treg NA28] + 24 Τῷ δὲ δυναμένῳ ὑμᾶς στηρίξαι κατὰ τὸ εὐαγγέλιόν μου καὶ τὸ κήρυγμα Ἰησοῦ Χριστοῦ, κατὰ ἀποκάλυψιν μυστηρίου χρόνοις αἰωνίοις σεσιγημένου, 25 φανερωθέντος δὲ νῦν διά τε γραφῶν προφητικῶν κατ᾽ ἐπιταγὴν τοῦ αἰωνίου θεοῦ εἰς ὑπακοὴν πίστεως εἰς πάντα τὰ ἔθνη γνωρισθέντος, 26 μόνῳ σοφῷ θεῷ, διὰ Ἰησοῦ χριστοῦ ᾧ ἡ δόξα εἰς τοὺς αἰῶνας· ἀμήν. RP

---

[1] TH: ἐν ᾧ, *by which measure.*
[2] δοκιμάζω, *I test, approve.*
[3] διακρίνω, *I separate, evaluate,* ***waver***.
[4] κατακρίνω, *I pronounce sentence,* ***condemn***. MH: perf. tense stem drops the ν.
[5] TH: pred. nom. to πᾶν.

ROMANS 15

New Vocabulary by Frequency [Chapter, Book, SBLGNT Occurrences]

ἀγαθωσύνη, ης, ἡ, *goodness* [1, 1, 4]
ἁγιάζω, *I sanctify, make holy* [1, 1, 28]
ἀδύνατος, ον, *powerless, impossible* [1, 2, 10]
αἰνέω, *I praise* [1, 1, 8]
ἀλλότριος, α, ον, *someone else's, belonging to another* [1, 2, 14]
ἀναγγέλλω, *I report, proclaim* [1, 1, 14]
ἀπειθέω, *I disobey, am disobedient* [1, 5, 14]
ἀρέσκω, *I please* [3, 4, 17]
ἀσθένημα, ατος, τό, *weakness* [1, 1, 1]
Ἀχαΐα, ας, ἡ, *Achaia* [1, 1, 10]
βαστάζω, *I bear, lift up* [1, 2, 27]
βεβαιόω, *I confirm, establish* [1, 1, 8]
γνῶσις, εως, ἡ, *knowledge* [1, 3, 29]
διακονέω, *I serve* [1, 1, 37]
διακονία, ας, ἡ, *ministry, service* [1, 4, 34]
διάκονος, ου, ὁ, *servant, minister* [1, 4, 29]
διαπορεύομαι, *I pass through* [1, 1, 5]
διδασκαλία, ας, ἡ, *teaching, instruction* [1, 2, 21]
δυνατός, ή, όν, *able, capable* [1, 5, 32]
ἐγκόπτω, *I hinder, oppose* [1, 1, 5]
ἔλεος, ους, τό, *mercy, compassion* [1, 3, 27]
ἐλπίζω, *I hope* [2, 4, 31]
ἐμπίπλημι, *I fill* [1, 1, 5]
ἐξομολογέω, *I confess, acknowledge, give thanks* [1, 2, 10]
ἐπαινέω, *I praise* [1, 1, 6]
ἐπαναμιμνῄσκω, *I remind* [1, 1, 1]
ἐπιπίπτω, *I fall on* [1, 1, 11]
ἐπιποθία, ας, ἡ, *longing, desire* [1, 1, 1]
ἐπιτελέω, *I complete, finish* [1, 1, 10]
ἔτος, ους, τό, *year* [1, 1, 49]
εὐδοκέω, *I am pleased* [2, 2, 21]
εὐλογία, ας, ἡ, *praise, blessing* [1, 2, 16]
εὐπρόσδεκτος, ον, *acceptable* [2, 2, 5]
εὐφραίνω, *I am glad, rejoice* [1, 1, 14]
ἡμέτερος, α, ον, *our* [1, 1, 7]
Ἠσαΐας, *Isaiah* [1, 5, 22]

θεάομαι, *I see, visit* [1, 1, 23]
θεμέλιος, ου, ὁ, *foundation* [1, 1, 12]
ἱερουργέω, *I serve as a priest* [1, 1, 1]
Ἰεσσαί, ὁ, *Jesse* [1, 1, 5]
ἱκανός, ή, όν, *sufficient* [1, 1, 40]
Ἰλλυρικόν, οῦ, τό, *Illyricum* [1, 1, 1]
Ἰουδαία, ας, ἡ, *Judea* [1, 1, 43]
κατεργάζομαι, *I do, commit, bring about* [1, 11, 22]
καύχησις, εως, ἡ, *boasting* [1, 2, 11]
κλίμα, ατος, τό, *district, region* [1, 1, 3]
κοινωνέω, *I share, participate* [1, 2, 8]
κοινωνία, ας, ἡ, *association, fellowship* [1, 1, 19]
κύκλῳ, *around* [1, 1, 8]
λειτουργέω, *I serve* [1, 1, 3]
λειτουργός, οῦ, ὁ, *servant, minister* [1, 2, 5]
Μακεδονία, ας, ἡ, *Macedonia* [1, 1, 22]
μέρος, ους, τό, *part* [2, 3, 42]
μεστός, ή, όν, *full* [1, 2, 9]
μέχρι, *until, as far as* [1, 2, 18]
μηκέτι, *no longer* [1, 3, 22]
νουθετέω, *I admonish, instruct* [1, 1, 8]
νυνί, *now* [2, 6, 20]
οἰκοδομέω, *I build* [1, 1, 40]
οἰκοδομή, ῆς, ἡ, *building* [1, 2, 18]
ὁμοθυμαδόν, *together, with one accord* [1, 1, 11]
ὀνειδίζω, *I insult, reproach* [1, 1, 10]
ὀνειδισμός, οῦ, ὁ, *insult, reproach* [1, 1, 5]
ὀνομάζω, *I name, call* [1, 1, 9]
ὀφειλέτης, ου, ὁ, *debtor, one who is under obligation* [1, 3, 7]
ὀφείλω, *I owe* [2, 3, 35]
παράκλησις, εως, ἡ, *exhortation, encouragement* [2, 3, 29]
περισσεύω, *I abound, overflow* [1, 3, 39]
περιτομή, ῆς, ἡ, *circumcision* [1, 15, 36]
πλήρωμα, ατος, τό, *fullness* [1, 4, 17]
πλησίον, *near* [1, 3, 17]
πνευματικός, ή, όν, *spiritual* [1, 3, 26]
προγράφω, *I write beforehand* [1, 1, 4]
προπέμπω, *I send forward, accompany* [1, 1, 9]
προσευχή, ῆς, ἡ, *prayer* [1, 3, 36]
προσλαμβάνω, *I receive, take in* [2, 4, 12]
προσφορά, ᾶς, ἡ, *offering* [1, 1, 9]

πτωχός, ή, όν, *poor* [1, 1, 34]
ῥίζα, ης, ἡ, *root* [1, 5, 17]
ῥύομαι, *I save, rescue, deliver* [1, 3, 17]
σαρκικός, ή, όν, *material, fleshly* [1, 1, 7]
Σπανία, ας, ἡ, *Spain* [2, 2, 2]
συναγωνίζομαι, *I contend along with* [1, 1, 1]
συναναπαύομαι, *I rest with, am refreshed* [1, 1, 1]
συνίημι, *I understand* [1, 2, 26]
σφραγίζω, *I seal* [1, 1, 15]
τέρας, ατος, τό, *wonder, sign* [1, 1, 16]
τολμάω, *I dare, show courage* [1, 2, 16]
τολμηρός, ά, όν, *bold* [1, 1, 1]
ὑπακοή, ῆς, ἡ, *obedience* [1, 6, 14]
ὑπομονή, ῆς, ἡ, *endurance, perseverance* [2, 6, 34]
φιλοτιμέομαι, *I am ambitious, aspire* [1, 1, 3]
φρονέω, *I think, am intent on* [1, 9, 26]
ψάλλω, *I sing praise* [1, 1, 5]

15.1 Ὀφείλομεν[1] δὲ ἡμεῖς οἱ δυνατοὶ[2] τὰ ἀσθενήματα[3]
τῶν ἀδυνάτων[4] βαστάζειν,[5] καὶ μὴ ἑαυτοῖς ἀρέσκειν.[6]
2 ἕκαστος ἡμῶν τῷ πλησίον[7] ἀρεσκέτω[8] εἰς τὸ ἀγαθὸν
πρὸς οἰκοδομήν·[9] **3** καὶ γὰρ ὁ Χριστὸς οὐχ ἑαυτῷ
ἤρεσεν·[10] ἀλλὰ καθὼς γέγραπται·[11] Οἱ ὀνειδισμοὶ[12] τῶν
ὀνειδιζόντων[13] σε ἐπέπεσαν[14] ἐπ᾽ ἐμέ. **4** ὅσα γὰρ
προεγράφη,[15] ⸀εἰς τὴν ἡμετέραν[16] διδασκαλίαν[17] ⸀ἐγράφη,[18]
ἵνα διὰ τῆς ὑπομονῆς[19] καὶ διὰ τῆς παρακλήσεως[20] τῶν
γραφῶν τὴν ἐλπίδα ἔχωμεν. **5** ὁ δὲ θεὸς τῆς ὑπομονῆς[21]
καὶ τῆς παρακλήσεως[22] δῴη[23] ὑμῖν τὸ αὐτὸ[24] φρονεῖν[25]

---

[1] ὀφείλω, *I owe*, ***ought***.
[2] δυνατός, ή, όν, *able, capable*. TH: subst. adj. in app. to ἡμεῖς; *we, the capable*.
[3] ἀσθένημα, ατος, τό, *weakness*.
[4] ἀδύνατος, ον, *powerless, impossible*.
[5] βαστάζω, *I bear, lift up*. TH: complementary inf. with Ὀφείλομεν.
[6] ἀρέσκω, *I please*. TH: complementary inf. with Ὀφείλομεν.
[7] πλησίον, *near*, ***neighbor***.
[8] ἀρέσκω, *I please*. TH: ἀρέσκω often takes a dat. dir. obj.
[9] οἰκοδομή, ῆς, ἡ, *building*, ***edification***.
[10] ἀρέσκω, *I please*. MH: aor. tense stem is ἀρε. TH: ἀρέσκω often takes a dat. dir. obj.
[11] MH: pf. pass. indic. 3rd sg.; occurs 3 times in Rom 15.
[12] ὀνειδισμός, οῦ, ὁ, *insult, reproach*.
[13] ὀνειδίζω, *I insult, reproach*.
[14] ἐπιπίπτω, *I fall on*. MH: aor. stem of ἐπιπίπτω = ἐπιπετ (root) › ἐπεπετ (aug.) › ἐπέπεσαν (τ immediately before σ drops out).
[15] προγράφω, *I write beforehand*. MH: 2nd aor. pass. does not include θ in the tense formative.
[16] ἡμέτερος, α, ον, *our*.
[17] διδασκαλία, ας, ἡ, *teaching, instruction*.
[18] MH: 2nd aor. pass. does not include θ in the tense formative.
[19] ὑπομονή, ῆς, ἡ, *endurance, perseverance*.
[20] παράκλησις, εως, ἡ, *exhortation, encouragement*.
[21] ὑπομονή, ῆς, ἡ, *endurance, perseverance*.
[22] παράκλησις, εως, ἡ, *exhortation, encouragement*.
[23] MH: aor. act. opt. 3rd sg. TH: *may he give*.
[24] TH: τὸ αὐτὸ is intensive; *the same*.
[25] φρονέω, *I think, am intent on*.

ἐν ἀλλήλοις[1] κατὰ ⸂Χριστὸν Ἰησοῦν⸃, **6** ἵνα ὁμοθυμαδὸν[2] ἐν
ἑνὶ στόματι δοξάζητε τὸν θεὸν καὶ πατέρα τοῦ κυρίου
ἡμῶν Ἰησοῦ Χριστοῦ.

7 Διὸ προσλαμβάνεσθε[3] ἀλλήλους, καθὼς καὶ
ὁ Χριστὸς προσελάβετο[4] ⸀ὑμᾶς, εἰς δόξαν ⸀τοῦ θεοῦ.
8 λέγω ⸀γὰρ ⸀Χριστὸν[5] διάκονον[6] ⸀γεγενῆσθαι[7] περιτομῆς[8]
ὑπὲρ ἀληθείας θεοῦ, εἰς τὸ βεβαιῶσαι[9] τὰς ἐπαγγελίας
τῶν πατέρων, **9** τὰ δὲ ἔθνη[10] ὑπὲρ ἐλέους[11] δοξάσαι[12] τὸν
θεόν· καθὼς γέγραπται· Διὰ τοῦτο ἐξομολογήσομαί[13]
σοι ἐν ἔθνεσι, καὶ τῷ ὀνόματί σου ψαλῶ.[14] **10** καὶ πάλιν
λέγει· Εὐφράνθητε,[15] ἔθνη, μετὰ τοῦ λαοῦ αὐτοῦ. **11** καὶ
πάλιν· Αἰνεῖτε,[16] ⸂πάντα τὰ ἔθνη, τὸν κύριον⸃, καὶ
⸀ἐπαινεσάτωσαν[17] αὐτὸν πάντες οἱ λαοί. **12** καὶ πάλιν
Ἠσαΐας[18] λέγει· Ἔσται[19] ἡ ῥίζα[20] τοῦ Ἰεσσαί,[21] καὶ

---

[1] TH: τὸ αὐτὸ φρονεῖν ἐν ἀλλήλοις, *to think the same among one another.*

[2] ὁμοθυμαδόν, *together, with one accord.*

[3] προσλαμβάνω, *I receive, take in.* MH: pres. mid. impv. 2nd pl.

[4] προσλαμβάνω, *I receive, take in.* MH: 2nd aor.; root is προσλαβ.

[5] TH: acc. subject of the inf. γεγενῆσθαι.

[6] διάκονος, ου, ὁ, *servant, minister.*

[7] MH: aor. pass. inf. from γίνομαι; root is γεν.

[8] περιτομή, ῆς, ἡ, *circumcision,* ***circumcised.***

[9] βεβαιόω, *I confirm, establish.* MH: aor. act. inf. TH: εἰς τὸ + inf. indicates purpose; *in order to confirm.*

[10] TH: acc. subject of the inf. δοξάσαι.

[11] ἔλεος, ους, τό, *mercy, compassion.*

[12] MH: aor. act. inf. of δοξάζω. The root ends in δ; δ + σ = σ.

[13] ἐξομολογέω, *I confess, acknowledge, give thanks.*

[14] ψάλλω, *I sing praise.* MH: fut. act. indic. 1st sg. = ψαλ (fut. tense stem) + εσω (tense formative) › ψαλεσω › ψαλεω (intervocalic σ drops out) › ψαλῶ (ε + ω = ω).

[15] εὐφραίνω, *I am glad, rejoice.*

[16] αἰνέω, *I praise.* MH: the root (αἰνε) ends in a vowel, so the connecting vowel contracts (ε + ε = ει).

[17] ἐπαινέω, *I praise.* MH: aor. act. impv. 3rd pl.

[18] Ἠσαΐας, ου, ὁ, *Isaiah.*

[19] TH: *will come.*

[20] ῥίζα, ης, ἡ, *root.*

[21] Ἰεσσαί, ὁ, *Jesse.*

ὁ ἀνιστάμενος[1] ἄρχειν ἐθνῶν· ἐπ' αὐτῷ ἔθνη ἐλπιοῦσιν.[2]
13 ὁ δὲ θεὸς τῆς ἐλπίδος πληρώσαι[3] ὑμᾶς πάσης χαρᾶς καὶ
εἰρήνης ἐν τῷ πιστεύειν,[4] εἰς τὸ περισσεύειν[5] ὑμᾶς[6] ἐν τῇ
ἐλπίδι ἐν[7] δυνάμει πνεύματος ἁγίου.

14 Πέπεισμαι[8] δέ, ἀδελφοί μου, καὶ αὐτὸς[9] ἐγὼ περὶ
ὑμῶν, ὅτι καὶ αὐτοὶ[10] μεστοί[11] ἐστε ἀγαθωσύνης,[12]
πεπληρωμένοι[13] ⸀πάσης[14] γνώσεως,[15] δυνάμενοι καὶ
⸀ἀλλήλους νουθετεῖν.[16] **15** ⸀τολμηρότερον[17] δὲ ἔγραψα[18]
⸀ὑμῖν ἀπὸ μέρους,[19] ὡς ἐπαναμιμνῄσκων[20] ὑμᾶς, διὰ τὴν
χάριν τὴν δοθεῖσάν[21] μοι ⸀ὑπὸ τοῦ θεοῦ **16** εἰς τὸ εἶναί[22]
με[23] λειτουργὸν[24] ⸂Χριστοῦ Ἰησοῦ⸃ εἰς τὰ ἔθνη,

---

[1] MH: pres. mid. prtc. nom. sg. masc. from ἀνίστημι.

[2] ἐλπίζω, *I hope*. MH: fut. act. indic. 3rd pl.

[3] MH: aor. act. opt. 3rd sg. TH: *may he fill*.

[4] TH: ἐν τῷ + inf. indicates contemporaneous time; *as you believe*.

[5] περισσεύω, *I abound, overflow*. TH: εἰς τὸ + inf. indicates result; *so that you will abound*.

[6] TH: acc. subject of the inf. περισσεύειν.

[7] TH: ἐν is instrumental; *by*.

[8] MH: root is πείθω; θ + μ = σμ.

[9] TH: αὐτὸς is intensive; αὐτὸς ἐγὼ, *I myself*.

[10] TH: αὐτοὶ is intensive; with ἐστε, *you yourselves are*.

[11] μεστός, ή, όν, *full*. TH: pred. adj. to the subject implied by ἐστε.

[12] ἀγαθωσύνη, ης, ἡ, *goodness*.

[13] MH: the ο lengthens to ω before the tense formative.

[14] NA has τῆς after πάσης, though τῆς is in brackets, indicating the questionable nature of its inclusion.

[15] γνῶσις, εως, ἡ, *knowledge*.

[16] νουθετέω, *I admonish, instruct*.

[17] τολμηρός, ά, όν, *bold*. MH: τολμηρότερον is the comp. form. Here it is used adv.; *more boldly*.

[18] MH: from γράφω; φ + σ = ψ.

[19] μέρος, ους, τό, *part*.

[20] ἐπαναμιμνῄσκω, *I remind*.

[21] MH: aor. pass. prtc. acc. sg. fem. of δίδωμι; root is δο.

[22] TH: εἰς τὸ + inf. indicates purpose; *in order that I would be*.

[23] TH: acc. subject of the inf. εἶναί.

[24] λειτουργός, οῦ, ὁ, *servant, minister*.

ἱερουργοῦντα[1] τὸ εὐαγγέλιον τοῦ θεοῦ, ἵνα γένηται[2] ἡ
προσφορὰ[3] τῶν ἐθνῶν εὐπρόσδεκτος,[4] ἡγιασμένη[5] ἐν[6]
πνεύματι ἁγίῳ. **17** ἔχω οὖν ⸀τὴν καύχησιν[7] ἐν Χριστῷ
Ἰησοῦ τὰ πρὸς τὸν θεόν·[8] **18** οὐ γὰρ τολμήσω[9] ⸂τι λαλεῖν[10]⸃
ὧν οὐ[11] κατειργάσατο[12] Χριστὸς δι᾽ ἐμοῦ εἰς ὑπακοὴν[13]
ἐθνῶν, λόγῳ καὶ ἔργῳ, **19** ἐν δυνάμει σημείων καὶ
τεράτων,[14] ἐν δυνάμει ⸀πνεύματος·[15] ὥστε[16] με[17] ἀπὸ
Ἰερουσαλὴμ καὶ κύκλῳ[18] μέχρι[19] τοῦ Ἰλλυρικοῦ[20]
πεπληρωκέναι τὸ εὐαγγέλιον τοῦ Χριστοῦ, **20** οὕτως δὲ
⸀φιλοτιμούμενον[21] εὐαγγελίζεσθαι[22] οὐχ ὅπου ὠνομάσθη[23]

---

[1] ἱερουργέω, *I serve as a priest*. MH: the root (ἱερουργε) ends in a vowel, so the connecting vowel contracts (ε + ο = ου).

[2] MH: 2nd aor. of γίνομαι; root is γεν.

[3] προσφορά, ᾶς, ἡ, *offering*.

[4] εὐπρόσδεκτος, ον, *acceptable*.

[5] ἁγιάζω, *I sanctify, make holy*. MH: perf. pass. prtc. nom. sg. fem.

[6] TH: ἐν is instrumental; *by*.

[7] καύχησις, εως, ἡ, *boasting*.

[8] TH: τὰ substantivizes the prep. phrase πρὸς τὸν θεόν; *the things pertaining to God*.

[9] τολμάω, *I dare, show courage*. MH: the α lengthens to η before the tense formative.

[10] TH: complementary inf. with τολμήσω.

[11] TH: ὧν οὐ, *except what*.

[12] κατεργάζομαι, *I do, commit, bring about*. MH: aor. mid. indic. 3rd sg.

[13] ὑπακοή, ῆς, ἡ, *obedience*.

[14] τέρας, ατος, τό, *wonder, sign*.

[15] NA has θεοῦ after πνεύματος, though θεοῦ is in brackets, indicating the questionable nature of its inclusion.

[16] TH: ὥστε + inf. indicates result. The inf. (πεπληρωκέναι) occurs later in the verse.

[17] TH: acc. subject of the inf.

[18] κύκλῳ, *around*.

[19] μέχρι, *until, as far as*.

[20] Ἰλλυρικόν, οῦ, τό, *Illyricum*.

[21] φιλοτιμέομαι, *I am ambitious, aspire*. MH: the root (φιλοτιμε) ends in a vowel, so the connecting vowel contracts (ε + ο = ου).

[22] TH: complementary inf. with φιλοτιμούμενον.

[23] ὀνομάζω, *I name, call*. MH: root ends in δ; δ + θ = σθ.

Χριστός, ἵνα μὴ ἐπ' ἀλλότριον[1] θεμέλιον[2] οἰκοδομῶ,[3]
21 ἀλλὰ καθὼς γέγραπται· ⸂Οἷς οὐκ ἀνηγγέλη[4] περὶ αὐτοῦ
ὄψονται[5]⸃, καὶ οἳ[6] οὐκ ἀκηκόασιν[7] συνήσουσιν.[8]

22 Διὸ καὶ ἐνεκοπτόμην[9] τὰ πολλὰ[10] τοῦ ἐλθεῖν[11] πρὸς
ὑμᾶς· **23** νυνὶ[12] δὲ μηκέτι[13] τόπον ἔχων ἐν τοῖς κλίμασι[14]
τούτοις, ἐπιποθίαν[15] δὲ ἔχων τοῦ ἐλθεῖν πρὸς ὑμᾶς ἀπὸ
⸀ἱκανῶν[16] ἐτῶν,[17] **24** ὡς ⸀ἂν πορεύωμαι εἰς τὴν ⸀Σπανίαν,[18]
ἐλπίζω[19] γὰρ διαπορευόμενος[20] θεάσασθαι[21] ὑμᾶς καὶ ὑφ'
ὑμῶν προπεμφθῆναι[22] ἐκεῖ ἐὰν ὑμῶν[23] πρῶτον ἀπὸ
μέρους[24] ἐμπλησθῶ—[25] **25** νυνὶ[26] δὲ πορεύομαι εἰς

---

[1] ἀλλότριος, α, ον, *someone else's, belonging to another.*

[2] θεμέλιος, ου, ὁ, *foundation.*

[3] οἰκοδομέω, *I build.*

[4] ἀναγγέλλω, *I report, proclaim.* MH: 2nd aor. pass. does not include θ in the tense formative.

[5] MH: fut. mid. indic. 3rd pl. of ὁράω.

[6] TH: rel. pron.; *those who.*

[7] MH: pf. stem of ἀκούω is ἀκηκο.

[8] συνίημι, *I understand.* MH: fut. act. indic. 3rd pl.

[9] ἐγκόπτω, *I hinder, oppose.* MH: compound of ἐν + κοπτ (ν + κ = γκ); when the aug. is added, γ reverts to ν.

[10] TH: adv. acc.; *often.*

[11] TH: τοῦ ἐλθεῖν, *from coming.*

[12] νυνί, *now.*

[13] μηκέτι, *no longer.*

[14] κλίμα, ατος, τό, *district, region.*

[15] ἐπιποθία, ας, ἡ, *longing, desire.*

[16] ἱκανός, ή, όν, *sufficient,* ***many***. NA has πολλῶν instead of ἱκανῶν.

[17] ἔτος, ους, τό, *year.*

[18] Σπανία, ας, ἡ, *Spain.*

[19] ἐλπίζω, *I hope.*

[20] διαπορεύομαι, *I pass through.*

[21] θεάομαι, *I see, visit.* TH: complementary inf. with ἐλπίζω.

[22] προπέμπω, *I send forward, accompany,* ***assist***. TH: complementary inf. with ἐλπίζω.

[23] TH: agent of pass. verb; *by you.*

[24] μέρος, ους, το, *part,* ***time***. TH: πρῶτον ἀπὸ μέρους, *first for a time.*

[25] ἐμπίπλημι, *I fill,* ***enjoy***. MH: aor. pass. subj. 1st sg.

[26] νυνί, *now.*

Ἰερουσαλὴμ διακονῶν[1] τοῖς ἁγίοις. **26** εὐδόκησαν[2] γὰρ
Μακεδονία[3] καὶ Ἀχαΐα[4] κοινωνίαν[5] τινὰ ποιήσασθαι[6] εἰς
τοὺς πτωχοὺς[7] τῶν ἁγίων τῶν ἐν Ἰερουσαλήμ.
27 εὐδόκησαν[8] γάρ, καὶ ὀφειλέται[9] ⸂εἰσὶν αὐτῶν⸃· εἰ γὰρ
τοῖς πνευματικοῖς[10] αὐτῶν ἐκοινώνησαν[11] τὰ ἔθνη,
ὀφείλουσιν[12] καὶ ἐν τοῖς σαρκικοῖς[13] λειτουργῆσαι[14]
αὐτοῖς. **28** τοῦτο οὖν ἐπιτελέσας,[15] καὶ σφραγισάμενος[16]
αὐτοῖς τὸν καρπὸν τοῦτον, ἀπελεύσομαι[17] δι᾽ ὑμῶν ⸀εἰς
Σπανίαν·[18] **29** οἶδα δὲ ὅτι ἐρχόμενος πρὸς ὑμᾶς ἐν
πληρώματι[19] ⸀εὐλογίας[20] Χριστοῦ ἐλεύσομαι.[21]

---

[1] διακονέω, *I serve.*

[2] εὐδοκέω, *I am pleased.* MH: the ε lengthens to η before the tense formative.

[3] Μακεδονία, ας, ἡ, *Macedonia.*

[4] Ἀχαΐα, ας, ἡ, *Achaia.*

[5] κοινωνία, ας, ἡ, *association, fellowship,* ***contribution***.

[6] MH: the ε lengthens to η before the tense formative. TH: complementary inf. with εὐδόκησαν.

[7] πτωχός, ή, όν, *poor.*

[8] εὐδοκέω, *I am pleased.* MH: the ε lengthens to η before the tense formative.

[9] ὀφειλέτης, ου, ὁ, *debtor, one who is under obligation.* TH: pred. nom. to the implied subject of εἰσὶν.

[10] πνευματικός, ή, όν, *spiritual.* TH: subst. adj.; *spiritual things.*

[11] κοινωνέω, *I share, participate.* MH: the ε lengthens to η before the tense formative.

[12] ὀφείλω, *I owe,* ***am obligated***.

[13] σαρκικός, ή, όν, *material, fleshly.* TH: subst. adj.; *material things.*

[14] λειτουργέω, *I serve.* TH: complementary inf. with ὀφείλουσιν.

[15] ἐπιτελέω, *I complete, finish.*

[16] σφραγίζω, *I seal.* MH: root ends in δ; δ + σ = σ.

[17] MH: from ἀπέρχομαι. Fut. tense stem is ἀπελευθ; θ + σ = σ.

[18] Σπανία, ας, ἡ, *Spain.*

[19] πλήρωμα, ατος, τό, *fullness.*

[20] εὐλογία, ας, ἡ, *praise, blessing.*

[21] MH: from ἔρχομαι. Fut. tense stem is ἐλευθ; θ + σ = σ.

30 Παρακαλῶ δὲ ὑμᾶς, ἀδελφοί, διὰ τοῦ κυρίου ἡμῶν
Ἰησοῦ Χριστοῦ καὶ διὰ τῆς ἀγάπης τοῦ πνεύματος
συναγωνίσασθαί[1] μοι[2] ἐν ταῖς προσευχαῖς[3] ὑπὲρ ἐμοῦ
πρὸς τὸν θεόν, **31** ἵνα ῥυσθῶ[4] ἀπὸ τῶν ἀπειθούντων[5] ἐν τῇ
Ἰουδαίᾳ[6] ⸀καὶ ἡ διακονία[7] μου ἡ[8] εἰς Ἰερουσαλὴμ
εὐπρόσδεκτος[9] ⸂τοῖς ἁγίοις γένηται⸃,[10] **32** ἵνα ἐν[11] χαρᾷ
⸀ἐλθὼν[12] πρὸς ὑμᾶς διὰ θελήματος ⸀θεοῦ συνανα-
παύσωμαι[13] ὑμῖν.[14] **33** ὁ δὲ θεὸς τῆς εἰρήνης μετὰ πάντων
ὑμῶν· ἀμήν.

---

[1] συναγωνίζομαι, *I contend along with*. TH: complementary inf. with Παρακαλῶ.

[2] TH: dat. of association; *with*.

[3] προσευχή, ῆς, ἡ, *prayer*.

[4] ῥύομαι, *I save, rescue, deliver*. MH: aor. pass. subj. 1st sg.

[5] ἀπειθέω, *I disobey, am disobedient*. MH: the root (ἀπειθε) ends in a vowel, so the connecting vowel contracts (ε + ο = ου).

[6] Ἰουδαία, ας, ἡ, *Judea*.

[7] διακονία, ας, ἡ, *ministry, service*.

[8] TH: ἡ substantivizes the prep. phrase εἰς Ἰερουσαλήμ.

[9] εὐπρόσδεκτος, ον, *acceptable*. TH: pred. adj. to διακονία.

[10] MH: 2nd aor. of γίνομαι; root is γεν.

[11] TH: ἐν is indicating manner; *with*.

[12] MH: from ἔρχομαι; root is ἐλθ.

[13] συναναπαύομαι, *I rest with, am refreshed*.

[14] TH: dat. of agency; *by*.

15:4 εἰς Treg NA28 RP] πάντα εἰς WH
- **ἐγράφη** WH Treg NA28] προεγράφη RP

5 Χριστὸν Ἰησοῦν WH NA28 RP] Ἰησοῦν Χριστὸν Treg
5 Χριστὸν Ἰησοῦν WH NA28 RP] Ἰησοῦν Χριστὸν Treg
7 ὑμᾶς Treg NA28 RP] ἡμᾶς WH
- **τοῦ** WH Treg NA28] – RP

8 γὰρ WH Treg NA28] δέ RP
- **Χριστὸν** WH Treg NA28] + Ἰησοῦν RP
- **γεγενῆσθαι** WH NA28 RP] γένεσθαι Treg

11 πάντα τὰ ἔθνη τὸν κύριον WH Treg NA28] τὸν κύριον πάντα τὰ ἔθνη RP
11 πάντα τὰ ἔθνη τὸν κύριον WH Treg NA28] τὸν κύριον πάντα τὰ ἔθνη RP
- **ἐπαινεσάτωσαν** WH Treg NA28] ἐπαινέσατε RP

14 πάσης Treg RP] + τῆς WH NA28
- **ἀλλήλους** WH Treg NA28] ἄλλους RP

15 τολμηρότερον NA28 RP] τολμηροτέρως WH Treg
- **ὑμῖν** WH Treg NA28] + ἀδελφοί RP
- **ὑπὸ** NA28 RP] ἀπὸ WH Treg

16 Χριστοῦ Ἰησοῦ WH Treg NA28] Ἰησοῦ Χριστοῦ RP
16 Χριστοῦ Ἰησοῦ WH Treg NA28] Ἰησοῦ Χριστοῦ RP
17 τὴν WH Treg NA28] – RP
18 τι λαλεῖν WH Treg NA28] λαλεῖν τι RP
18 τι λαλεῖν WH Treg NA28] λαλεῖν τι RP
19 πνεύματος NIV] + ἁγίου WH Treg; + θεοῦ RP NA28
20 φιλοτιμούμενον WH NA28 RP] φιλοτιμοῦμαι Treg
21 Οἷς … αὐτοῦ ὄψονται Treg NA28 RP] Ὄψονται οἷς … αὐτοῦ WH
21 Οἷς … αὐτοῦ ὄψονται Treg NA28 RP] Ὄψονται οἷς … αὐτοῦ WH
23 ἱκανῶν WH Treg] πολλῶν NA28 RP
24 ἂν WH Treg NA28] ἐὰν RP
- **Σπανίαν** WH Treg NA28] + ἐλεύσομαι πρὸς ὑμᾶς RP

27 εἰσὶν αὐτῶν WH Treg NA28] αὐτῶν εἰσὶν RP
27 εἰσὶν αὐτῶν WH Treg NA28] αὐτῶν εἰσὶν RP
28 εἰς WH Treg NA28] + τὴν RP
29 εὐλογίας WH Treg NA28] + τοῦ εὐαγγελίου τοῦ RP
31 καὶ WH Treg NA28] + ἵνα RP
- **τοῖς ἁγίοις γένηται** WH Treg NA28] γένηται τοῖς ἁγίοις RP
- **τοῖς ἁγίοις γένηται** WH Treg NA28] γένηται τοῖς ἁγίοις RP

32 ἐλθὼν WH NA28] ἔλθω Treg RP
- **θεοῦ** WH NA28] + καὶ Treg RP

ROMANS 16

New Vocabulary by Frequency [Chapter, Book, SBLGNT Occurrences]

ἀδελφή, ῆς, ἡ, *sister* [2, 2, 25]
ἄκακος, ον, *innocent* [1, 1, 2]
ἀκέραιος, ον, *pure, innocent* [1, 1, 3]
Ἀκύλας, ὁ *Aquila* [1, 1, 6]
Ἀμπλιᾶτος, ου, ὁ, *Ampliatus* [1, 1, 1]
Ἀνδρόνικος, ου, ὁ, *Andronicus* [1, 1, 1]
ἀξίως, *worthily* [1, 1, 6]
ἀπαρχή, ῆς, ἡ, *first fruit* [1, 3, 9]
Ἀπελλῆς, οῦ, ὁ, *Apelles* [1, 1, 1]
Ἀριστόβουλος, ου, ὁ, *Aristobulus* [1, 1, 1]
Ἀσία, ας, ἡ, *Asia* [1, 1, 18]
Ἀσύγκριτος, ου, ὁ, *Asyncritus* [1, 1, 1]
ἀφικνέομαι, *I reach, arrive* [1, 1, 1]
Γάϊος, ου, ὁ, *Gaius* [1, 1, 5]
διάκονος, ου, ὁ, *servant, minister* [1, 4, 29]
διδαχή, ῆς, ἡ, *teaching* [1, 2, 30]
διχοστασία, ας, ἡ, *dissension, division* [1, 1, 2]
δόκιμος, ον, *approved* [1, 2, 7]
δουλεύω, *I serve, am a slave* [1, 7, 25]
ἐκκλίνω, *I avoid, turn away* [1, 2, 3]
ἐκλεκτός, ή, όν, *chosen* [1, 2, 23]
ἐξαπατάω, *I deceive* [1, 2, 6]
Ἐπαίνετος, ου, ὁ, *Epaenetus* [1, 1, 1]
ἐπίσημος, ον, *prominent, outstanding* [1, 1, 2]
ἐπιστολή, ῆς, ἡ, *letter, epistle* [1, 1, 24]
Ἔραστος, ου, ὁ, *Erastus* [1, 1, 3]
Ἑρμᾶς, οῦ, ὁ, *Hermas* [1, 1, 1]
Ἑρμῆς, οῦ, ὁ, *Hermes* [1, 1, 2]
εὐλογία, ας, ἡ, *praise, blessing* [1, 2, 16]
εὐχαριστέω, *I give thanks* [1, 5, 38]
Ἡρῳδίων, ωνος, ὁ, *Herodion* [1, 1, 1]
Ἰάσων, ονος, ὁ, *Jason* [1, 1, 5]
Ἰουλία, ας, ἡ, *Julia* [1, 1, 1]
Ἰουνιᾶς, ᾶ, ὁ, *Junias* [1, 1, 1]
Κεγχρεαί, ῶν, αἱ, *Cenchreae* [1, 1, 2]
κοιλία, ας, ἡ, *belly, stomach* [1, 1, 23]

κοπιάω, *I work hard, toil* [3, 3, 23]
Κούαρτος, ου, ὁ, *Quartus* [1, 1, 1]
Λούκιος, ου, ὁ, *Lucius* [1, 1, 2]
μανθάνω, *I learn* [1, 1, 25]
Μαρία, ας, ἡ, *Mary* [1, 1, 27]
Νάρκισσος, ου, ὁ, *Narcissus* [1, 1, 1]
Νηρεύς, έως, ὁ, *Nereus* [1, 1, 1]
ξένος, η, ον, *strange, foreign* [1, 1, 14]
οἰκονόμος, ου, ὁ, *steward, administrator* [1, 1, 10]
Ὀλυμπᾶς, ᾶ, ὁ, *Olympas* [1, 1, 1]
Οὐρβανός, οῦ, ὁ, *Urbanus* [1, 1, 1]
παρίστημι, *I present, demonstrate* [1, 8, 41]
Πατροβᾶς, οῦ, ὁ, *Patrobas* [1, 1, 1]
Περσίς, ίδος, ἡ, *Persis* [1, 1, 1]
πρᾶγμα, ατος, τό, *thing, matter* [1, 1, 11]
Πρίσκα, ης, ἡ, *Prisca* [1, 1, 3]
πρό, *before* [1, 1, 47]
προσδέχομαι, *I receive, welcome* [1, 1, 14]
προστάτις, ιδος, ἡ, *patron* [1, 1, 1]
Ῥοῦφος, ου, ὁ, *Rufus* [1, 1, 2]
Σατανᾶς, ᾶ, ὁ, *Satan* [1, 1, 36]
σκάνδαλον, ου, τό, *trap, stumbling block* [1, 4, 15]
σκοπέω, *I look out for, pay attention to* [1, 1, 6]
σοφός, ή, όν, *wise, intelligent* [1, 3, 19]
Στάχυς, υος, ὁ, *Stachys* [1, 1, 1]
συγγενής, ές, *related, of the same race* [3, 4, 11]
συναιχμάλωτος, ου, ὁ, *fellow prisoner* [1, 1, 3]
συνεργός, όν, *working together* [3, 3, 13]
συνίστημι, *I bring together* [1, 3, 6]
συντρίβω, *I crush, shatter* [1, 1, 7]
Σωσίπατρος, ου, ὁ, *Sosipater* [1, 1, 1]
τάχος, ους, τό, *speed* [1, 1, 8]
Τέρτιος, ου, ὁ, *Tertius* [1, 1, 1]
Τιμόθεος, ου, ὁ, *Timothy* [1, 1, 24]
τράχηλος, ου, ὁ, *neck* [1, 1, 7]
Τρύφαινα, ης, ἡ, *Tryphena* [1, 1, 1]
Τρυφῶσα, ης, ἡ, *Tryphosa* [1, 1, 1]
ὑπακοή, ῆς, ἡ, *obedience* [1, 6, 14]
ὑποτίθημι, *I lay down* [1, 1, 2]
φίλημα, ατος, τό, *kiss* [1, 1, 7]
Φιλόλογος, οῦ, ὁ, *Philologus* [1, 1, 1]

Φλέγων, οντος, ὁ, *Phlegon* [1, 1, 1]
Φοίβη, ης, ἡ, *Phoebe* [1, 1, 1]
χρῄζω, *I need* [1, 1, 5]
χρηστολογία, ας, ἡ, *smooth talk* [1, 1, 1]

16.1 Συνίστημι[1] δὲ ὑμῖν Φοίβην[2] τὴν ἀδελφὴν[3] ἡμῶν,
οὖσαν[4] ⸀καὶ διάκονον[5] τῆς ἐκκλησίας τῆς[6] ἐν Κεγχρεαῖς,[7]
2 ἵνα ⸂αὐτὴν προσδέξησθε[8]⸃ ἐν κυρίῳ ἀξίως[9] τῶν ἁγίων, καὶ
παραστῆτε[10] αὐτῇ ἐν ᾧ ἂν[11] ὑμῶν χρῄζῃ[12] πράγματι,[13] καὶ
γὰρ αὐτὴ προστάτις[14] πολλῶν ἐγενήθη[15] καὶ ⸂ἐμοῦ
αὐτοῦ[16]⸃.

3 Ἀσπάσασθε[17] Πρίσκαν[18] καὶ Ἀκύλαν[19] τοὺς
συνεργούς[20] μου ἐν Χριστῷ Ἰησοῦ, **4** οἵτινες ὑπὲρ τῆς
ψυχῆς μου τὸν ἑαυτῶν τράχηλον[21] ὑπέθηκαν,[22] οἷς οὐκ
ἐγὼ μόνος εὐχαριστῶ[23] ἀλλὰ καὶ πᾶσαι αἱ ἐκκλησίαι τῶν
ἐθνῶν, **5** καὶ τὴν κατ᾽ οἶκον αὐτῶν ἐκκλησίαν.
ἀσπάσασθε Ἐπαίνετον[24] τὸν ἀγαπητόν μου, ὅς ἐστιν

---

[1] συνίστημι, *I bring together*, ***commend***.
[2] Φοίβη, ης, ἡ, *Phoebe*.
[3] ἀδελφή, ῆς, ἡ, *sister*.
[4] MH: pres. act. prtc. acc. fem. sg. of εἰμί. TH: *who is*.
[5] διάκονος, ου, ὁ, *servant, minister*.
[6] TH: τῆς substantivizes the prep. phrase ἐν Κεγχρεαῖς.
[7] Κεγχρεαί, ῶν, αἱ, *Cenchreae*.
[8] προσδέχομαι, *I receive, welcome*. MH: χ + σ › ξ.
[9] ἀξίως, *worthily*, ***in a manner worthy (of)***.
[10] παρίστημι, *I present, demonstrate*. MH: aor. act. subj. 2nd pl.; root is παραστα.
[11] TH: ἐν ᾧ ἂν, *in whatever*.
[12] χρῄζω, *I need*.
[13] πρᾶγμα, ατος, τό, *thing, matter*. TH: ἐν ᾧ ἂν ὑμῶν … πράγματι, *in whatever of your things*.
[14] προστάτις, ιδος, ἡ, *patron*. TH: προστάτις is a pred. nom. to αὐτή.
[15] MH: 2nd aor. of γίνομαι; root is γεν.
[16] TH: αὐτοῦ is intensive; ἐμοῦ αὐτοῦ, *myself*.
[17] MH: from ἀσπάζομαι. The root is ἀσπαδ; δ + σ = σ. This aor. mid. impv. form occurs 16 times in Rom 16.
[18] Πρίσκα, ης, ἡ, *Prisca*.
[19] Ἀκύλας, ὁ *Aquila*.
[20] συνεργός, όν, *working together*, ***fellow worker***.
[21] τράχηλος, ου, ὁ, *neck*.
[22] ὑποτίθημι, *I lay down*, ***risk***. MH: aor. act. indic. 3rd pl.
[23] εὐχαριστέω, *I give thanks*.
[24] Ἐπαίνετος, ου, ὁ, *Epaenetus*.

ἀπαρχὴ[1] τῆς ⸀Ἀσίας[2] εἰς Χριστόν. **6** ἀσπάσασθε ⸀Μαριάμ,[3]
ἥτις πολλὰ ἐκοπίασεν [4] εἰς ⸀ὑμᾶς. **7** ἀσπάσασθε
Ἀνδρόνικον [5] καὶ ⸀Ἰουνίαν [6] τοὺς συγγενεῖς [7] μου καὶ
συναιχμαλώτους[8] μου, οἵτινές εἰσιν ἐπίσημοι [9] ἐν τοῖς
ἀποστόλοις, οἳ καὶ πρὸ [10] ἐμοῦ ⸀γέγοναν [11] ἐν Χριστῷ.
8 ἀσπάσασθε ⸀Ἀμπλιᾶτον[12] τὸν ἀγαπητόν μου ἐν κυρίῳ.
9 ἀσπάσασθε Οὐρβανὸν[13] τὸν συνεργὸν[14] ἡμῶν ἐν Χριστῷ
καὶ Στάχυν[15] τὸν ἀγαπητόν μου. **10** ἀσπάσασθε Ἀπελλῆν[16]
τὸν δόκιμον [17] ἐν Χριστῷ. ἀσπάσασθε τοὺς ἐκ τῶν [18]
Ἀριστοβούλου. [19] **11** ἀσπάσασθε Ἡρῳδίωνα [20] τὸν
⸀συγγενῆ [21] μου. ἀσπάσασθε τοὺς ἐκ τῶν Ναρκίσσου [22]
τοὺς ὄντας [23] ἐν κυρίῳ. **12** ἀσπάσασθε Τρύφαιναν [24] καὶ

---

[1] ἀπαρχή, ῆς, ἡ, *first fruit.*
[2] Ἀσία, ας, ἡ, *Asia.*
[3] Μαρία, ας, ἡ, *Mary.* NA has Μαρίαν.
[4] κοπιάω, *I work hard, toil.*
[5] Ἀνδρόνικος, ου, ὁ, *Andronicus.*
[6] Ἰουνιᾶς, ᾶ, ὁ, *Junias.* NA has Ἰουνιᾶν.
[7] συγγενής, ές, *related, of the same race,* ***compatriot.***
[8] συναιχμάλωτος, ου, ὁ, *fellow prisoner.*
[9] ἐπίσημος, ον, *prominent, outstanding.*
[10] πρό, *before.*
[11] MH: 2nd pf. of γίνομαι. The root (γεν) becomes γον due to ablaut.
[12] Ἀμπλιᾶτος, ου, ὁ, *Ampliatus.*
[13] Οὐρβανός, οῦ, ὁ, *Urbanus.*
[14] συνεργός, όν, *working together,* ***fellow worker.***
[15] Στάχυς, υος, ὁ, *Stachys.*
[16] Ἀπελλῆς, οῦ, ὁ, *Apelles.*
[17] δόκιμος, ον, *approved.*
[18] TH: τοὺς ἐκ τῶν, *those from the house/family of.* This construction occurs 2 times in Rom 16.
[19] Ἀριστόβουλος, ου, ὁ, *Aristobulus.*
[20] Ἡρῳδίων, ωνος, ὁ, *Herodion.*
[21] συγγενής, ές, *related, of the same race,* ***compatriot.***
[22] Νάρκισσος, ου, ὁ, *Narcissus.*
[23] MH: pres. act. prtc. acc. masc. pl. of εἰμί. TH: *who are.*
[24] Τρύφαινα, ης, ἡ, *Tryphena.*

Τρυφῶσαν [1] τὰς κοπιώσας [2] ἐν κυρίῳ. ἀσπάσασθε
Περσίδα [3] τὴν ἀγαπητήν, ἥτις πολλὰ ἐκοπίασεν [4] ἐν
κυρίῳ. **13** ἀσπάσασθε Ῥοῦφον[5] τὸν ἐκλεκτὸν[6] ἐν κυρίῳ καὶ
τὴν μητέρα αὐτοῦ καὶ ἐμοῦ. **14** ἀσπάσασθε Ἀσύγκριτον,[7]
Φλέγοντα,[8] ˹Ἑρμῆν,[9] Πατροβᾶν,[10] Ἑρμᾶν[11]˺ καὶ τοὺς σὺν
αὐτοῖς ἀδελφούς. **15** ἀσπάσασθε Φιλόλογον [12] καὶ
Ἰουλίαν, [13] Νηρέα [14] καὶ τὴν ἀδελφὴν [15] αὐτοῦ, καὶ
Ὀλυμπᾶν [16] καὶ τοὺς σὺν αὐτοῖς πάντας ἁγίους.
16 Ἀσπάσασθε ἀλλήλους ἐν φιλήματι[17] ἁγίῳ. Ἀσπάζονται
ὑμᾶς αἱ ἐκκλησίαι ˹πᾶσαι τοῦ Χριστοῦ.

17 Παρακαλῶ δὲ ὑμᾶς, ἀδελφοί, σκοπεῖν[18] τοὺς[19] τὰς
διχοστασίας[20] καὶ τὰ σκάνδαλα[21] παρὰ τὴν διδαχὴν[22] ἣν
ὑμεῖς ἐμάθετε[23] ποιοῦντας[19], καὶ ˹ἐκκλίνετε[24] ἀπ᾽ αὐτῶν·

---

[1] Τρυφῶσα, ης, ἡ, *Tryphosa.*
[2] κοπιάω, *I work hard, toil.*
[3] Περσίς, ίδος, ἡ, *Persis.*
[4] κοπιάω, *I work hard, toil.*
[5] Ῥοῦφος, ου, ὁ, *Rufus.*
[6] ἐκλεκτός, ή, όν, *chosen.*
[7] Ἀσύγκριτος, ου, ὁ, *Asyncritus.*
[8] Φλέγων, οντος, ὁ, *Phlegon.*
[9] Ἑρμῆς, οῦ, ὁ, *Hermes.*
[10] Πατροβᾶς, οῦ, ὁ, *Patrobas.*
[11] Ἑρμᾶς, οῦ, ὁ, *Hermas.*
[12] Φιλόλογος, οῦ, ὁ, *Philologus.*
[13] Ἰουλία, ας, ἡ, *Julia.*
[14] Νηρεύς, έως, ὁ, *Nereus.*
[15] ἀδελφή, ῆς, ἡ, *sister.*
[16] Ὀλυμπᾶς, ᾶ, ὁ, *Olympas.*
[17] φίλημα, ατος, τό, *kiss.*
[18] σκοπέω, *I look out for, pay attention to.*
[19] TH: A great distance exists: τοὺς … ποιοῦντας, *the ones doing* or *making.*
[20] διχοστασία, ας, ἡ, *dissension, division.*
[21] σκάνδαλον, ου, τό, *trap, offense,* ***stumbling block.***
[22] διδαχή, ῆς, ἡ, *teaching.*
[23] μανθάνω, *I learn.* MH: 2nd aor. verb; aor. tense stem is μαθ.
[24] ἐκκλίνω, *I avoid, turn away.*

18 οἱ γὰρ τοιοῦτοι τῷ κυρίῳ ⸀ἡμῶν Χριστῷ οὐ δουλεύουσιν[1]
ἀλλὰ τῇ ἑαυτῶν κοιλίᾳ,[2] καὶ διὰ τῆς χρηστολογίας[3] καὶ
εὐλογίας[4] ἐξαπατῶσι[5] τὰς καρδίας τῶν ἀκάκων.[6] **19** ἡ γὰρ
ὑμῶν ὑπακοὴ[7] εἰς πάντας ἀφίκετο·[8] ⸂ἐφ᾽ ὑμῖν οὖν χαίρω⸃,
θέλω δὲ ὑμᾶς ⸀σοφοὺς[9] εἶναι[10] εἰς τὸ ἀγαθόν, ἀκεραίους[11]
δὲ εἰς τὸ κακόν. **20** ὁ δὲ θεὸς τῆς εἰρήνης συντρίψει[12] τὸν
Σατανᾶν[13] ὑπὸ τοὺς πόδας ὑμῶν ἐν τάχει.[14] ἡ χάρις τοῦ
κυρίου ἡμῶν Ἰησοῦ ⸀Χριστοῦ[15] μεθ᾽ ὑμῶν.

21 ⸆Ἀσπάζεται ὑμᾶς Τιμόθεος[16] ὁ συνεργός[17] μου, καὶ
Λούκιος[18] καὶ Ἰάσων[19] καὶ Σωσίπατρος[20] οἱ συγγενεῖς[21]
μου. **22** ἀσπάζομαι ὑμᾶς ἐγὼ Τέρτιος[22] ὁ γράψας τὴν
ἐπιστολὴν[23] ἐν κυρίῳ. **23** ἀσπάζεται ὑμᾶς Γάϊος[24] ὁ ξένος[25]

---

[1] δουλεύω, *I serve, am a slave*. TH: δουλεύω takes a dat. dir. obj.

[2] κοιλία, ας, ἡ, *belly, stomach,* ***appetite***.

[3] χρηστολογία, ας, ἡ, *smooth talk*.

[4] εὐλογία, ας, ἡ, *praise, blessing,* ***flattery***.

[5] ἐξαπατάω, *I deceive*. MH: the root (ἐξαπατα) ends in a vowel, so the connecting vowel contracts (α + ου = ω)

[6] ἄκακος, ον, *innocent*.

[7] ὑπακοή, ῆς, ἡ, *obedience*.

[8] ἀφικνέομαι, *I reach, arrive*. MH: root is ἀφικ. TH: ἡ γὰρ ὑμῶν ὑπακοὴ εἰς πάντας ἀφίκετο, *for your obedience is known to all*.

[9] σοφός, ή, όν, *wise, intelligent*.

[10] TH: complementary inf. with θέλω.

[11] ἀκέραιος, ον, *pure, innocent*.

[12] συντρίβω, *I crush, shatter*. MH: β + σ = ψ.

[13] Σατανᾶς, ᾶ, ὁ, *Satan*.

[14] τάχος, ους, τό, *speed*. TH: ἐν τάχει, *soon*.

[15] NA omits Χριστοῦ.

[16] Τιμόθεος, ου, ὁ, *Timothy*.

[17] συνεργός, όν, *working together,* ***fellow worker***.

[18] Λούκιος, ου, ὁ, *Lucius*.

[19] Ἰάσων, ονος, ὁ, *Jason*.

[20] Σωσίπατρος, ου, ὁ, *Sosipater*.

[21] συγγενής, ές, *related, of the same race,* ***compatriot***.

[22] Τέρτιος, ου, ὁ, *Tertius*. TH: app. to ἐγὼ and followed by another app. phrase

[23] ἐπιστολή, ῆς, ἡ, *letter, epistle*.

[24] Γάϊος, ου, ὁ, *Gaius*.

[25] ξένος, η, ον, *strange, foreign;* ***host***.

μου καὶ ⸂ὅλης τῆς ἐκκλησίας⸃. ἀσπάζεται ὑμᾶς Ἔραστος[1]
ὁ οἰκονόμος[2] τῆς πόλεως καὶ Κούαρτος[3] ὁ ἀδελφός.[4]
24 ⸂Ἡ χάρις τοῦ κυρίου ἡμῶν Ἰησοῦ Χριστοῦ μετὰ
πάντων ὑμῶν.⸃ ⸀Ἀμήν.[5]

⸀ **16:1 καὶ** WH NA28] – Treg RP
⸂ **2 αὐτὴν προσδέξησθε** NA28 RP] προσδέξησθε αὐτὴν WH Treg
⸃ **2 αὐτὴν προσδέξησθε** NA28 RP] προσδέξησθε αὐτὴν WH Treg
- **ἐμοῦ αὐτοῦ** WH Treg NA28] αὐτοῦ ἐμοῦ RP
- **ἐμοῦ αὐτοῦ** WH Treg NA28] αὐτοῦ ἐμοῦ RP

5 Ἀσίας WH Treg NA28] Ἀχαΐας RP
6 Μαριάμ RP] Μαρίαν WH Treg NA28
- **ὑμᾶς** WH Treg NA28] ἡμᾶς RP

7 Ἰουνίαν WH Treg RP] Ἰουνιᾶν NA28
- **γέγοναν** WH Treg NA28] γεγόνασιν RP

8 Ἀμπλιᾶτον WH NA28 Treg] Ἀμπλίαν RP
11 συγγενῆ WH NA28 RP] συγγενῆν Treg
14 Ἑρμῆν Πατροβᾶν Ἑρμᾶν WH Treg NA28] Ἑρμᾶν Πατρόβαν Ἑρμῆν RP
14 Ἑρμῆν Πατροβᾶν Ἑρμᾶν WH Treg NA28] Ἑρμᾶν Πατρόβαν Ἑρμῆν RP
16 πᾶσαι WH Treg NA28] – RP
17 ἐκκλίνετε WH Treg NA28] ἐκκλίνατε RP
18 ἡμῶν WH Treg NA28] + Ἰησοῦ RP
19 ἐφ' ὑμῖν οὖν χαίρω WH Treg NA28] Χαίρω οὖν τὸ ἐφ' ὑμῖν RP
19 ἐφ' ὑμῖν οὖν χαίρω WH Treg NA28] Χαίρω οὖν τὸ ἐφ' ὑμῖν RP
- **σοφοὺς** Treg NA28] + μὲν WH RP

20 Χριστοῦ Treg RP] – WH NA28
21 Ἀσπάζεται WH Treg NA28] Ἀσπάζονται RP
23 ὅλης τῆς ἐκκλησίας WH Treg NA28] τῆς ἐκκλησίας ὅλης RP
23 ὅλης τῆς ἐκκλησίας WH Treg NA28] τῆς ἐκκλησίας ὅλης RP
24 Ἡ χάρις ... ὑμῶν RP] – WH Treg NA28
24 Ἡ χάρις ... ὑμῶν RP] – WH Treg NA28
- **Ἀμήν** RP] 25 Τῷ δὲ δυναμένῳ ὑμᾶς στηρίξαι κατὰ τὸ εὐαγγέλιόν μου καὶ τὸ κήρυγμα Ἰησοῦ Χριστοῦ, κατὰ ἀποκάλυψιν μυστηρίου χρόνοις αἰωνίοις σεσιγημένου, 26 φανερωθέντος δὲ νῦν διά τε γραφῶν προφητικῶν κατ' ἐπιταγὴν τοῦ αἰωνίου θεοῦ εἰς ὑπακοὴν πίστεως εἰς πάντα τὰ ἔθνη γνωρισθέντος, 27 μόνῳ σοφῷ θεῷ διὰ Ἰησοῦ Χριστοῦ ᾧ ἡ δόξα εἰς τοὺς αἰῶνας· ἀμήν. WH Treg NA28

---

[1] Ἔραστος, ου, ὁ, *Erastus*.
[2] οἰκονόμος, ου, ὁ, *steward, administrator*.
[3] Κούαρτος, ου, ὁ, *Quartus*.
[4] TH: app. to Κούαρτος.
[5] NA omits v. 24 and adds another paragraph (16:25–27), for which see the text critical notes immediately above for 16:24.

APPENDICES

Appendix I

VOCABULARY 50 TIMES OF MORE SORTED BY FREQUENCY

19796	ὁ, ἡ, τό	*the; (sub.) he, she, thing*
8984	καί	*and; (adv.) also, even*
5569	αὐτός, ή, ό	*he, she, it; (adj.) -self, same*
2899	σύ, σοῦ; ὑμεῖς, ὑμῶν	*you; you all*
2777	δέ	*but, rather, and, now*
2737	ἐν	*(+dat) in, with, among*
2582	ἐγώ, (ἐ)μοῦ; ἡμεῖς, ἡμῶν	*I; we*
2458	εἰμί	*I am, exist, happen*
2352	λέγω	*I say, speak, claim*
1857	εἰς	*(+acc) to, into*
1621	οὐ, οὐκ, οὐχ	*not, no*
1407	ὅς, ἥ, ὅ	*who, which, that*
1387	οὗτος, αὕτη, τοῦτο	*this; (sub.) he, she, this one*
1307	θεός, οῦ, ὁ and ἡ	*God, god, divine one*
1294	ὅτι	*that, because*
1243	πᾶς, πᾶσα, πᾶν	*every, each, all, whole*
1039	γάρ	*for, because, since*
1038	μή	*not, no; (+subj.) in order that…not*
913	ἐκ, ἐξ	*(+gen) from, out from*
911	Ἰησοῦς, οῦ, ὁ	*Joshua, Jesus*
887	ἐπί	*(+gen/dat/acc) on, near, toward*
714	κύριος, ου, ὁ	*Lord, master, owner*
707	ἔχω	*I have, am*
698	πρός	*(+acc) to, toward, with*
667	γίνομαι	*I am, become, happen*
666	διά	*(+gen) through; (+acc) because of*
663	ἵνα	*in order that, so that*

645	ἀπό	*(+gen) from, away from*
638	ἀλλά	*but, yet, rather*
633	ἔρχομαι	*I come, go*
568	ποιέω	*I make, do*
551	τίς, τί	*who? which? what?*
550	ἄνθρωπος, ου, ὁ	*man, human*
534	τις, τι	*someone, something*
528	Χριστός, οῦ, ὁ	*Messiah, Anointed One, Christ*
504	ὡς	*as, like*
502	εἰ	*if, whether*
495	οὖν	*therefore, then*
470	κατά	*(+gen) against, down; (+acc) according to*
470	μετά	*(+gen) with; (+acc) after, behind*
453	ὁράω	*I see, perceive, experience*
428	ἀκούω	*I hear, obey, listen*
415	πολύς, πολλή, πολύ	*much, many*
415	δίδωμι	*I give, entrust*
413	πατήρ, πατρός, ὁ	*father*
389	ἡμέρα, ας, ἡ	*day, time*
379	πνεῦμα, ατος, τό	*spirit, breath*
375	υἱός, οῦ, ὁ	*son*
346	ἤ	*or, than*
344	εἷς, μία, ἕν	*one, single*
342	ἀδελφός , οῦ, ὁ	*brother*
332	περί	*(+gen) concerning; (+acc) around*
330	ἐάν	*if, whenever*
330	λόγος, ου, ὁ	*word, speech, matter*
321	ἑαυτοῦ, ῆς, οῦ	*himself, herself, itself*
320	οἶδα	*I know, understand*
297	λαλέω	*I speak*
273	οὐρανός, οῦ, ὁ	*sky, heaven*
262	μαθητής, οῦ, ὁ	*disciple, student*

258	λαμβάνω	*I take, receive*
250	γῆ, γῆς, ἡ	*land, earth*
243	ἐκεῖνος, η, ο	*that; (sub.) he, she, that one*
243	μέγας, μεγάλη, μέγα	*large, great*
242	πίστις, εως, ἡ	*belief, faithfulness, trust, fidelity, faith*
241	πιστεύω	*I believe, trust*
233	ἅγιος, ία, ον	*holy, pure, devout; (sub.) Saint*
232	ἀποκρίνομαι	*I answer*
229	ὄνομα, ατος, τό	*name*
227	οὐδείς, οὐδεμία, οὐδέν	*no; (sub.) no one, nothing*
221	γινώσκω	*I know, understand, learn*
221	ὑπό	*(+gen) by; (+acc) underneath*
217	ἐξέρχομαι	*I go out, exit*
216	ἀνήρ, ἀνδρός, ὁ	*man, husband*
216	γυνή, αικός, ἡ	*woman, wife*
213	τέ	*and, so*
209	δύναμαι	*I am able*
208	θέλω	*I wish, want*
207	οὕτω/οὕτως	*thus, so*
200	ἰδού	*Look!, Notice!, See!*
195	Ἰουδαῖος, αία, αῖον	*Jewish; (sub.) Jew*
194	νόμος, ου, ὁ	*law, custom*
193	εἰσέρχομαι	*I go into, enter*
193	παρά	*(+gen) along side, from; (+dat) beside, near; (+acc) out from, by*
192	γράφω	*I write*
185	κόσμος, ου, ὁ	*world, universe, order*
182	καθώς	*as, just as*
178	μέν	*however, but, indeed*
176	χείρ, χειρός, ἡ	*hand*
176	εὑρίσκω	*I find, discover*

175	ἄγγελος, ου, ὁ	*messenger, envoy, angel*
174	ὄχλος, ου, ὁ	*crowd, multitude*
172	ἁμαρτία, ίας, ἡ	*sin, guilt, failure*
170	ἄν	*ever [conditional particle, indicates possibility]*
169	ἔργον, ου, τό	*work, accomplishment*
165	δόξα, ης, ἡ	*splendor, glory; reputation*
163	πόλις, εως, ἡ	*town, city*
162	βασιλεία, ας, ἡ	*kingdom, providence, dominion*
160	ἔθνος, ους, τό	*nation, culture group, people*
159	τότε	*at that time, then*
158	ἐσθίω	*I eat, drink, consume*
158	Παῦλος, ου, ὁ	*Paul*
156	καρδία, ας, ἡ	*heart*
156	Πέτρος, ου, ὁ	*Peter*
155	πρῶτος, η, ον	*first, most prominent*
155	χάρις, ιτος, ἡ	*grace, thankfulness, kindness*
154	ἄλλος, η, ο	*other, another*
154	ἵστημι	*I set, place, establish*
153	πορεύομαι	*I go, walk*
150	ὑπέρ	*(+gen) on behalf of, for; (+acc) over, beyond*
148	καλέω	*I call, summon, invite*
147	σάρξ, σαρκός, ἡ	*flesh, muscle, body*
145	νῦν	*now, currently, presently*
145	ἕως	*while, until, up to the point of, as far as*
144	ὅστις, ἥτις, ὅ τι	*whoever, whichever, any one who*
144	προφήτης, ου, ὁ	*prophet*
143	ἐγείρω	*I rise, raise*
143	ἀγαπάω	*I love, adore*

143	ἀφίημι	*I release, forgive, reprieve; depart*
143	οὐδέ	*but not, nor, neither*
142	λαός, οῦ, ὁ	*people, populace, multitude*
142	σῶμα, ατος, τό	*body*
141	πάλιν	*again*
140	ζάω	*I live*
139	φωνή, ῆς, ἡ	*voice, sound, communication*
135	δύο	*two*
135	ζωή, ῆς, ἡ	*life, existence*
135	Ἰωάν(ν)ης, ου, ὁ	*John*
133	βλέπω	*I see, observe, notice*
131	ἀποστέλλω	*I send (off)*
129	σύν	*(+dat) with, along with*
128	ἀμήν	*certainly, truly, indeed*
128	νεκρός, ά, όν	*dead*
126	δοῦλος, ου, ὁ	*slave, bondservant*
123	ὅταν	*whenever, when*
122	αἰών, ῶνος, ὁ	*age, era, lifetime*
122	ἀρχιερεύς, έως, ὁ	*high priest, chief priest*
122	βάλλω	*I throw, place*
120	θάνατος, ου, ὁ	*death*
119	δύναμις, εως, ἡ	*power, strength, ability*
119	παραδίδωμι	*I hand over, deliver, grant*
118	μένω	*I remain, continue*
117	ἀπέρχομαι	*I depart, go away*
117	ζητέω	*I seek, search, inquire*
116	ἀγάπη, ης, ἡ	*love, adoration*
115	βασιλεύς, έως, ὁ	*king*
115	κρίνω	*I judge, decide, choose*
114	ἐκκλησία, ας, ἡ	*assembly, gathering, community, church*
114	ἴδιος, ία, ον	*one's own*
113	μόνος, η, ον	*alone, only*

113	οἶκος, ου, ὁ	*house, dwelling, family*
111	ἀποθνῄσκω	*I die, perish*
111	ὅσος, η, ον	*as many as, as much as, as great as*
109	ἀλήθεια, ας, ἡ	*truth, reality*
109	μέλλω	*I am about to, intend*
109	παρακαλέω	*I encourage, call, request*
108	ὅλος, η, ον	*whole, entire*
108	ἀνίστημι	*I raise, resurrect, establish*
106	σῴζω	*I save, rescue, keep safe*
106	ὥρα, ας, ἡ	*hour, time, period, season*
105	πῶς	*how?*
102	ὅτε	*when*
102	ψυχή, ῆς, ἡ	*soul, life*
102	ἐξουσία, ας, ἡ	*authority, capability*
101	ἀγαθός, ή, όν	*good, beneficial*
101	αἴρω	*I lift up, raise up, take away*
101	δεῖ	*I must, am required, ought*
101	ὁδός, οῦ, ἡ	*road, way, path, trip*
101	καλός, ή, όν	*beautiful, good, noble*
100	ἀλλήλων	*one another*
100	ὀφθαλμός, οῦ,	*eye*
100	τίθημι	*I put, place, lay*
99	τέκνον, ου, τό	*child*
97	ἕτερος, α, ον	*other, another*
97	Φαρισαῖος, ου, ὁ	*Pharisee, Separatist*
97	αἷμα, ατος, τό	*blood, bloodshed*
97	ἄρτος, ου, ὁ	*bread, food*
97	γεννάω	*I beget, give birth, parent*
97	διδάσκω	*I teach, instruct*
95	ἐκεῖ	*there*
95	περιπατέω	*I walk (about), live, behave*

95	φοβέω	*I fear, respect; I flee frightened*
94	ἐνώπιον	*before, face to face, in the view of*
94	τόπος, ου, ὁ	*place, position*
93	ἔτι	*yet, still, even now*
93	οἰκία, ας, ἡ	*house, building, family*
93	πούς, ποδός, ὁ	*foot*
91	δικαιοσύνη, ης, ἡ	*righteousness, justice*
91	εἰρήνη, ης, ἡ	*peace, well-being*
91	θάλασσα, ης, ἡ	*lake, sea*
91	κάθημαι	*I sit, settle, reside*
91	μηδείς, μηδεμία, μηδέν	*no, no one, nothing*
90	ἀπόλλυμι	*ruin, destroy, perish*
90	πίπτω	*I fall, collapse*
89	ἀκολουθέω	*I follow, obey*
88	ἑπτά	*seven*
87	οὔτε	*and not, nor, neither*
86	ἄρχω	*I rule, lead, begin*
86	πληρόω	*I fill, complete, fulfill*
85	προσέρχομαι	*I go to, visit, approach*
85	καιρός, οῦ, ὁ	*time, period, season*
85	προσεύχομαι	*I pray, petition a deity*
83	κἀγώ	*and I, I too (crasis καὶ ἐγώ)*
83	μήτηρ, τρός, ἡ	*mother*
83	ὥστε	*so that, therefore, consequently*
82	ἕκαστος, η, ον	*every, each*
81	ἀναβαίνω	*I go up, ascend*
81	ὅπου	*where, whereas, whenever*
81	ἐκβάλλω	*I throw out, expel, reject*
81	μᾶλλον	*more, exceedingly, rather*
80	καταβαίνω	*I go down, descend*
80	Μωϋσῆς, ὁ	*Moses*

79	ἀπόστολος, ου, ὁ	*delegate, ambassador, apostle*
79	δίκαιος, αία, ον	*just, righteous, fair*
79	πέμπω	*I send, despatch*
79	ὑπάγω	*I withdraw, go away*
78	πονηρός, ά, όν	*evil, bad, worthless, sick*
78	στόμα, ατος, τό	*mouth, opening*
77	ἀνοίγω	*I open*
77	βαπτίζω	*I soak, submerge, wash, baptize*
77	Ἰερουσαλήμ, ἡ	*Jerusalem*
77	σημεῖον, ου, τό	*sign, mark, signal, miracle*
76	μαρτυρέω	*I give evidence, witness, testify*
76	πρόσωπον, ου, τό	*face, appearance, expression, presence*
76	ὕδωρ, ατος, τό	*water, rain*
75	εὐαγγέλιον, ου, τό	*good news, gospel*
75	δώδεκα	*twelve*
75	κεφαλή, ῆς, ἡ	*head*
75	Σίμων, ωνος, ὁ	*Simon*
74	ἀποκτείνω, ἀποκτέννω	*I kill, slay*
74	χαίρω	*I am glad, rejoice, welcome*
73	Ἀβραάμ, ὁ	*Abraham*
72	πίνω	*I drink*
72	φῶς, φωτός, τό	*light, torch*
72	ἱερόν, οῦ, τό	*temple, holy place*
71	πῦρ, ός, τό	*fire*
71	τηρέω	*I watch over, guard, keep*
70	αἰτέω	*I ask, demand*
69	αἰώνιος, ον	*long-lasting, eternal*
69	ἄγω	*I lead, carry, arrest, observe*
68	ἐμός, ή, όν	*my, mine*
68	τρεῖς, τρία	*three*

68	Ἰσραήλ, ὁ	*Israel*
68	σάββατον, ου, τό	*Sabbath*
67	ῥῆμα, ατος, τό	*word, saying, thing*
67	πιστός, ή, όν	*faithful, trustworthy, believing*
67	πλοῖον, ου, τό	*boat, ship, vessel*
67	ἀπολύω	*I release, pardon, dismiss*
66	ἐντολή, ῆς, ἡ	*command, order, commandment*
66	κάρπος, ου, ὁ	*fruit, produce, profit*
66	πρεσβύτερος, α, ον	*aged, old;* (Subst.) *elder*
66	φέρω	*I carry, bring, lead*
65	φημί	*I say, declare*
65	εἴτε	*if, either, or, whether*
63	γραμματεύς, έως, ὁ	*scribe, law expert, high official*
63	δαιμόνιον, ου, τό	*demon, evil spirit, inferior divinity*
63	ἐρωτάω	*I ask, inquire, question*
63	ὄρος, ους, τό	*mountain, hill*
62	ἔξω	*outside, out*
62	δοκέω	*I think, suppose, form an opinion; I seem, suppose*
62	θέλημα, ατος, τό	*will, want*
62	θρόνος, ου, ὁ	*chair, seat, throne*
62	Ἱεροσόλυμα, τά	*Jerusalem (city or its inhabitants)*
61	ἀγαπητός, ή, όν	*beloved, dearly loved*
61	Γαλιλαία, ας, ἡ	*Galilee*
61	δοξάζω	*I honor, esteem in high regard, exalt, glorify*
61	κηρύσσω	*I preach, proclaim, announce*
61	νύξ, νυκτός, ἡ	*night (often metaph.)*
61	ὧδε	*here, thus, in this way, exceedingly so*

60	ἤδη	*already, now; by this time*
60	ἱμάτιον, ου, τό	*garment; outer garment*
60	προσκυνέω	*I worship, prostrate myself*
60	ὑπάρχω	*I am present, at one's disposal; I am, exist*
59	ἀσπάζομαι	*I greet, welcome*
59	Δαυίδ, ὁ	*David*
59	διδάσκαλος, ου, ὁ	*teacher, master*
59	λίθος, ου, ὁ	*stone*
59	συνάγω	*I gather together, collect; receive as a guest*
59	χαρά, ᾶς, ἡ	*joy, delight, gladness*
59	εὐθύς, εῖα, ύ	*immediately, straight, proper*
58	θεωρέω	*I view (as a spectator), behold, observe, see*
58	μέσος, η, ον	*middle, in the midst*
57	τοιοῦτος, αύτη, οῦτον	*such as this, of such a kind*
56	δέχομαι	*I take, receive; welcome*
56	ἐπερωτάω	*I ask, inquire*
56	μηδέ	*but not, nor; not even, not either*
56	συναγωγή, ῆς, ἡ	*assembly, gathering; synagogue*
56	τρίτος, η, ον	*third*
55	ἀρχή, ῆς, ἡ	*beginning; power; rule*
55	κράζω	*I call out, cry out, scream*
55	λοιπός, ή, όν	*rest, remaining; from now on*
55	Πιλᾶτος, ου, ὁ	*Pilate*
54	δεξιός, ά, όν	*right (directional; often metph.); true*
54	εὐαγγελίζω	*I bring/proclaim (the) good news*

54	οὐχί	*not, no, in no way (intensified οὐ)*
53	χρόνος, ου, ὁ	*time, occasion*
53	διό	*therefore, for this reason*
53	ἐλπίς, ίδος, ἡ	*expectation, hope*
53	ὅπως	*how; in order that*
52	ἐπαγγελία, ας, ἡ	*promise, offer*
52	ἔσχατος, η, ον	*last, farthest, least*
52	παιδίον, ου, τό	*child; young servant/slave*
52	πείθω	*I persuade, win over; depend on*
52	σπείρω	*I sow seed, scatter*
51	σοφία, ας, ἡ	*wisdom, sound judgement*
50	γλῶσσα, ης, ἡ	*tongue; language; joyful speech*
50	κακός, ή, όν	*evil, bad; incorrect*
50	μακάριος, ία, ιον	*favored, blessed*
50	παραβολή, ῆς, ἡ	*parable, illustration; type, embodiment*
50	τυφλός, ή, όν	*blind (often metaph.)*
49	γραφή, ῆς, ἡ	*scripture, writing*[1]

[1] Though γραγή occurs 49 times in the SBLGNT, this word occurs 50 times in the NA. As such, many resources include γραφή in their most frequently occurring word list and retention requirements. To retain this standard, it has also been included in this most frequently occurring vocabulary list. Γραγή is not included in the General Reader's footnotes or chapter vocabulary helps.

Appendix II

VOCABULARY 50 TIMES OF MORE ARRANGED ALPHABETICALLY

Α α

Ἀβραάμ, ὁ	*Abraham*
ἀγαθός, ή, όν	*good, beneficial*
ἀγαπάω	*I love, adore*
ἀγάπη, ης, ἡ	*love, adoration*
ἀγαπητός, ή, όν	*beloved, dearly loved*
ἄγγελος, ου, ὁ	*messenger, envoy, angel*
ἅγιος, ία, ον	*holy, pure, devout; (Subst.) Saint*
ἄγω	*I lead, carry, arrest, observe*
ἀδελφός , οῦ, ὁ	*brother*
αἷμα, ατος, τό	*blood, bloodshed*
αἴρω	*I lift up, raise up, take away*
αἰτέω	*I ask, demand*
αἰών, ῶνος, ὁ	*age, era, lifetime*
αἰώνιος, ον	*long-lasting, eternal*
ἀκολουθέω	*I follow, obey*
ἀκούω	*I hear, obey, listen*
ἀλήθεια, ας, ἡ	*truth, reality*
ἀλλά	*but, yet, rather*
ἀλλήλων	*one another*
ἄλλος, η, ο	*other, another*
ἁμαρτία, ίας, ἡ	*sin, guilt, failure*
ἀμήν	*certainly, truly, indeed*
ἄν	*ever [conditional particle, indicates possibility]*
ἀναβαίνω	*I go up, ascend*
ἀνήρ, ἀνδρός, ὁ	*man, husband*
ἄνθρωπος, ου, ὁ	*man, human*
ἀνίστημι	*I raise, resurrect, establish*
ἀνοίγω	*I open*
ἀπέρχομαι	*I depart, go away*

ἀπό	*(+gen) from, away from*
ἀποθνῄσκω	*I die, perish*
ἀποκρίνομαι	*I answer*
ἀποκτείνω, ἀποκτέννω	*I kill, slay*
ἀπόλλυμι	*I ruin, destroy, perish*
ἀπολύω	*I release, pardon, dismiss*
ἀποστέλλω	*I send (off)*
ἀπόστολος, ου, ὁ	*delegate, ambassador, apostle*
ἄρτος, ου, ὁ	*bread, food*
ἀρχή, ῆς, ἡ	*beginning; power; rule*
ἀρχιερεύς, έως, ὁ	*high priest, chief priest*
ἄρχω	*I rule, lead, begin*
ἀσπάζομαι	*I greet, welcome*
αὐτός, ή, ό	*he, she, it; (adj.) -self, same*
ἀφίημι	*I release, forgive, reprieve; depart*

Β β

βάλλω	*I throw, place*
βαπτίζω	*I soak, submerge, wash, baptize*
βασιλεία, ας, ἡ	*kingdom, providence, dominion*
βασιλεύς, έως, ὁ	*king*
βλέπω	*I see, observe, notice*

Γ γ

Γαλιλαία, ας, ἡ	*Galilee*
γάρ	*for, because, since*
γεννάω	*I beget, give birth, parent*
γῆ, γῆς, ἡ	*land, earth*
γίνομαι	*I am, become, happen*
γινώσκω	*I know, understand, learn*
γλῶσσα, ης, ἡ	*tongue; language; joyful speech*
γραμματεύς, έως, ὁ	*scribe, law expert, high official*
γραφή, ῆς, ἡ	*scripture, writing*

γράφω	*I write*
γυνή, αικός, ἡ	*woman, wife*

Δ δ

δαιμόνιον, ου, τό	*demon, evil spirit, inferior divinity*
Δαυίδ, ὁ	*David*
δέ	*but, rather, and, now*
δεῖ	*I must, am required, ought*
δεξιός, ά, όν	*right (directional; often metph.); true*
δέχομαι	*I take, receive; welcome*
διά	*(+gen) through; (+acc) because of*
διδάσκαλος, ου, ὁ	*teacher, master*
διδάσκω	*I teach, instruct*
δίδωμι	*I give, entrust*
δίκαιος, αία, ον	*just, righteous, fair*
δικαιοσύνη, ης, ἡ	*righteousness, justice*
διό	*therefore, for this reason*
δοκέω	*I think, suppose, form an opinion; I seem, suppose*
δόξα, ης, ἡ	*splendor, glory; reputation*
δοξάζω	*I honor, esteem in high regard, exalt, glorify*
δοῦλος, ου, ὁ	*slave, bondservant*
δύναμαι	*I am able*
δύναμις, εως, ἡ	*power, strength, ability*
δύο	*two*
δώδεκα	*twelve*

Ε ε

ἐάν	*if, whenever*
ἑαυτοῦ, ῆς, οῦ	*himself, herself, itself*
ἐγείρω	*I rise, raise*

ἐγώ, (ἐ)μοῦ; ἡμεῖς, ἡμῶν	*I; we*
ἔθνος, ους, τό	*nation, culture group, people*
εἰ	*if, whether*
εἰμί	*I am, exist, happen*
εἰρήνη, ης, ἡ	*peace, well-being*
εἷς, μία, ἕν	*one, single*
εἰς	*(+acc) to, into*
εἰσέρχομαι	*I go into, enter*
εἴτε	*if, either, or, whether*
ἐκ, ἐξ	*(+gen) from, out from*
ἕκαστος, η, ον	*every, each*
ἐκβάλλω	*I throw out, expel, reject*
ἐκεῖ	*there*
ἐκεῖνος, η, ο	*that; (Subst.) he, she, that one*
ἐκκλησία, ας, ἡ	*assembly, gathering, community, church*
ἐλπίς, ίδος, ἡ	*expectation, hope*
ἐμός, ἡ, όν	*my, mine*
ἐν	*(+dat) in, with, among*
ἐντολή, ῆς, ἡ	*command, order, commandment*
ἐνώπιον	*before, face to face, in the view of*
ἐξέρχομαι	*I go out, exit*
ἐξουσία, ας, ἡ	*authority, capability*
ἔξω	*outside, out*
ἐπαγγελία, ας, ἡ	*promise, offer*
ἐπερωτάω	*I ask, inquire*
ἐπί	*(+gen/dat/acc) on, near, toward*
ἑπτά	*seven*
ἔργον, ου, τό	*work, accomplishment*
ἔρχομαι	*I come, go*
ἐρωτάω	*I ask, inquire, question*
ἐσθίω	*I eat, drink, consume*
ἔσχατος, η, ον	*last, farthest, least*
ἕτερος, α, ον	*other, another*
ἔτι	*yet, still, even now*
εὐαγγελίζω	*I bring/proclaim (the) good news*
εὐαγγέλιον, ου, τό	*good news, gospel*

εὐθύς, εῖα, ύ	*immediately, straight, proper*
εὑρίσκω	*I find, discover*
ἔχω	*I have, am*
ἕως	*while, until, up to the point of, as far as*

Ζ ζ

ζάω	*I live*
ζητέω	*I seek, search, inquire*
ζωή, ῆς, ἡ	*life, existence*

Η η

ἤ	*or, than*
ἤδη	*already, now; by this time*
ἡμέρα, ας, ἡ	*day, time*

Θ ϑ

ϑάλασσα, ης, ἡ	*lake, sea*
ϑάνατος, ου, ὁ	*death*
ϑέλημα, ατος, τό	*will, want*
ϑέλω	*I wish, want*
ϑεός, οῦ, ὁ and ἡ	*God, god, divine one*
ϑεωρέω	*I view (as a spectator), behold, observe, see*
ϑρόνος, ου, ὁ	*chair, seat, throne*

Ι ι

ἴδιος, ία, ον	*one's own*
ἰδού	*Look!, Notice!, See!*

ἱερόν, οῦ, τό	*temple, holy place*
Ἱεροσόλυμα, τά	*Jerusalem (city or its inhabitants)*
Ἰερουσαλήμ, ἡ	*Jerusalem*
Ἰησοῦς, οῦ, ὁ	*Joshua, Jesus*
ἱμάτιον, ου, τό	*garment; outer garment*
ἵνα	*in order that, so that*
Ἰουδαῖος, αία, αῖον	*Jewish; (Subst..) Jew*
Ἰσραήλ, ὁ	*Israel*
ἵστημι	*I set, place, establish*
Ἰωάν(ν)ης, ου, ὁ	*John*

Κ κ

κἀγώ	*and I, I too (crasis καὶ ἐγώ)*
κάθημαι	*I sit, settle, reside*
καθώς	*as, just as*
καί	*and; (adv.) also, even*
καιρός, οῦ, ὁ	*time, period, season*
κακός, ή, όν	*evil, bad; incorrect*
καλέω	*I call, summon, invite*
καλός, ή, όν	*beautiful, good, noble*
καρδία, ας, ἡ	*heart*
κάρπος, ου, ὁ	*fruit, produce, profit*
κατά	*(+gen) against, down; (+acc) according to*
καταβαίνω	*I go down, descend*
κεφαλή, ῆς, ἡ	*head*
κηρύσσω	*I preach, proclaim, announce*
κόσμος, ου, ὁ	*world, universe, order*
κράζω	*I call out, cry out, scream*
κρίνω	*I judge, decide, choose*
κύριος, ου, ὁ	*Lord, master, owner*

Λ λ

λαλέω	*I speak*
λαμβάνω	*I take, receive*
λαός, οῦ, ὁ	*people, populace, multitude*
λέγω	*I say, speak, claim*
λίθος, ου, ὁ	*stone*
λόγος, ου, ὁ	*word, speech, matter*
λοιπός, ή, όν	*rest, remaining; from now on*

Μ μ

μαθητής, οῦ, ὁ	*disciple, student*
μακάριος, ία, ιον	*favored, blessed*
μᾶλλον	*more, exceedingly, rather*
μαρτυρέω	*I give evidence, witness, testify*
μέγας, μεγάλη, μέγα	*large, great*
μέλλω	*I am about to, intend*
μέν	*however, but, indeed*
μένω	*I remain, continue*
μέσος, η, ον	*middle, in the midst*
μετά	*(+gen) with; (+acc) after, behind*
μή	*not, no; (+subj.) in order that…not*
μηδέ	*but not, nor; not even, not either*
μηδείς, μηδεμία, μηδέν	*no, no one, nothing*
μήτηρ, τρός, ἡ	*mother*
μόνος, η, ον	*alone, only*
Μωϋσῆς, ὁ	*Moses*

Ν ν

νεκρός, ά, όν	*dead*
νόμος, ου, ὁ	*law, custom*
νῦν	*now, currently, presently*
νύξ, νυκτός, ἡ	*night (often metaph.)*

Ο ο

ὁ, ἡ, τό	*the; (Subst.) he, she, thing*
ὁδός, οῦ, ἡ	*road, way, path, trip*
οἶδα	*I know, understand*
οἰκία, ας, ἡ	*house, building, family*
οἶκος, ου, ὁ	*house, dwelling, family*
ὅλος, η, ον	*whole, entire*
ὄνομα, ατος, τό	*name*
ὅπου	*where, whereas, whenever*
ὅπως	*how; in order that*
ὁράω	*I see, perceive, experience*
ὄρος, ους, τό	*mountain, hill*
ὅς, ἥ, ὅ	*who, which, that*
ὅσος, η, ον	*as many as, as much as, as great as*
ὅστις, ἥτις, ὅ τι	*whoever, whichever, any one who*
ὅταν	*whenever, when*
ὅτε	*when*
ὅτι	*that, because*
οὐ, οὐκ, οὐχ	*not, no*
οὐδέ	*but not, nor, neither*
οὐδείς, οὐδεμία, οὐδέν	*no; (Subst.) no one, nothing*
οὖν	*therefore, then*
οὐρανός, οῦ, ὁ	*sky, heaven*
οὔτε	*and not, nor, neither*
οὗτος, αὕτη, τοῦτο	*this; (Subst.) he, she, this one*
οὕτω/οὕτως	*thus, so*
οὐχί	*not, no, in no way (intensified οὐ)*
ὀφθαλμός, οῦ,	*eye*
ὄχλος, ου, ὁ	*crowd, multitude*

Π π

παιδίον, ου, τό	*child; young servant/slave*
πάλιν	*again*

VOCABULARY
50 TIMES OR MORE
ARRANGED ALPHABETICALLY

παρά	*(+gen) along side, from; (+dat) beside, near; (+acc) out from, by*
παραβολή, ῆς, ἡ	*parable, illustration; type, embodiment*
παραδίδωμι	*I hand over, deliver, grant*
παρακαλέω	*I encourage, call, request*
πᾶς, πᾶσα, πᾶν	*every, each, all, whole*
πατήρ, πατρός, ὁ	*father*
Παῦλος, ου, ὁ	*Paul*
πείθω	*I persuade, win over; depend on*
πέμπω	*I send, despatch*
περί	*(+gen) concerning; (+acc) around*
περιπατέω	*I walk (about), live, behave*
Πέτρος, ου, ὁ	*Peter*
Πιλᾶτος, ου, ὁ	*Pilate*
πίνω	*I drink*
πίπτω	*I fall, collapse*
πιστεύω	*I believe, trust*
πίστις, εως, ἡ	*belief, faithfulness, trust, fidelity, faith*
πιστός, ή, όν	*faithful, trustworthy, believing*
πληρόω	*I fill, complete, fulfill*
πλοῖον, ου, τό	*boat, ship, vessel*
πνεῦμα, ατος, τό	*spirit, breath*
ποιέω	*I make, do*
πόλις, εως, ἡ	*town, city*
πολύς, πολλή, πολύ	*much, many*
πονηρός, ά, όν	*evil, bad, worthless, sick*
πορεύομαι	*I go, walk*
πούς, ποδός, ὁ	*foot*
πρεσβύτερος, α, ον	*aged, old;* (Subst.) *elder*
πρός	*(+acc) to, toward, with*
προσέρχομαι	*I go to, visit, approach*
προσεύχομαι	*I pray, petition a deity*
προσκυνέω	*I worship, prostrate myself*
πρόσωπον, ου, τό	*face, appearance, expression, presence*

προφήτης, ου, ὁ	*prophet*
πρῶτος, η, ον	*first, most prominent*
πῦρ, ός, τό	*fire*
πῶς	*how?*

Ρ ρ

ῥῆμα, ατος, τό	*word, saying, thing*

Σ σ

σάββατον, ου, τό	*Sabbath*
σάρξ, σαρκός, ἡ	*flesh, muscle, body*
σημεῖον, ου, τό	*sign, mark, signal, miracle*
Σίμων, ωνος, ὁ	*Simon*
σοφία, ας, ἡ	*wisdom, sound judgement*
σπείρω	*I sow seed, scatter*
στόμα, ατος, τό	*mouth, opening*
σύ, σοῦ; ὑμεῖς, ὑμῶν	*you; you all*
σύν	*(+dat) with, along with*
συνάγω	*I gather together, collect; receive as a guest*
συναγωγή, ῆς, ἡ	*assembly, gathering; synagogue*
σῴζω	*I save, rescue, keep safe*
σῶμα, ατος, τό	*body*

Τ τ

τέ	*and, so*
τέκνον, ου, τό	*child*
τηρέω	*I watch over, guard, keep*
τίθημι	*I put, place, lay*
τις, τι	*someone, something*
τίς, τί	*who? which? what?*
τοιοῦτος, αύτη, οῦτον	*such as this, of such a kind*

τόπος, ου, ὁ	*place, position*
τότε	*at that time, then*
τρεῖς, τρία	*three*
τρίτος, η, ον	*third*
τυφλός, ή, όν	*blind (often metaph.)*

Υ υ

ὕδωρ, ατος, τό	*water, rain*
υἱός, οῦ, ὁ	*son*
ὑπάγω	*I withdraw, go away*
ὑπάρχω	*I am present, at one's disposal; I am, exist*
ὑπέρ	*(+gen) on behalf of, for; (+acc) over, beyond*
ὑπό	*(+gen) by; (+acc) underneath*

Φ φ

Φαρισαῖος, ου, ὁ	*Pharisee, Separatist*
φέρω	*I carry, bring, lead*
φημί	*I say, declare*
φοβέω	*I fear, respect; I flee frightened*
φωνή, ῆς, ἡ	*voice, sound, communication*
φῶς, φωτός, τό	*light, torch*

Χ χ

χαίρω	*I am glad, rejoice, welcome*
χαρά, ᾶς, ἡ	*joy, delight, gladness*
χάρις, ιτος, ἡ	*grace, thankfulness, kindness*
χείρ, χειρός, ἡ	*hand*
Χριστός, οῦ, ὁ	*Messiah, Anointed One, Christ*
χρόνος, ου, ὁ	*time, occasion,*

Ψ ψ

ψυχή, ῆς, ἡ	*soul, life*

Ω ω

ὧδε	*here, thus, in this way, exceedingly so*
ὥρα, ας, ἡ	*hour, time, period, season*
ὡς	*as, like*
ὥστε	*so that, therefore, consequently*

Appendix III

PARADIGMS

Athematic (μι) Stems: no connecting vowels

	Primary Tense				Secondary/Historical Tense			
	Active		Middle/Passive		Active		Middle/Passive	
	Singular	Plural	Singular	Plural	Singular	Plural	Singular	Plural
1st	μι	μεν	μαι	μεθα	ν	μεν	μην	μεθα
2nd	ς	τε	σαι	σθε	ς	τε	σο	σθε
3rd	σι(ν)	ασι(ν)	ται	νται	-	σαν	το	ντο

Thematic (ω) Stems: connecting vowel included

	Primary Tense				Secondary/Historical Tense			
	Active		Middle/Passive		Active		Middle/Passive	
	Singular	Plural	Singular	Plural	Singular	Plural	Singular	Plural
1st	ω	ομεν	ομαι	ομεθα	ον	ομεν	ομην	ομεθα
2nd	εις	ετε	ῃ	εσθε	ες	ετε	ου	εσθε
3rd	ει	ουσι	εται	ονται	- / ε	ον	ετο	οντο

Imperative (using λύω)

			Active	Middle	Passive
Present	Singular	2nd	λῦε	λύου	
		3rd	λυέτω	λυέσθω	
	Plural	2nd	λύετε	λύεσθε	
		3rd	λυέτωσαν	λυέσθωσαν	
Aorist	Singular	2nd	λῦσον	λῦσαι	λύθητι
		3rd	λυσάτω	λυσάσθω	λυθήτω
	Plural	2nd	λύσατε	λύσασθε	λύθητε
		3rd	λυσάτωσαν	λυσάσθωσαν	λυθήτωσαν

Infinitive (using λύω)

	Active	Middle	Passive
Present	λυείν	λύεσθαι	
Aorist	λῦσαι	λύσασθαι	λυθῆναι
Perfect	λελυκέναι	λελύσθαι	

Participle (using λύω)

			Present		Aorist			Perfect	
			Act.	Mid./Pass.	Act.	Mid.	Pass.	Act.	Mid./Pass.
Masculine	Singular	Nom.	λύων	λυόμενος	λύσας	λυσάμενος	λυθείς	λελυκώς	λελυμένος
		Gen.	λύοντος	λυομένου	λύσαντος	λυσαμένου	λυθέντος	λελυκότος	λελυμένου
		Dat.	λύοντι	λυομένῳ	λύσαντι	λυσαμένῳ	λυθέντι	λελυκότι	λελυμένῳ
		Acc.	λύοντα	λυόμενον	λύσαντα	λυσάμενον	λυθέντα	λελυκότα	λελυμένον
	Plural	Nom.	λύοντες	λυόμενοι	λύσαντες	λυσάμενοι	λυθέντες	λελυκότες	λελυμένοι
		Gen.	λυόντων	λυομένων	λυσάντων	λυσαμένων	λυθέντων	λελυκότων	λελυμένων
		Dat.	λύουσι(ν)	λυομένοις	λύσασι(ν)	λυσαμένοις	λυθεῖσι(ν)	λελυκόσι(ν)	λελυμένοις
		Acc.	λύοντας	λυομένους	λύσαντας	λυσαμένους	λυθέντας	λελυκότας	λελυμένους
Feminine	Singular	Nom.	λύουσα	λυομένη	λύσασα	λυσαμένη	λυθεῖσα	λελυκυῖα	λελυμένη
		Gen.	λυούσης	λυομένης	λυσάσης	λυσαμένης	λυθείσης	λελυκυίας	λελυμένης
		Dat.	λυούσῃ	λυομένῃ	λυσάῃ	λυσαμένῃ	λυθείσῃ	λελυκυίᾳ	λελυμένῃ
		Acc.	λύουσαν	λυομένην	λύσασαν	λυσαμένην	λυθεῖσαν	λελυκυῖαν	λελυμένην
	Plural	Nom.	λύουσαι	λυόμεναι	λύσασαι	λυσάμεναι	λυθεῖσαι	λελυκυῖαι	λελυμέναι
		Gen.	λυουσῶν	λυομένων	λυσασῶν	λυσαμένων	λυθεισῶν	λελυκυιῶν	λελυμένων
		Dat.	λυούσαις	λυομέναις	λυσάσαις	λυσαμέναις	λυθείσαις	λελυκυίαις	λελυμέναις
		Acc.	λυούσας	λυομένας	λυσάσας	λυσαμένας	λυθείσας	λελυκυίας	λελυμένας
Neuter	Singular	Nom.	λῦον	λυόμενον	λῦσαν	λυσάμενον	λυθέν	λελυκός	λελυμένον
		Gen.	λύοντος	λυομένου	λύσαντος	λυσαμένου	λυθέντος	λελυκότος	λελυμένου
		Dat.	λύοντι	λυομένῳ	λύσαντι	λυσαμένῳ	λυθέντι	λελυκότι	λελυμένῳ
		Acc.	λῦον	λυόμενον	λῦσαν	λυσάμενον	λυθέν	λελυκός	λελυμένον
	Plural	Nom.	λύοντα	λυόμενα	λύσαντα	λυσάμενα	λυθέντα	λελυκότα	λελυμένα
		Gen.	λυόντων	λυομένων	λυσάντων	λυσαμένων	λυθέντων	λελυκότων	λελυμένων
		Dat.	λύουσι(ν)	λυομένοις	λύσασι(ν)	λυσαμένοις	λυθεῖσι(ν)	λελυκόσι(ν)	λελυμένοις
		Acc.	λύοντα	λυόμενα	λύσαντα	λυσάμενα	λυθέντα	λελυκότα	λελυμένα

Subjunctive

(Aor Act. add -σ-; Aor Pass. add -θ-)

	Active		Middle/Passive	
	Sing.	Plur.	Sing.	Plur.
1st	ω	ωμεν	ωμαι	ωμεθα
2nd	ῃς	ητε	ῃ	ησθε
3rd	ῃ	ωσι(ν)	ηται	ωνται

Optative

	Active		Middle/Passive	
	Sing.	Plur.	Sing.	Plur.
1st	μι / ν	μεν	μην	μεθα
2nd	ς	τε	σο	σθε
3rd	-	εν / σαν	το	ντο

Thematic Formation:
Pres: -οι + ending
Aor A/M: -σαιη + ending
Aor P: -θειη + ending

Athematic Formation:
Pres: -ιη or -ι + ending
Aor A/M/P: -ιη or -ι + ending

Present Indicative

	Sing.	Plur.
1st	εἰμί	ἐσμέν
2nd	εἶ	ἐστέ
3rd	ἐστί(ν)	εἰσί(ν)

Imperfect Indicative

	Sing.	Plur.
1st	ἤμην	ἦμεν
2nd	ἦς	ἦτε
3rd	ἦν	ἦσαν

Future Indicative

	Sing.	Plur.
1st	ἔσομαι	ἐσόμεθα
2nd	ἔσῃ	ἔσεσθε
3rd	ἔσται	ἔσονται

Present Subjunctive

	Sing.	Plur.
1st	ὦ	ὦμεν
2nd	ᾖς	ἦτε
3rd	ᾖ	ὦσι(ν)

Present Imperative

	Sing.	Plur.
2nd	ἴσθι	ἔστε
3rd	ἔστω	ἔστωσαν

Present Optative

	Sing.	Plur.
1st	εἴην	εἶμεν/εἴημεν
2nd	εἴης	εἶτε/εἴητε
3rd	εἴη	εἶεν/εἴησαν

Infinitive

Present	εἶναι
Future	ἔσεσθαι

Present Participle

		Masc.	Fem.	Neut.
Singular	Nom.	ὤν	οὖσα	ὄν
	Gen.	ὄντος	οὔσης	ὄντος
	Dat.	ὄντι	οὔσῃ	ὄντι
	Acc.	ὄντα	οὖσαν	ὄν
Plural	Nom.	ὄντες	οὖσαι	ὄντα
	Gen.	ὄντων	οὐσῶν	ὄντων
	Dat.	οὖσι(ν)	οὔσαις	οὖσι(ν)
	Acc.	ὄντας	οὔσας	ὄντα

Definite Article

	Singular			Plural		
	Masc.	Fem.	Neut.	Masc.	Fem.	Neut.
Nom.	ὁ	ἡ	τό	οἱ	αἱ	τά
Gen.	τοῦ	τῆς	τοῦ		τῶν	
Dat.	τῷ	τῇ	τῷ	τοῖς	ταῖς	τοῖς
Acc.	τόν	τήν	τό	τούς	τάς	τά

1st Declension Endings

	Singular				Plur.
	ε, ι, ρ	σ, ζ, ξ, ψ	all other	Masc.	
Nom.	α	α	η	ης	αι
Gen.	ας	ης	ης	ου	ων
Dat.	ᾳ	ῃ	ῃ	ῃ	αις
Acc.	αν	αν	ην	ην	ας

2nd Declension Endings

	Singular			Plural		
	Masc.	Fem.	Neut.	Masc.	Fem.	Neut.
Nom.	ος		ον	οι		α
Gen.	ου			ων		
Dat.	ῳ			οις		
Acc.	ον			ους		α

3rd Declension Endings

	Singular			Plural		
	Masc.	Fem.	Neut.	Masc.	Fem.	Neut.
Nom.	ς / -		-	ες		α
Gen.	ος			ων		
Dat.	ι			σι(ν)		
Acc.	α / ν		-	ας / ες		α

πᾶς, πᾶσα, πᾶν | 3-1-3

	Singular			Plural		
	Masc.	Fem.	Neut.	Masc.	Fem.	Neut.
Nom.	πᾶς	πᾶσα	πᾶν	πάντες	πᾶσαι	πάντα
Gen.	παντός	πάσης	παντός	πάντων	πασῶν	πάντων
Dat.	παντί	πάσῃ	παντί	πᾶσι(ν)	πάσαις	πᾶσι(ν)
Acc.	πάντα	πᾶσαν	πᾶν	πάντας	πάσας	πάντα

πολύς, πολλή, πολύ | 2-1-2

	Singular			Plural		
	Masc.	Fem.	Neut.	Masc.	Fem.	Neut.
Nom.	πολύς	πολλή	πολύ	πολλοί	πολλαί	πολλά
Gen.	πολλοῦ	πολλῆς	πολλοῦ	πολλῶν		
Dat.	πολλῷ	πολλῇ	πολλῷ	πολλοῖς	πολλαῖς	πολλοῖς
Acc.	πολύν	πολλήν	πολύ	πολλούς	πολλάς	πολλά

Personal Pronouns: *I, we, you, she, he, it, they*

	1st		2nd	
	Sing.	Plur.	Sing.	Plur.
Nom.	ἐγώ	ἡμεῖς	σύ	ὑμεῖς
Gen.	(ἐ)μοῦ	ἡμῶν	σοῦ	ὑμῶν
Dat.	(ἐ)μοί	ἡμῖν	σοί	ὑμῖν
Acc.	(ἐ)μέ	ἡμᾶς	σέ	ὑμᾶς

	3rd					
	Singular			Plural		
	Masc.	Fem.	Neut.	Masc.	Fem.	Neut.
Nom.	αὐτός	αὐτή	αὐτό	αὐτοί	αὐταί	αὐτά
Gen.	αὐτοῦ	αὐτῆς	αὐτοῦ		αὐτῶν	
Dat.	αὐτῷ	αὐτῇ	αὐτῷ	αὐτοῖς	αὐταῖς	αὐτοῖς
Acc.	αὐτόν	αὐτήν	αὐτό	αὐτοῦς	αὐτᾶς	αὐτά

Proximal (Near) Demonstrative: *this, these*

	Singular			Plural		
	Masc.	Fem.	Neut.	Masc.	Fem.	Neut.
Nom.	οὗτος	αὕτη	τοῦτο	οὗτοι	αὗται	ταῦτα
Gen.	τούτου	ταύτης	τούτου		τούτων	
Dat.	τούτῳ	ταύτῃ	τούτῳ	τούτοις	ταύταις	τούτοις
Acc.	τοῦτον	ταύτην	τοῦτο	τούτους	ταύτας	ταῦτα

Distal (Far) Demonstrative: *that, those*

	Singular			Plural		
	Masc.	Fem.	Neut.	Masc.	Fem.	Neut.
Nom.	ἐκεῖνος	ἐκείνη	ἐκεῖνο	ἐκεῖνοι	ἐκεῖναι	ἐκεῖνα
Gen.	ἐκείνου	ἐκείνης	ἐκείνου		ἐκείνων	
Dat.	ἐκείνῳ	ἐκείνῃ	ἐκείνῳ	ἐκείνοις	ἐκείναις	ἐκείνοις
Acc.	ἐκεῖνον	ἐκεῖνην	ἐκεῖνο	ἐκείνους	ἐκείνας	ἐκεῖνα

Interrogative Pronouns: *who? which? what?*

	Singular			Plural		
	Masc.	Fem.	Neut.	Masc.	Fem.	Neut.
Nom.	τίς		τί	τίνες		τίνα
Gen.		τίνος			τίνων	
Dat.		τίνι			τίσι(ν)	
Acc.	τίνα		τί	τίνας		τίνα

Indefinite Pronouns: *someone, something*

	Singular			Plural		
	Masc.	Fem.	Neut.	Masc.	Fem.	Neut.
Nom.	τις		τι	τινες		τινα
Gen.		τινος			τινων	
Dat.		τινι			τισι(ν)	
Acc.	τινα		τι	τινας		τινα

Indefinite Relative Pronouns: *whoever, whichever, every one who*

	Singular			Plural		
	Masc.	Fem.	Neut.	Masc.	Fem.	Neut.
Nom.	ὅστις	ἥτις	ὅ τι / ὅτι	οἵτινες	αἵτινες	ἅτινα
Gen.	οὗτινος	ἧστινος	οὗτινος	ὧντινων		
Dat.	ᾧτινι	ᾗτινι	ᾧτινι	οἷστισι(ν)	αἷστισι(ν)	οἷστισι(ν)
Acc.	ὅντινα	ἥντινα	ὅ τι / ὅτι	οὕστινας	ἅστινας	ἅτινα

Relative Pronouns: *who, which, that*

	Singular			Plural		
	M	F	N	M	F	N
Nom.	ὅς	ἥ	ὅ	οἵ	αἵ	ἅ
Gen.	οὗ	ἧς	οὗ	ὧν		
Dat.	ᾧ	ᾗ	ᾧ	οἷς	αἷς	οἷς
Acc.	ὅν	ἥν	ὅ	οὕς	ἅς	ἅ

Reciprocal Pronouns: *one another*

	Plural
Gen.	ἀλλήλων
Dat.	ἀλλήλοις
Acc.	ἀλλήλους

Reflexive Pronouns: *myself, yourself, herself, himself, itself*

		1st		2nd		3rd		
		Masc.	Fem.	Masc.	Fem.	Masc.	Fem.	Neut.
Singular	Gen.	ἐμαυτοῦ	ἐμαυτῆς	σεαυτοῦ	σεαυτῆς	ἑαυτοῦ	ἑαυτῆς	ἑαυτοῦ
	Dat.	ἐμαυτῷ	ἐμαυτῇ	σεαυτῷ	σεαυτῇ	ἑαυτῷ	ἑαυτῇ	ἑαυτῷ
	Acc.	ἐμαυτόν	ἐμαυτήν	σεαυτόν	σεαυτήν	ἑαυτόν	ἑαυτήν	ἑαυτό
Plural	Gen.	ἑαυτῶν		ἑαυτῶν		ἑαυτῶν		
	Dat.	ἑαυτοῖς	ἑαυταῖς	ἑαυτοῖς	ἑαυταῖς	ἑαυτοῖς	ἑαυταῖς	ἑαυτοῖς
	Acc.	ἑαυτούς	ἑαυτάς	ἑαυτούς	ἑαυτάς	ἑαυτούς	ἑαυτάς	ἑαυτά

NOTES

NOTES

Made in the USA
Monee, IL
10 September 2026

62770615R00115